The Christian Imagination

ESSAYS ON LITERATURE AND THE ARTS

Leland Ryken

BAKER BOOK HOUSE

Grand Rapids, Michigan 49506

Copyright 1981 by
Baker Book House Company

ISBN: 0-8010-7702-8

Library of Congress Catalog Card Number: 80-70154

Printed in the United States of America

The editor wishes to express his appreciation:

To Cambridge University Press, for permission to print C. S. Lewis' essay "How the Few and the Many Use Pictures and Music," pages 14-26 in *An Experiment in Criticism*, copyright 1961 by Cambridge University Press. Used by permission.

To Chad Walsh, for permission to print excerpts from "A Hope for Literature," originally published in *The Climate of Faith in Modern Literature*, ed. Nathan A. Scott, Jr., by Seabury Press, 1964; copyright presently held by Chad Walsh. Used by permission.

To *Christian Herald*, for permission to print "Christian Imagination," by Clyde S. Kilby, copyright 1969 by *Christian Herald*. Used by permission.

To Farrar, Straus & Giroux, Inc., for permission to print "Novelist and Believer," from *Mystery and Manners* by Flannery O'Connor. Selected and edited by Sally and Robert Fitzgerald. Copyright 1963, 1969 by the Estate of Mary Flannery O'Connor. Reprinted by permission of Farrar, Straus and Giroux, Inc.

To Harcourt Brace Jovanovich, Inc., for permission to print "Literature and Religion," from *Selected Essays, New Edition* by T. S. Eliot, copyright 1932 by Harcourt Brace Jovanovich, Inc.; copyright 1960 by T. S. Eliot. Reprinted by permission of Harcourt Brace Jovanovich, Inc.

To InterVarsity Press, for permission to print excerpts taken from *Art and the Bible* by Francis A. Schaeffer. Copyright 1973 by L'Abri Fellowship and used by permission of InterVarsity Press.

To The National Council of Churches of Christ in the U.S.A., for permission to quote from the Revised Standard Version of the Bible, copyright 1946, 1952, 1971, 1973.

To Nelvin Vos, for permission to print excerpts from *The Drama of Comedy: Victim and Victor*, originally published by John Knox Press in 1966; copyright presently held by Nelvin Vos. Used by permission.

To Pantheon Books, Inc., a Division of Random House, Inc., for permission to quote from pages 40-43 of *Leisure, The Basis of Culture*, by Josef Pieper, copyright 1952 by Pantheon Books, Inc., and 1965 by Random House, Inc.

To Westminster Press, for permission to print excerpts from Chapter 2: "Literature and the Greatness of Man" from *Perspective on Man: Literature and the Christian Tradition*, by Roland Mushat Frye. Copyright 1961 by W. L. Jenkins. Used by permission of The Westminster Press.

To William B. Eerdmans Publishing Company, for permission to print "Christianity and Culture," by C. S. Lewis, originally published in *Christian Reflections*, copyright 1967 by William B. Eerdmans. Used by permission.

To *Christianity Today*, for permission to print the following copyrighted articles: "Approach to Modern Literature," by Virginia Ramey Mollenkott, February 16, 1959, copyrighted 1959 and used by permission; "The Christian Novel and the Evangelical Dilemma," by James Wesley Ingles, September 26, 1960, copyrighted 1960 and used by permission; "Shakespeare and Christianity," by Steve J. Van Der Weele, September 25, 1961, copyrighted 1961 and used by permission; "Music in Christian Education," by Frank Gaebelein, February 16, 1962, copyrighted 1962 and used by permission; "The Place of Music in Christian Life," by Robert Elmore, January 31, 1964, copyrighted 1964 and used by permission; "Letter to a Christian Artist," by H. R. Rookmaaker, September 2, 1966, copyrighted 1966 and used by permission; "Toward a Biblical View of Aesthetics," by Frank E. Gaebelein, August 30, 1968, copyrighted 1968 and used by permission; "Homer, Dante, and All That," by Thomas Howard, October 25, 1968, copyrighted 1968 and used by permission; "Art Is Long," by Addison H. Leitch, October 10, 1969, copyrighted 1969 and used by permission; "On Evil in Art," by Thomas Howard, December 17, 1971, copyrighted 1971 and used by permission; "The Arts: A Bridge Between the Natural and Spiritual Realms," by C. Nolan Huizenga, October 12, 1973, copyrighted 1973 and used by permission; "The Christian Reader," by Nancy M. Tischler, June 8, 1973, copyrighted 1973 and used by permission; "A Biblical View of the Novel," by Rolland N. Hein, January 5, 1973, copyrighted 1973 and used by permission; "The Play's the Thing—Or Is It?" by Gordon C. Bennett, May 10, 1974, copyrighted 1974 and used by permission; "Unwelcoming the Christian Poet," by John Leax, April 12, 1974, copyrighted 1974 and used by permission; "There Is More to Redemption Than Meets the Ear," by Harold M. Best, July 26, 1974, copyrighted 1974 and used by permission; "Good Reading in the Good Book," by Leland Ryken, January 17, 1975, copyrighted 1975 and used by permission; "Would Augustine Have Enjoyed Picasso?" by Mark Marchak, May 7, 1976, copyrighted 1976 and used by permission; "What Is Truth in Art?" by Frank E. Gaebelein, August 27, 1976, copyrighted 1976 and used by permission; "Poems Should Stay Across the Street from the Church," by Rod Jellema, June 4, 1976, copyrighted 1976 and used by permission; "The Price of Praise," by Virginia Stem Owens, November 18, 1977, copyrighted 1977 and used by permission; "An Uneasy Smile for Satire," by Harry Boonstra, June 23, 1978, copyrighted 1978 and used by permission.

To *The Banner*, for permission to print "Christian Art," by Calvin Seerveld, copyright 1969 by *The Banner*. Used by permission.

For Mary

Notes on Contributors

E. Beatrice Batson is Professor of English at Wheaton College. She is widely known for her articles and lectures on literature, the humanities, and liberal education. She is the author of *A Reader's Guide to Religious Literature*.

Gordon C. Bennett is a teacher-playwright at Eastern College. He is the author of five published plays and numerous unpublished plays. He is also cofounder of The King's Players, a Christian theatre group founded in 1965.

Harold M. Best is Director of the Conservatory of Music at Wheaton College. He is a composer and organist. As a musical theorist he has been concerned with the role of music in the Christian community, and with the nature of music as an act of worship.

Harry Boonstra is director of libraries at Hope College. Before assuming that position he was a college teacher of literature. His fields of expertise include satire and the Bible as literature.

E. Margaret Clarkson is a teacher, free-lance writer, and hymn writer. In recent years she has lectured on Christian hymnology at Regent College, and she has written the conference hymn at recent Inter-Varsity Urbana conferences.

Mark Coppenger is Associate Professor of Philosophy at Wheaton College. He has taught courses in aesthetics, and film is a special interest of his.

T. S. Eliot is perhaps the most influential figure in twentieth-century English and American literature. His numerous works fall chiefly into the categories of poetry, drama, and literary criticism. In all of these fields his mature viewpoint was Christian, sometimes overtly, sometimes implicitly.

Robert S. Elmore has had a varied musical career. His work as a college professor of music has included teaching at the University of Pennsylvania, and his role as a church musician has included work in the Central Moravian Church of Bethlehem, Pennsylvania, and the Tenth Presbyterian Church of Philadelphia.

Roland M. Frye is Felix E. Schelling Professor of English Literature at the University of Pennsylvania. He has published books on Shakespeare, Milton, Bunyan, and the Bible as literature, as well as a book of literary theory entitled *Perspective on Man: Literature and the Christian Tradition.*

Frank E. Gaebelein is Headmaster Emeritus of Stony Brook School of New York. He has been a noted lecturer on the place of the arts in Christian education and the Christian's life. His books and articles have dealt with the Bible, education, and the arts, especially music.

Rolland N. Hein is Professor of English at Wheaton College. He has edited four volumes of the works of George MacDonald.

Thomas Howard is Professor of English at Gordon College. He is a prolific writer and frequent lecturer on the arts, the imagination, C. S. Lewis, and Christian apologetics. *Christ the Tiger* is the book that made him famous, and many more have followed on a variety of topics.

C. Nolan Huizenga is professor of piano and music history at Houghton College. As an aesthetic theorist his interests have included the significance of Christ's Incarnation for the arts, including music and the dance.

James Wesley Ingles has taught English at several schools, including Eastern College. He is the author of five novels (including *Silver Trumpet* and *A Woman of Samaria*), as well as numerous short stories and poems.

Rod Jellema teaches writing and literature at the University of Maryland. He has edited a volume of Dorothy Sayers' essays entitled *Christian Letters to a Post-Christian World,* and he was a general editor of Eerdmans' Contemporary Writers in Christian Perspective series. He has written several volumes of poetry.

Clyde S. Kilby was for many years Professor of English at Wheaton College. He is best known for having established what is now known as the Marion E. Wade Collection of the books and papers of C. S. Lewis and six other British authors. He is the author of numerous books, including several on C. S. Lewis.

John Leax is a member of the English Department at Houghton College. He is a leading figure among contemporary Christian poets, and his publications include a volume entitled *Reaching into Silence.*

Addison H. Leitch was a professor of theology at Gordon-Conwell Theological Seminary. He authored several theological books and was a regular contributor to a column in *Christianity Today* entitled "Current Religious Thought." He had a keen interest in literature and often wrote on literary topics.

C. S. Lewis was by profession a tutor of English literature at Oxford and Cambridge Universities in England. His voluminous work as a writer covered a wide range of topics, including literary criticism, Christian apologetics, fiction, and poetry.

Mark Marchak exemplifies a major focus of this book. By vocation he is involved in an inner-city Christian ministry, and by avocation he is a painter and enthusiast for art.

Virginia Ramey Mollenkott is Professor of English at William Patterson College of New Jersey. She is best known in scholarly circles as an authority on John Milton, Robert Herrick, and George Herbert. She has also been prominent as a contributor to the Conference on Christianity and Literature.

Flannery O'Connor is one of the best known fiction writers of the twentieth century. A Catholic by theological persuasion, her greatest literary subject was the rural, Protestant South. She is nearly as well known for her comments about the writer's craft as for her fiction; her books in this area are *Mystery and Manners* and *The Habit of Being*.

Virginia Stem Owens is a free-lance writer. She has written on such subjects as Christian living, the arts, and communications. Her books include *A Taste of Creation*.

H. R. Rookmaaker was Professor of the History of Art at the Free University of Amsterdam. His views on the relationship between Christianity and art have been most fully expressed in his book *Modern Art and the Death of a Culture*.

Leland Ryken is Professor of English at Wheaton College. His books include *The Literature of the Bible* and *Triumphs of the Imagination: Literature in Christian Perspective*.

Francis A. Schaeffer is director of L'Abri Fellowship in Switzerland. In his numerous books he has attempted to relate the Christian faith to a wide range of intellectual disciplines. His monograph *Art and the Bible* deals specifically with the arts.

Calvin Seerveld is Senior Member in Philosophical Aesthetics at the Institute for Christian Studies in Toronto. In addition to his numerous articles on the topic of aesthetics, he has authored books entitled *A Christian Critique of Art and Literature* and *Rainbows for the Fallen World*.

Nancy M. Tischler is Professor of English and Humanities at Pennsylvania State University. Her most recent books include *Legacy of Eve: Women of the Bible* and *Dorothy L. Sayers: A Pilgrim Soul.*

Steve J. Van Der Weele is Professor of English at Calvin College. His areas of expertise include C. S. Lewis, the Bible as literature, and Shakespeare.

Nelvin Vos is Professor of English at Muhlenberg College. An authority on drama and comedy, his books include *The Drama of Comedy: Victim and Victor, For God's Sake Laugh*, and *Eugene Ionesco and Edward Albee.*

Chad Walsh, now retired, was Professor of English at Beloit College until 1977. He has published books on C. S. Lewis, Christian apologetics, the Bible, and utopian literature. He is perhaps best known for his numerous volumes of poetry.

Preface

This book is an exploration of the ways of the imagination. Although the essays will discuss this topic in detail, I would ask the reader to accept just one initial definition of the imagination: the imagination is what enables us to produce and enjoy the arts.

There are two main themes in this volume. The first is that the imagination is one way we know the truth. For truth—including religious truth—is not solely the province of the reason or intellect. For example, one can experience the truth about God and salvation while listening to Handel's *Messiah*. But how? Not primarily through reason, but through the senses (hearing), emotions, and the combination of mind, senses, and emotions that I call the imagination.

A pastor friend of mine recalls the moment when he first knew that Jesus rose from the grave. That moment came during an Easter sunrise service in California. It occurred, not during the sermon, but with the sound of the trumpets that concluded the service. Many have experienced truth about God's creation when walking on a sunny autumn or spring afternoon. How? Not, surely, with the intellect, but with the senses, feelings, and imagination. Truth, I repeat, does not come to us solely through the reason and intellect.

Consider the way truth comes to us in the Bible. If you asked an adult Sunday school class what topics are covered in the Old Testament Psalms, the list would look something like this: God, providence, guilt, forgiveness, joy, worship, suffering, godliness. Such a list leans decidedly toward the abstract, the rational, and the theological side of things. But consider an equally valid list of topics also found in the Psalms: dogs, honey, grass, thunder, snow, broken arms, butter, sparrows. This list appeals largely to the senses, and it touches our emotions and imaginations far more vividly than the first list does. In the Bible, truth does not address only the rational intellect.

To say that truth is the province of the imagination as well as the intellect is not a revolutionary claim. An examination of our church services reveals that we do not limit truth to the intellect. We experience religious truth through the senses when we hear and make music in a church service, observe the symbolic decoration of the sanctuary, partake of the bread and wine of communion or the water of baptism. The reading from the Bible (especially if it is from a literary part of the Bible) speaks to us in quite a different way from the exposition of the passage in a sermon. In the moment of silent commitment to God we "know" the truth primarily with our wills.

Our daily lives, as well as our specifically religious acts, are full of reminders that truth cannot be limited to the reason or intellect. The problem is that we do not pay attention to the other ways in which we know the truth that sets us free. One aim of this book is to awaken our Christian sensibilities to the ways the imagination can lead us in the paths of truth—truth about God, the world, and ourselves.

But, someone may protest, do we not associate the imagination with untruth rather than truth? After all, the poet tells us that his love is like a red, red rose, when in fact we know that she does not resemble a flower. Music brings together sounds in a way that we would never hear in nature. And what the painter puts on a canvas does not simply duplicate what we see around us. But despite these elements of the imaginary, the arts deal with the human issues that make up our daily reality. In the words of Picasso, "We all know that Art is not truth. Art is a lie that makes us realize truth."[1]

The second great theme of this book is that people do not live by knowledge or truth alone. They also stand in need of beauty. In our best moments we know this. We know that Handel's *Messiah* is as important to us as a Christmas sermon, and that an autumn sunset, though not "useful" in the utilitarian sense, is nevertheless necessary to a full life. Genesis 2:9 tells us that when God formed Paradise he "made to grow every tree that is pleasant to the sight and good for food." A perfect human world, in other words, is both beautiful and functional. In this regard, too, our church services and our Bibles show us the truth, but we too often overlook it. The beauty of color or harmony or metaphor is not less valuable because it does not put money into our pockets or food into our mouths.

The essays in this volume represent the essays that I have found essential to my own thinking about Christianity and the arts. Unlike similar collections that have appeared in recent years, this volume accepts the Bible as the ultimate authority for Christian doctrine. The essays represent the materials from which anyone can build a solid Christian approach to the arts.

Six of the essays are here printed for the first time. The remainder have previously appeared in either books or journals (twenty-two of them in *Christianity Today*). I have supplied the subtitles that appear in most of the essays, and I have also written brief introductions to the main sections of the book and the individual essays. These introductions provide a context and organizing framework for the material that follows, and

1. *The Arts*, May, 1923.

taken together they provide a comprehensive overview of the perennial issues of Christian aesthetics.

Leland Ryken
Wheaton College

Preparation of this book was assisted by a grant from the Wheaton College Faculty Development Fund.

Contents

15

Part 4   Christian Perspectives on Eight Literary Forms

Part 5   The Christian Writer

Part 6 Christian Perspectives on the Visual Arts

Part 7 Christian Perspectives on Music

part 1

Toward a Christian Philosophy of the Arts

Introduction

"If we commit ourselves to saying that the Christian revelation discovers to us the nature of *all* truth," Dorothy Sayers once wrote, "then it must discover to us the nature of the truth about Art among other things." That premise is the moving spirit behind this entire book, which is an attempt to discover and apply the Christian principles that should govern a Christian's involvement in the arts.

A Christian philosophy of the arts must begin with an identification of the biblical doctrines that apply most directly to the arts, such as the creation, the fall, the incarnation, redemption and sanctification, common grace, stewardship, and the Christian's purpose of glorifying God. Use this list as a framework to organize the essays in part 1, noting what the authors say about these doctrines in relation to the arts.

Christianity and Culture

C. S. Lewis

The question of whether the arts are worthwhile is part of the bigger question of the value of culture in general. Unless culture itself is worthy of a Christian's attention, we need not bother with the arts. If, on the other hand, culture is worthy, we can proceed to assess the relative value of the arts when placed beside other cultural pursuits.

Christians throughout the centuries have disagreed on this question of culture. The rejection of culture was expressed in Tertullian's famous aphorism, "What indeed has Athens to do with Jerusalem?" The other extreme, of equating culture with religion, has become popular in recent centuries with the increased secularization of Western civilization. The great spokesman for this view was Matthew Arnold, who believed that because the Christian religion has waned as a force in modern society we should turn increasingly to culture "to interpret life for us, to console us, to sustain us."

In the following essay, C. S. Lewis steers a balanced middle course between the extremes of the total rejection of culture and the elevation of culture to a substitute religion. Writing in his engaging personal style, Lewis makes significant comments along the way about the biblical data, the traditional Christian answers to the problem of Christ and culture, the influence (good and bad) that the arts have on people, and the importance of the arts as a repository of human values.

Is Culture Good for a Christian?

At an early age I came to believe that the life of culture (that is, of intellectual and aesthetic activity) was very good for its own sake, or even that it was the good for man. After my conversion, which occurred in my later twenties, I continued to hold this belief without consciously asking how it could be reconciled with my new belief that the end of human life was salvation in Christ and the glorifying of God. I was awakened from this confused state of mind by finding that the friends of culture seemed to me to be exaggerating. In my reaction against what seemed exaggerated I was driven to the other extreme, and began, in my own mind, to belittle the claims of culture. As soon as I did this I was faced with the question, "If it is a thing of so little value, how are you justified in spending so much of your life on it?"

In the heat of the moment I rushed to the opposite extreme. I felt, with some spiritual pride, that I had been saved in the nick of time from being "sensitive." The "sentimentality and cheapness" of much Christian hymnody had been a strong point in my own resistance to conversion. Now I felt almost thankful for the bad hymns. It was good that we should have to lay down our precious refinement at the very doorstep of the church; good that we should be cured at the outset of our inveterate confusion between nature and supernature. The glory of God, and, as our only means to glorifying Him, the salvation of human souls, is the real business of life. What, then, is the value of culture? It is, of course, no new question; but as a living question it was new to me.

Culture in the New Testament

I naturally turned first to the New Testament. Here I found, in the first place, a demand that whatever is most highly valued on the natural level is to be held, as it were, merely on sufferance, and to be abandoned without mercy the moment it conflicts with the service of God. The organs of sense (Matt. v, 29) and of virility (Matt. xix, 12) may have to be sacrificed. And I took it that the least these words could mean was that a life, by natural standards, crippled and thwarted was not only no bar to salvation, but might easily be one of its conditions. The text about hating father and mother (Luke xiv, 26) and our Lord's apparent belittling even of His own natural relation to the Blessed Virgin (Matt. xii, 48) were even more discouraging. I took it for granted that anyone in his senses would hold it better to be a good son than a good critic, and that whatever was said of natural affection was implied *a fortiori* of culture. The worst of all was Philippians iii, 8, where something obviously more relevant to spiritual life than culture can be— "blameless" conformity to the Jewish Law—was described as "muck."

In the second place I found a number of emphatic warnings against every kind of superiority. We were told to become as children (Matt. xviii, 3), not to be called Rabbi (Matt. xxiii, 8), to dread reputation (Luke vi, 26). We are reminded that few of the intelligentsia are called (I Cor. i, 26); that a man must become a fool by secular standards before he can attain real wisdom (I Cor. iii, 18).

Against all this I found some passages that could be interpreted in a sense more favourable to culture. I argued that secular learning might be embodied in the Magi; that the Talents in the parable might conceivably include "talents" in the modern sense of the word; that the miracle at Cana in Galilee by sanctifying an innocent, sensuous pleasure could be taken to sanctify at least a recreational use of culture—mere "entertainment"; and that aesthetic enjoyment of nature was certainly hallowed by our Lord's praise of the lilies. At least some use of science was implied in St Paul's demand that we should perceive the Invisible through the visible (Rom. i, 20). But I was more than doubtful whether his exhortation, "Be not children in mind" (I Cor. xiv, 20), and his boast of "wisdom" among the initiate, referred to anything that we should recognize as secular culture.

On the whole, the New Testament seemed, if not hostile, yet unmistakably cold to culture. I think we can still believe culture to be innocent after we have read the New Testament; I cannot see that we are encouraged to think it important.

Culture in the Christian Tradition

It might be important none the less, for Hooker has finally answered the contention that Scripture must contain everything important or even everything necessary. Remembering this, I continued my researches. If my selection of authorities seems arbitrary, that is due not to a bias but to my ignorance. I used such authors as I happened to know.

Of the great pagans Aristotle is on our side. Plato will tolerate no culture that does not directly or indirectly conduce either to the intellectual vision of the good or the military efficiency of the commonwealth. Joyce and D. H. Lawrence would have fared ill in the Republic.

St Augustine regarded the liberal education which he had undergone in his boyhood as a *dementia*, and wondered why it should be considered *honestior et uberior* than the really useful "primary" education which preceded it (*Conf.* I, xiii). He is extremely distrustful of his own delight in church music (*ibid.*, X, xxxiii). Tragedy is for St Augustine a kind of sore.

Let none reply that the Fathers were speaking of polytheistic literature at a time when polytheism was still a danger. The scheme of values presupposed in most imaginative literature has not become very much more Christian since the time of St Jerome. In *Hamlet* we see everything questioned *except* the duty of revenge. In all Shakespeare's works the conception of good really operative—whatever the characters may say—seems to be purely worldly. In medieval romance, honour and sexual love are the true values; in nineteenth-century fiction, sexual love and material prosperity. In romantic poetry, either the enjoyment of nature (ranging from pantheistic mysticism at one end of the scale to mere innocent sensuousness at the other) or else the indulgence of a *Sehnsucht* [longing] awakened by the past, the distant, and the imagined, but not believed, supernatural. In modern literature, the life of liberated instinct. There are, of course, exceptions: but to study these exceptions would not be to study literature as such, and as a whole. "All literatures," as Newman has said,[1] "are one; they are the voices of the natural man . . . if Literature is to be made a study of human nature, you cannot have a Christian Literature. It is a contradiction in terms to attempt a sinless Literature of sinful man." And I could not doubt that the sub-Christian or anti-Christian values implicit in most literature did actually infect many readers. Only a few days ago I was watching, in some scholarship papers, the results of this infection in a belief that the crimes of such Shakespearian characters as Cleopatra and Macbeth were somehow compensated for by a quality described as their "greatness." This very morning I have read in a critic the remark that if the wicked lovers in Webster's *White Devil* had repented we should hardly have forgiven them. And many people certainly draw from Keats's phrase about negative capability or "love of good and evil" (if the reading which attributes to him such meaningless words is correct) a strange doctrine that experience *simpliciter* is good. I do not say that the sympathetic reading of literature must produce such results, but that it may and often does. If we are to answer the Fathers' attack on pagan literature we must not ground our answer on a belief that literature as a whole has become, in any important sense, more Christian since their days.

In Thomas Aquinas I could not find anything directly bearing on my problem; but I am a very poor Thomist and shall be grateful for correction on this point.

Thomas a Kempis I take to be definitely on the anti-cultural side. In the *Theologia Germanica* (cap. xx) I found that nature's

---

1. *Scope and Nature of University Education*. Discourse 8.

refusal of the life of Christ "happeneth most of all where there are high natural gifts of reason, for that soareth upwards in its own light and by its own power, till at last it cometh to think itself the true Eternal Light." But in a later chapter (xlii) I found the evil of the false light identified with its tendency to love knowledge and discernment more than the object known and discerned. This seemed to point to the possibility of a knowledge which avoided that error.

The cumulative effect of all this was very discouraging to culture. On the other side—perhaps only through the accidental distribution of my ignorance—I found much less.

I found the famous saying, attributed to Gregory, that our use of secular culture was comparable to the action of the Israelites in going down to the Philistines to have their knives sharpened. This seems to me a most satisfactory argument as far as it goes, and very relevant to modern conditions. If we are to convert our heathen neighbours, we must understand their culture. We must "beat them at their own game." But of course, while this would justify Christian culture (at least for some Christians whose vocation lay in that direction) at the moment, it would come very far short of the claims made for culture in our modern tradition. On the Gregorian view culture is a weapon; and a weapon is essentially a thing we lay aside as soon as we safely can.

In Milton I found a disquieting ally. His *Areopagitica* troubled me. He seemed to make too little of the difficulties; and his glorious defence of freedom to explore all good and evil seemed, after all, to be based on an aristocratic preoccupation with great souls and a contemptuous indifference to the mass of mankind which, I suppose, no Christian can tolerate.

Newman's View of Culture

Finally I came to that book of Newman's from which I have already quoted, the lectures on *University Education*. Here at last I found an author who seemed to be aware of both sides

of the question; for no one ever insisted so eloquently as Newman on the beauty of culture for its own sake, and no one ever
so sternly resisted the temptation to confuse it with things
spiritual. The cultivation of the intellect, according to him, is
"for this world";[2] between it and "genuine religion" there is a
"radical difference";[3] it makes "not the Christian . . . but the
gentleman", and looks like virtue "only at a distance";[4] he "will
not for an instant allow" that it makes men better.[5] The "pastors of the Church" may indeed welcome culture because it
provides innocent distraction at those moments of spiritual
relaxation which would otherwise very likely lead to sin; and
in this way it often "draws the mind off from things which
will harm it to subjects worthy of a rational being." But even
in so doing "it does not raise it above nature, nor has any
tendency to make us pleasing to our Maker."[6] In some instances
the cultural and the spiritual value of an activity may even be
in inverse ratio. Theology, when it ceases to be part of liberal
knowledge, and is pursued for purely pastoral ends, gains in
"meritoriousness" but loses in liberality "just as a face worn by
tears and fasting loses its beauty."[7] On the other hand Newman
is certain that liberal knowledge is an end in itself; the whole
of the fourth Discourse is devoted to this theme. The solution
of this apparent antinomy lies in his doctrine that everything,
including, of course, the intellect, "has its own perfection. Things
animate, inanimate, visible, invisible, all are good in their kind,
and have a *best* of themselves, which is an object of pursuit."[8]
To perfect the mind is "an object as intelligible as the cultivation of virtue, while, at the same time, it is absolutely distinct
from it."[9]

2. *Op. cit.*, VIII, p. 227, in Everyman Edition.
3. VII, p. 184, 5.
4. IV, p. 112.
5. IV, p. 111.
6. VII, p. 180.
7. IV, p. 100.
8. IV, p. 113.
9. IV, p. 114.

Whether because I am too poor a theologian to understand the implied doctrine of grace and nature, or for some other reason, I have not been able to make Newman's conclusion my own. I can well understand that there is a kind of goodness which is not moral; as a well-grown healthy toad is "better" or "more perfect" than a three-legged toad, or an archangel is "better" than an angel. In this sense a clever man is "better" than a dull one, or any man than any chimpanzee. The trouble comes when we start asking how much of our time and energy God wants us to spend in becoming "better" or "more perfect" in this sense. If Newman is right in saying that culture has *no* tendency "to make us pleasing to our Maker," then the answer would seem to be, "None." And that is a tenable view: as though God said, "Your *natural* degree of perfection, your place in the chain of being, is my affair: do you get on with what I have explicitly left as your task—righteousness." But if Newman had thought this he would not, I suppose, have written the discourse on "Liberal Knowledge its Own End." On the other hand, it would be possible to hold (perhaps it is pretty generally held) that one of the moral duties of a rational creature was to attain to the highest non-moral perfection it could. But if this were so, then (a) The perfecting of the mind would not be "absolutely distinct" from virtue but part of the content of virtue; and (b) It would be very odd that Scripture and the tradition of the Church have little or nothing to say about this duty. I am afraid that Newman has left the problem very much where he found it. He has clarified our minds by explaining that culture gives us a non-moral "perfection." But on the real problem—that of relating such non-moral values to the duty or interest of creatures who are every minute advancing either to heaven or hell—he seems to help little. "Sensitivity" may be a perfection: but if by becoming sensitive I neither please God nor save my soul, why should I become sensitive? Indeed, what exactly is meant by a "perfection" compatible with utter loss of the end for which I was created?

Christianity and Culture

My researches left me with the impression that there could be no question of restoring to culture the kind of status which I had given it before my conversion. If any constructive case for culture was to be built up it would have to be of a much humbler kind; and the whole tradition of educated infidelity from Arnold to *Scrutiny* appeared to me as but one phase in that general rebellion against God which began in the eighteenth century. In this mood I set about construction.

1. I begin at the lowest and least ambitious level. My own professional work, though conditioned by taste and talents, is immediately motivated by the need for earning my living. And on earning one's living I was relieved to note that Christianity, in spite of its revolutionary and apocalyptic elements, can be delightfully humdrum. The Baptist did not give the tax-gatherers and soldiers lectures on the immediate necessity of turning the economic and military system of the ancient world upside down; he told them to obey the moral law—as they had presumably learned it from their mothers and nurses—and sent them back to their jobs. St Paul advised the Thessalonians to stick to their work (1 Thess. iv, 11) and not to become busybodies (2 Thess. iii, 11). The need for money is therefore *simpliciter* an innocent, though by no means a splendid, motive for any occupation. The Ephesians are warned to work professionally at something that is "good" (Eph. iv, 28). I hoped that "good" here did not mean much more than "harmless," and I was certain it did not imply anything very elevated. Provided, then, that there was a demand for culture, and that culture was not actually deleterious, I concluded I was justified in making my living by supplying that demand—and that all others in my position (dons, schoolmasters, professional authors, critics, reviewers) were similarly justified; especially if, like me, they had few or no talents for any other career—if their "vocation" to a cultural profession consisted in the brute fact of not being fit for anything else.

2. But is culture even harmless? It certainly can be harmful and often is. If a Christian found himself in the position of one inaugurating a new society *in vacuo* he might well decide not to introduce something whose abuse is so easy and whose use is, at any rate, not necessary. But that is not our position. The abuse of culture is already there, and will continue whether Christians cease to be cultured or not. It is therefore probably better that the ranks of the "culture-sellers" should include some Christians—as an antidote. It may even be the duty of some Christians to be culture-sellers. Not that I have yet said anything to show that even the lawful use of culture stands very high. The lawful use might be no more than innocent pleasure; but if the abuse is common, the task of resisting that abuse might be not only lawful but obligatory. Thus people in my position might be said to be "working the thing which is good" in a stronger sense than that reached in the last paragraph.

In order to avoid misunderstanding, I must add that when I speak of "resisting the abuse of culture" I do not mean that a Christian should take money for supplying one thing (culture) and use the opportunity thus gained to supply a quite different thing (homiletics and apologetics). That is stealing. The mere presence of Christians in the ranks of the culture-sellers will inevitably provide an antidote.

It will be seen that I have now reached something very like the Gregorian view of culture as a weapon. Can I now go a step further and find any intrinsic goodness in culture for its own sake?

3. When I ask what culture has done to me personally, the most obviously true answer is that it has given me quite an enormous amount of pleasure. I have no doubt at all that pleasure is in itself a good and pain in itself an evil; if not, then the whole Christian tradition about heaven and hell and the passion of our Lord seems to have no meaning. Pleasure, then, is good; a "sinful" pleasure means a good offered, and accepted, under conditions which involve a breach of the moral

law. The pleasures of culture are not intrinsically bound up with such conditions—though of course they can very easily be so enjoyed as to involve them. Often, as Newman saw, they are an excellent diversion from guilty pleasures. We may, therefore, enjoy them ourselves, and lawfully, even charitably, teach others to enjoy them.

This view gives us some ease. We should, indeed, be justified in propagating good taste on the ground that cultured pleasure in the arts is more varied, intense, and lasting, than vulgar or "popular" pleasure. But we should not regard it as meritorious. In fact, much as we should differ from Bentham about value in general, we should have to be Benthamites on the issue between pushpin and poetry.

Culture as a Repository of Human Values

4. It was noticed above that the values assumed in literature were seldom those of Christianity. Some of the principal values actually implicit in European literature were described as (a) honour, (b) sexual love, (c) material prosperity, (d) pantheistic contemplation of nature, (e) *Sehnsucht* [longing] awakened by the past, the remote, or the (imagined) supernatural, (f) liberation of impulses. These were called "sub-Christian." This is a term of disapproval if we are comparing them with Christian values: but if we take "sub-Christian" to mean "immediately sub-Christian" (i.e., the highest level of merely natural value lying immediately below the lowest level of spiritual value) it may be a term of relative approval. Some of the six values I have enumerated may be sub-Christian in this (relatively) good sense. For (c) and (f) I can make no defence; whenever they are accepted by the reader with anything more than a "willing suspension of disbelief" they must make him worse. But the other four are all two-edged. I may symbolize what I think of them all by the aphorism "Any road out of Jerusalem must also be a road into Jerusalem." Thus:

(a) To the perfected Christian the ideal of honour is simply a temptation. His courage has a better root, and, being learned in Gethsemane, may have no honour about it. But to the man coming up from below, the ideal of knighthood may prove a schoolmaster to the ideal of martyrdom. Galahad is the *son* of Launcelot.

(b) The road described by Dante and Patmore is a dangerous one. But mere animalism, however disguised as "honesty," "frankness," or the like, is not dangerous, but fatal. And not all are qualified to be, even in sentiment, eunuchs for the Kingdom's sake. For some souls romantic love also has proved a schoolmaster.

(d) There is an easy transition from Theism to Pantheism; but there is also a blessed transition in the other direction. For some souls I believe, for my own I remember, Wordsworthian contemplation can be the first and lowest form of recognition that there is something outside ourselves which demands reverence. To return to Pantheistic errors about the nature of this something would, for a Christian, be very bad. But once again, for "the man coming up from below" the Wordsworthian experience is an advance. Even if he goes no further he has escaped the worst arrogance of materialism: if he goes on he will be converted.

(e) The dangers of romantic *Sehnsucht* are very great. Eroticism and even occultism lie in wait for it. On this subject I can only give my own experience for what it is worth. When we are first converted I suppose we think mostly of our recent sins; but as we go on, more and more of the terrible past comes under review. In this process I have not (or not yet) reached a point at which I can honestly repent of my early experiences of romantic *Sehnsucht*. That they were occasions to much that I do repent, is clear; but I still cannot help thinking that this was my abuse of them, and that the experiences themselves contained, from the very first, a wholly good element. Without them my conversion would have been more difficult.

I have dwelt chiefly on certain kinds of literature, not because I think them the only elements in culture that have this value as schoolmasters, but because I know them best; and on literature rather than art and knowledge for the same reason. My general case may be stated in Ricardian terms—that culture is a storehouse of the best (sub-Christian) values. These values are in themselves of the soul, not the spirit. But God created the soul. Its values may be expected, therefore, to contain some reflection or antepast of the spiritual values. They will save no man. They resemble the regenerate life only as affection resembles charity, or honour resembles virtue, or the moon the sun. But though "like is not the same," it is better than unlike. Imitation may pass into initiation. For some it is a good beginning. For others it is not; culture is not everyone's road into Jerusalem, and for some it is a road out.

There is another way in which it may predispose to conversion. The difficulty of converting an uneducated man nowadays lies in his complacency. Popularized science, the conventions or "unconventions" of his immediate circle, party programmes, etc., enclose him in a tiny windowless universe which he mistakes for the only possible universe. There are no distant horizons, no mysteries. He thinks everything has been settled. A cultured person, on the other hand, is almost compelled to be aware that reality is very odd and that the ultimate truth, whatever it may be, *must* have the characteristics of strangeness—*must* be something that would seem remote and fantastic to the uncultured. Thus some obstacles to faith have been removed already.

On these grounds I conclude that culture has a distinct part to play in bringing certain souls to Christ. Not all souls—there is a shorter, and safer, way which has always been followed by thousands of simple affectional natures who begin, where we hope to end, with devotion to the person of Christ.

Has it any part to play in the life of the converted? I think so, and in two ways. (a) If all the cultural values, on the way up to Christianity, were dim antepasts and ectypes of the truth, we can recognize them as such still. And since we must rest and play, where can we do so better than here—in the suburbs of Jerusalem? It is lawful to rest our eyes in moonlight—especially now that we know where it comes from, that it is only sunlight at second hand. (b) Whether the purely contemplative life is, or is not, desirable for any, it is certainly not the vocation of all. Most men must glorify God by doing to His glory something which is not *per se* an act of glorifying but which becomes so by being offered. If, as I now hope, cultural activities are innocent and even useful, then they also (like the sweeping of the room in Herbert's poem) can be done to the Lord. The work of a charwoman and the work of a poet become spiritual in the same way and on the same condition. There must be no return to the Arnoldian or Ricardian view. Let us stop giving ourselves airs.

I said that culture was a storehouse of the best sub-Christian *values*, not the best sub-Christian *virtues*. I meant by this that culture recorded man's striving for those ends which, though not the true end of man (the fruition of God), have nevertheless some degree of similarity to it, and are not so grossly inadequate to the nature of man as, say, physical pleasure, or money. This similarity, of course, while making it less evil to rest in them, makes the danger of resting in them greater and more subtle.

The salvation of souls is a means to the glorifying of God because only saved souls can duly glorify Him. The thing to which, on my view, culture must be subordinated, is not (though it includes) moral virtue, but the conscious direction of all will and desire to a transcendental Person in whom I believe all values to reside, and the reference to Him in every thought and act.

Christian Imagination

Clyde S. Kilby

Aristotle and the classical tradition generally slighted the concept of imagination. According to the classical theory, art is an imitation of what already exists in nature.

We owe our modern emphasis on the imagination as the human capacity responsible for the arts to the Romantic movement of two centuries ago. In this view the imagination is the human faculty that allows us to create something new, to see or feel something familiar in a fresh way, to express an old truth in a new manner, to make a new application of truth to life. Imagination is the great foe of the static and lifeless; its goal (to borrow a great phrase from Matthew Arnold) is to create "a stir and growth everywhere."

In the following essay, Clyde S. Kilby shares his amazement that there is so little evidence of imaginative stir and growth among evangelical Christians. Writing with prophetic fervor, Dr. Kilby marshals evidence that the most common failing of evangelical Christianity is not theological weakness but a failure to exercise the imagination; he argues that our imagination can be unleashed to create stir and growth in every area of our lives.

The Bible: A Work of the Imagination

I want to base what I have to say on three facts which I think indisputable.

The first is that the Bible belongs to literature; that is, it is a piece of art. Does it make any difference that the Book we look upon as holy comes to us in literary form rather than in the form of abstract doctrine or systematic theology? Is the poetry of the Bible a fact plus an artistic decoration? If we summarize the Twenty-third Psalm to declare that God cares for his children as a good shepherd cares for his sheep, do the poetry and the prose summary amount to the same thing? If so, why the poetry in the first place? What change takes place when a piece of poetry is turned into a piece of doctrine or of practical exhortation?

How is the divine inspiration of the Bible related to the great oddity that the longest of the Psalms was written in the form of an acrostic? Was the acrostic form from God or only from the poet? The best authority I know of on the Bible as literature, Richard G. Moulton, points out the large variety of literary forms in the Scripture—epic cycles, orations, dramatic anthems, war anthems, festal hymns, litanies, acrostics, elegies, national anthems, odes, sonnets, epigrams, rhapsodies, vision cycles, encomiums, and so forth. Did God inspire the form or only the content of the Bible? Is its form only a man-made incidental? Should Christian teachers ever encourage students to read the Bible as literature?

Why the "indirection" of saying that a godly man is like a tree planted by the rivers of water, and the extreme exaggeration of saying that the floods and the trees of the fields clap their hands and sing? Are such expressions to be dismissed as mere adornments, embroidery, as feathers—perhaps very pretty ones—that are to be removed from the turkey before its caloric and real meaning can come into existence?

Why isn't the Bible plain, expository, concrete? Why those numerous and difficult paradoxes flung at the reader, such as

Jeremiah 17:9—"The heart is deceitful above all things, and desperately wicked," and Romans 10:10—"With the heart man believeth unto righteousness"? Why the oddity of Paul's prayer in Ephesians 3:19, that Christians may *know* the love of Christ, which *passeth knowledge,* or of Hebrews 4:11, "*Labour . . . to enter into . . . rest,*" and the frequent wordplay even in our Lord's own language? All of which suggests the literary quality of the Bible.

The second indisputable fact is that, because one—and possibly the greatest—ingredient of literature is imagination, we must say that the Bible is an imaginative book. There is no literature without imagination—strong, honest, often daring imagination.

God, the Imaginer

The third indisputable fact is that the greatest artist of all, the greatest imaginer of all, is the one who appears at the opening of Genesis. Esthetics has to do with form, design, harmony, beauty. Perhaps the key word is "form." Now the earth, says Genesis, was without form. God shaped the creation into form—light and darkness, the heavens, the teeming waters, the multitudinous fauna and flora. He shaped birds and roses and morning glories and dandelions, the hippo and the alligator, the mammoth and the giraffe, and man in his own image. And we are told that he looked upon each thing he had shaped and saw that it was good. The whole he saw to be "*very* good." Even after the fall of man the Bible treats nature as beautiful, with God as its maker and wielder. Job, the Psalms and numerous other books celebrate—perhaps to a point a bit scary to some Christians—the intimate relationship of God and his creation. God did not, as so many of us, think that the esthetic was an incidental for leisure time.

And we can also add that God is an architect. The Scripture tells us in no uncertain detail that God put his spirit into the workmen who built Solomon's temple and that it required seventy thousand men to bear burdens and eighty thousand to hew timbers in the mountains, with thirty-three hundred supervisors, over a period of seven years. It is altogether proper, I think, to imagine God telling Solomon how to carve the magnificent lilies to go at the top of the great columns. More glorious still is the final fulfillment God promises in Ephesians 1 where he says (Phillips' translation): "He purposes in his sovereign will that all human history shall be consummated in Christ, that everything that exists in Heaven or earth shall find its perfection and fulfillment in him." No greater esthetic consummation is possible.

The Failure of Imagination in Evangelical Christianity

Now when we look from these three facts to contemporary evangelical Christianity we find a great oddity. The people who spend the most time with the Bible are in large numbers the "foes" of art and the sworn foes of imagination. And I grow in the feeling that these people have quite an astonishing indifference to the created world. Evangelicals hear the great "I am" of God but they are far less aware of the "I am" of his handiwork. Furthermore, when evangelicals dare attempt any art form it is generally done badly.

As to the evangelical's skittishness toward imagination, I have looked into the Scriptures and I cannot find such a prejudice there. One prominent evangelical holds that the triad of truth-goodness-beauty is Greek in origin and the Hebrew concept is only that of the true and the holy. I doubt it. I doubt it primarily because of the glorious beauty I see every day in God's handiwork, but I also doubt it from looking at Scripture. The Revised Standard Version shows ninety uses of the words *beauteous, beautiful, beautify* and *beauty* (the King James Version uses seventy-six of these words), and overwhelmingly in a favorable sense. I see no esthetic difference between God's word and his creative work. Even if his world were purely a functional one, the bee and the flower around which it buzzes would be equally glorious, equally fantastic, equally miraculous.

How can it be that with a God who created birds and the blue of the sky, and who before the foundation of the world wrought out a salvation more romantic than Cinderella, with a Christ who encompasses the highest heaven and deepest hell, with the very hairs of our heads numbered, with God closer than hands and feet, Christians often turn out to have an unenviable corner on the unimaginative and the commonplace?

God shamelessly flings out the rainbow, but some Christians paint the bumpers of their autos black or shun attractive clothing, apparently on the ground that whatever is shiny is sinful. An evangelical sees a picture of a mission board and writes a warning against the worldliness that is creeping in because some of the members have handkerchiefs tucked in their coat pockets. Yet when the Lord talks of espousing Israel (Ezekiel 16:10ff.), he says, "I clothed you also with embroidered cloth . . . I swathed you in fine linen and covered you with silk. And I decked you with ornaments, and put bracelets on your arms, and a chain on your neck. And I put . . . earrings in your ears, and a beautiful crown upon your head. . . . you were decked with gold and silver; and your raiment was of fine linen, and silk, and embroidered cloth."

Evangelical Christians have had one of the purest of motives and one of the worst of outcomes. The motive is never to mislead by the smallest fraction of an iota in the precise nature of salvation, to live it and state it in its utter purity. But the unhappy outcome has too often been to elevate the cliché. The motive is that the gospel shall not be misunderstood, not sullied, not changed in jot or tittle. The outcome has often been merely the reactionary, static and hackneyed.

Take evangelical poetry as an example. Some years ago I sent an inquiry to Christian editors. The all but unanimous response was that they published little or no poetry because what they received was simply trash. The same is more or less true of all our other creative efforts. I had given up the hope of ever seeing an evangelical novel that had any artistic merit when I came upon Olov Hartman's *The Holy Masquerade*.[1] When I began to praise it, someone asked me if the author really was an evangelical! I don't know.

But to come a little closer to home, it appears that the cliché has marked the evangelical's creative efforts because it first marked his thought and life. C. S. Lewis talks about the child who on Easter morning was heard whispering to himself, "Chocolate eggs and Jesus risen." In our desperate evangelical desire for a clear, logical depiction of Jesus risen we have tended to remove the chocolate eggs. P. T. Forsyth describes the glory and expectation that permeated early Christianity when, as he says: "Life received a horizon in place of a boundary. The Christian Faith introduced the witness of the true Infinite, not a mere mathematical infinity or extension, nor a dynamical infinity of energy, but the Infinite of spiritual thought, passion, purpose, and power—the thought and purpose of God, the passion of his holy redeeming love, and the power of the Holy Ghost."

For this expectant and viable Christianity we have somehow come to elevate the trite and the static as our rule. Our efforts to keep the Gospel pure and the way of salvation clear have led us almost exclusively to the expository, frontal, exegetical, functional and prosaic. We want the Word of God and everything pertaining to Christianity to be as simple as two times two, yet over against this stands the Bible itself as example, I believe, of another sort of thing.

There is a simplicity which diminishes and a simplicity which enlarges, and evangelicals have too often chosen the wrong one. The first is that of the cliché—simplicity with mind and heart removed. The other is that of art. The first falsifies by its exclusions, the second encompasses. The first silently denies the multiplicity and grandeur of creation, salvation and indeed all

---

1. Olov Hartman, *The Holy Masquerade* (Grand Rapids: Eerdmans, 1964).

things. The second symbolizes and celebrates them. The first tries to take the danger out of Christianity and with the danger often removes the actuality. The second suggests the creative and sovereign God of the universe with whom there are no impossibilities. The contrast suggests that *not* to imagine is what is sinful. The symbol, the figure, the image, the parable—in short, the artistic method—so pungent in the Lord's teaching and acting, are often noteworthy for their absence in ours. Is this not a case of humanism far more reprehensible than the sort of humanism we often decry?

In an article discussing religious writing, Sydney Harris told of seeing in *The Saturday Evening Post* a cartoon of a boy sitting at the piano. The boy's father was wincing and saying to the mother, "He's trustworthy, loyal, helpful, and friendly . . . and untalented." Harris says the religious manuscripts he receives are the most painful ones he looks at and that ninety-nine out of one hundred religious books are useless. And what applies to our writing very often also marks our whole way of life. One very wrong thing we have done is to see the unsaved as objects, something destitute not only of salvation but of any worthy thoughts about God. An adequate imagination would have saved us from the mistake of turning men into things.

Even the pulpit, or so it seems to me, is often marked by a strange negativism. I have known at least one devoted pastor who stated that he would never use an illustration other than those in the Scriptures. Did Christ ever by the least hint suggest any such method? Did he ever suggest that he meant to exhaust the parabolic and the illustrative? Did Christ not instead confirm the Arabian adage that the best teacher is the one who can change men's ears to eyes? Much of the preaching I have heard, though it faithfully repeats the Christian message, bears little resemblance to that of Christ. Phillips' translation of Mark 11:19 says that Christ's teaching had "captured the imagination of the people." I seldom have such an experience from the sermons I hear. I get the impression that Christ's parables generally developed from a quick look at whatever object was at hand—bushel measures, a house with a shaky foundation, dowry coins worn by a woman, sheep, a common flower. It seems to me no less astonishing how little of this sort of thing rubs off on men in our evangelical seminaries.

Pastors seem beset with the conviction that statement is the only correct way. I am starkly admonished, for instance, to love, as though I did not know this fully as well as the preacher, as though I had not already beaten myself a thousand times with this cudgel. What I need instead is the opening of some little door through which I can enter, some little path through the tangle of my own selfishness, some glimpse of a person who practiced love last week. But what is the use of repeating to me, as though my soul were blind, what my conscience and the Holy Spirit habitually tell me?

Learning to Live Imaginatively

One critic said that Robert Frost was good as a poet because he thought of himself as a farmer and that, had he ever once called himself a poet, he would at that moment have become a literary shoemaker. The phrase "esthetic distance" means that the human attitude must prevail over the professional one. We need esthetic distance in our Christian way of life. St. Paul tells us to be instant in season and out of season, but he also tells us to be anxious in nothing. Our excuse for our esthetic failure has often been that we must be about the Lord's business, the assumption being that the Lord's business is never esthetic.

We must not take something infinitely large, glorious and precious and, even unintentionally, diminish it to what is small, fixed and patent. As evangelicals we wish never to misrepresent God and salvation. Yet some of us have developed an ear as big as a barn door in our practice of pitching the coin on the counter and listening not only to its Christian ring but expecting also the tinkle of our own favorite evangelical language. The cliché deadens whatever it touches, however good or great. It is the call to indifference, to the slavery of the commonplace, to nonthought and nonfeeling. Evangelicalism, I believe, is greatly in need of fresh and meaningful imagination.

A great principle of art and esthetics is that of the necessity of renewal. The freshness of being, says Alfred North White- head, evaporates under mere repetition; a static value, however good, suffers from claustrophobia. God has created a world with the paradoxical qualities of utter law and utter unique- ness. Orthodox Christians accent the first but almost ignore the second. The fall of man can hardly be more forcefully felt than simply in noting what we all do with a fresh snowfall or the first buds of spring. On Monday they fill us with delight and meaning, and on Tuesday we ignore them. No amount of shouting to us that this is all wrong changes the fact for very long. Detachment and the upside-down view are a constant necessity to circumvent the ruts, the tags, the clichés every- where awaiting us. Only some esthetic power akin to God's own creativity has the capability for renewal, for giving us the power to see.

Art is a means of renewing our eyes and our hearts. I am not here talking simply about what goes on in the art or music department of a college; I am talking of a way, and I think a God-given way, for us to recognize his voice and his world. All institutions and practices tend to diminish their center and accent their periphery. The genuinely holy act of yesterday is only too easily hypostatized into the *act* minus the holiness, of today. One of Jonathan Blanchard's favorite phrases was *cor- ruptio optima pessima* —The best thing, when not used in the right way, becomes the most loathsome.

Perhaps our hymns are an example. We mummify them into books and most of us sing them without the least notice of their meaning. John Newton and William Cowper formed an agreement to write a hymn each Sunday night covering their experiences of the previous week. They accepted, as we do not, the exhortation of the psalmist to sing to the Lord a new song.

With this meager mention of the principle of renewal let me go on to another and final principle that I believe we should consider. Perhaps the deepest thrust of the esthetic is toward the expression of being. "Life is a petty thing," says Ortega, "unless it is moved by the indomitable urge to extend its boundaries. Only in proportion as we are desirous of living more do we really live." Artists tell us that the creative process is more of an exploration and a profound learning than it is the production of a canvas or a piece of music. It is an act filled at once with joy and pain.

In the best essay I've ever read on the creative act, Stephen Spender says: "I dread writing poetry . . . a poem is a terrible journey . . . the writing of a poem brings one face to face with one's own personality with all its familiar and clumsy limitations. In every other phase of existence, one can exercise the orthodoxy of a conventional routine. . . . In Poetry, one is wrestling with a god." If our evangelical preaching efforts at creativeness had this quality of search to the point of knowing really who we are, I think a different situation might prevail.

That man and life are almost pure mysteries ought to permeate our constant thoughts. Mark Van Doren says that man is "a nervous animal, straining to comprehend what he contains, straining even to contain it."

I think one implication of this is that we ought to assume that students know more than we estimate they do. Nothing is more destructive in the classroom than telling students what they already know. The same is true for the sermon. Life is never static. It is dynamic.

Keeping orthodox is a high and necessary aim. But one of the best ways, I think, of destroying our orthodoxy is to make "keeping orthodox" an all-encompassing and tight-lipped aim. Orthodoxy is better retained when regarded as a by-product of a far higher aim, the love of God and the expectant search into his truth.

Toward a Biblical View of Aesthetics

Frank E. Gaebelein

The Protestant Reformation bequeathed to the Christian tradition a great heritage when it established the principle that the Bible alone is the final authority for religious belief and practice. From this fountainhead has flowed an enduring legacy of scholarship in which the content of the Bible is allowed to permeate scholarly discourse in the disciplines of human thought.

That stream of biblically-based scholarship has not, however, flowed everywhere with equal abundance. I know of no area in which the Bible has been slighted as a source of truth more than in scholarly writing about the arts. The prominence given to biblical data in many of the essays that follow is atypical of published scholarship on the topic of aesthetics. The following essay by Frank E. Gaebelein is a roadmap to much of the territory that will be covered by subsequent essays.

The Relationship Between Christianity and the Arts

At the root of evangelical Christianity is its biblical heritage. The great company of Christians who hold the basic doctrines of the Gospel are pre-eminently people of the Book. For them, the written Word is the inspired source of knowledge of their divine Saviour and Lord; in its pages they find what they are to believe about God and what duty he requires of them. They are obligated to see every aspect of life in relation to the incarnate Word and to the written Word that bears witness to him.

"But," thoughtful Christians are asking, "what about the relation of our biblical heritage to literature and the arts?" What about it indeed, in these days when none of us is exempt from the influence of the mass media and other powerful aesthetic forces?

Some think commitment to the Holy Scriptures as the inspired Word of God and the rule for all of life is a hindrance to aesthetic expression and appreciation. Complete fidelity to Scripture, they say, leaves little place for anything but religious use of the arts; they consider the arts as generally worldly and thus outside the bounds of biblical truth, mere marginal activities for those determined to be about the Father's business. But this is wrong in principle, because it assumes a gap between sacred and secular truth and thus violates the unity of truth. Truth, though on its highest level incarnate in Christ and expressed in the Bible, is not confined to religion. All truth is God's.

In a baccalaureate sermon entitled "Secularism and the Joy of Belief," President Nathan Pusey of Harvard spoke of *"the cultural ignorance* [italics added] which comes from neglect of the Scriptures, unexamined persistence in immature conceptions of God . . . above all perhaps the loss of the practice of prayer."[1] If anything, the biblical heritage of evangelical Christianity affords a head start in the arts; it does not inhibit their practice and appreciation. Through the ages Scripture has been the single greatest influence on art. It sheds more light upon the creative process and the use of the arts than any other

---

1. Nathan M. Pusey, *The Age of the Scholar* (Cambridge: Harvard University Press, 1963).

source, because in it are found the great truths about man as well as God that are at the wellsprings of art.

This leads to a challenge. Among the rank and file of evangelical Christians, aesthetic standards are generally low. The evidence is abundant. The pictures on the walls, the books on the shelves, the records played—so many of these things are products of a sentimental, pietistic dilution of the aesthetic integrity that should mark the Christian use of art. But, and this also must be said, evangelicals are not alone in their habituation to the mediocre in art and literature. A similar kind of cultural illiteracy runs through much of liberal Protestantism and indeed through most of American life today.

The need among Christians is not for avoidance of literature and art they do not like or understand but for responsible criticism of it by believers who know the Scriptures and who also know the arts. T. S. Eliot has said, "What I believe to be incumbent upon all Christians is the duty of maintaining consciously certain standards and criteria of criticism over and above those applied by the rest of the world. . . ." And he adds: "We must remember that the greater part of our current reading matter is written for us by people who have no real belief in a supernatural order."[2] Eliot's words apply, of course, to forms of art other than literature. Observe that he says, not that Christians should not read what is written out of a purely naturalistic context, but rather that they should measure it by Christian criteria. The condemnation out of ignorance in which some Christians indulge simply is not honest.

The Bible: Basis for a Christian Philosophy of the Arts

This leads to the all-important question of Christian criteria for the practice and criticism of art. Here the basic document

2. T. S. Eliot, "Religion and Literature," reprinted in the present volume.

is the Bible. Not that the classical writers like Plato, Aristotle, and Longinus, and all the other non-Christian critics down through the centuries should be neglected. Under common grace these thinkers have some very important and even indispensable things to say. But an essential requirement of good scholarship is the use of primary sources. And for a Christian aesthetic, the primary source is Scripture. Surely the chief reason for our confusion about the meaning and use of art is the neglect of the biblical pattern for art through a one-sided emphasis on secondary, extra-biblical sources.

There are two approaches to the Bible as the basis for a Christian aesthetic. The first is to examine all its references to art, most of which are to music. It is significant, by the way, that according to the Book of Revelation, which John Milton called "a seven-fold chorus of Hallelujahs and harping symphonies," artistic beauty is prominent in heaven.

The other approach is through biblical doctrine. Consider, then, the very beginning of everything. This we must do because true art is not merely imitative, as the Greeks taught, but also in its creaturely way creative. And it is not Plato or Aristotle or any other non-biblical writer but *only* Scripture that gives us authoritative knowledge about origins and the creation of man.

What the Bible says about God's creative activity and man's origin and fall and redemption is centrally related to a Christian aesthetic. But to understand that relationship we must look closely at the concept of God as the great Maker of all things and of man as his creation.

The Doctrinal Foundations: Creation, Fall, and Redemption

In a remarkable book about the relation of the human to the divine creative process, Dorothy Sayers reminds us that the author of Genesis points in his first chapter to one basic thing about God: that he creates. "The characteristic common to God and man is apparently just this: The desire and the ability to make things."[3] Moreover, the pattern for this making is the relation of Father, Son, and Spirit in the Trinity. So the image of God in man has its creative, its "making" implications. God is the great Maker, the only true Creator, from whom all other creative activity is derived. That we are made in his image is probably the greatest thing ever said of man, and takes us deep into the nature of our human creative ability. For one of the marks of the image of God that we bear is that we, too, in our creaturely way, are makers. And in no human activity is this aspect of God's image more evident than in our making of art.

Six times the first chapter of Genesis tells us that God looked upon what he had made and "it was good." Then we read that when Creation was finished "God saw everything that he had made and it was very good." God is, as the ancient creed says, the "Maker of heaven and earth," and what he made was "very good."

There are great spiritual depths in the Hebrew word for "good" in Genesis 1, and its connotations surely include the concept of beauty. Some contemporary artists and critics today are inclined to downgrade the place of beauty in art. The cult of the ugly has its disciples. But Scripture links beauty to God and approves the beautiful. Moreover, by very definition aesthetics is the philosophy of beauty. Art cannot possibly be divorced from beauty. Beauty is inherent in the universe. If "the heavens declare the glory of God and the firmament showeth his handiwork," as they so gloriously do, it is with a beauty that transcends in majesty, power, and diversity all the works of men. The problem is that there are many, some Christians among them, whose idea of beauty is not broad enough to include dissonance in music or big enough to go beyond what is merely pretty in painting or blandly nice in poetry and literature. Beauty has various manifestations. It can be strong

---

3. Dorothy L. Sayers, *The Mind of the Maker* (1941; reprint ed., Westport, Conn.: Greenwood Press), p. 17.

and astringent; it has disturbing and shocking as well as calm and peaceful moods.

Man in his making of things follows the pattern of the mind of the triune Maker of all things. This concept shows us the incarnational aspect of art—its down-to-earth here-and-now-ness, in which the idea takes to itself a real body, an actual form, whatever the aesthetic medium may be. In his making of art man does indeed reflect the image of God. To hold this firmly is the best answer to the irresponsibility of those Christians who turn their backs upon the arts as mere luxuries, frivolous side issues that are not to be taken seriously in these urgent days.

Nevertheless, some of the distinguished Anglican and Catholic thinkers (like Dorothy Sayers) who have written so helpfully about the incarnational aspect of art and the analogy of human to divine creation are open to the criticism of not giving enough attention to the relation between man's creative faculty and his sinfulness. They stress Genesis 1 with insufficient reference to Genesis 3.

For there is another side to the idea of man's aesthetic capability as a reflection of the image of God. This side has to do with man's fall through sin, the primordial tragedy that resulted in the marring of God's image in man. No biblical thinker, whether in aesthetics or in any other field, can afford to slight the fact that, because of the fall, man has an innate bent toward sin, and that this bent is reflected in what he does. Christians know how God has provided for the redemption of fallen man through our Lord Jesus Christ. They also know that the redeemed are not now exempt from sin and that, while in the inner man they have been restored, they too bear the marks of the fall in their lives—and in their art.

To be sure, God in his grace enables artists, including some great non-Christian ones, to produce glorious works. Yet there is among us finite men no perfect artist. The only perfect artist is God, and the only perfect works of art are his original creation and his written Word, and the only perfection in art is exemplified by Christ, the God-man, who in his mastery of spoken word spoke as never man spoke. Knowing these things should keep us from arrogant pride, of which artists have their share.

Most of us, evangelicals included, use the words "create" and "creative" too loosely. God is the only true Creator, and his Son is the only truly creative man. For all others, the words "create" and "creative" must be used with reservations and with the awareness that their application to man is only an accommodation. To say, as Dr. Rosemary Park did in her inaugural address as president of Barnard College in 1963, that "truth not only is to be uncovered but created" is a perilous misconception akin to the Promethean error.

Consider, then, fallen man—the artist included—and his redemption. It is not art—music, painting, poetry, drama, or whatever it may be—that can be redeemed but only the man or woman who makes it. Christ did not die for things; he died for persons. Yet redemption does make a difference in art through the kind of person it makes the artist. Bach was a Christian. No one knows just what his work would have been if he were an unbeliever, but it is safe to say that it would not have reached so high as it does in the *St. Matthew Passion* and in the B-Minor Mass. Or take Rembrandt. Would the largest category of his works (including some of his very greatest) have been on biblical and religious subjects had he been an atheist? And what about Milton? Could an unbelieving man have written *Paradise Lost?* Or, to look at a modern example, what of T. S. Eliot?

The point must not be pressed too hard, lest we become involved in judging the faith of others. Only God knows those who are his. And we must always grant that the sovereign God is great enough to allow unredeemed men to achieve supremacy in the arts; that he has indeed done this is a fact of which all of us, Christians and non-Christians, are beneficiaries. The honest thing for the Christian student of the arts is simply to say that the God who "makes his sun rise on the evil and on the good and sends rain on the just and on the unjust" does as he wills, and then to rejoice in the special qualities of the work of the redeemed artist that might not be there were he not a Christian.

Whether art is made by Christians or non-Christians, all aesthetic achievement that has integrity comes from God, who gives men talent as he wills. Therefore, it is to be enjoyed with gratitude to the great Giver of every good and perfect gift. Art, though it has tragic depths, is not in itself tragic. The artist reflects the mind of the Divine Maker, and when he created, "the morning stars sang together and all the sons of God shouted for joy." Art may be, as Calvin Seerveld says, a happy act of praise to the Creator, a humble celebration of his greatness. In that way it makes its own noble contribution to man's chief end, which is "to glorify God and enjoy him forever."

In the Beginning, God Created

Leland Ryken

The Book of Genesis is the Bible's "book of beginnings." Its overall purpose is to tell us how the world and the human race first appeared, how evil began, and how God's dealings with people and a nation became established.

Regarding a Christian philosophy of the arts we can also say un-equivocally that it all started with Genesis. In Genesis 1–3 we find an impressive (though not complete) foundation for a biblical aesthetic. The main pillars of that foundation are the doctrines of creation, the image of God in people, recreation or leisure, and the fall.

Creation

The Bible begins with a truly impressive artistic perform-ance. It is the story of creation, filled with mystery and divine creative power. Even in its form, the story is an artistic wonder. Each of the six days of creation falls into a discernible pattern: announcement ("and God said . . ."), command ("let there be . . . ," "let it be gathered . . . ," "let it bring forth . . ."), re-port ("and it was so," "and God made"), evaluation ("and God saw that it was good"), and placement in a temporal frame ("And there was evening and there was morning, a . . . day").

There is also an abundance of repeated words and phrases in the story. And there is artistic balance between three pairs of items: on the first three days God creates, respectively, light, sky and sea, and dry land and vegetation; on the next three days he fills each setting with its corresponding agents, in the same sequence of the first three days—light bearers, birds and sea creatures, land animals and man.

The telling of the story is so artistic, in fact, that commentators have found it natural to talk about Genesis 1 in terms of music and painting. Genesis 1, we are told, strikes us "like a mysterious song," like "a symphony," "a festal celebration," "a litany," "a divine liturgy." And like a painter working on a canvas, God assembles one detail after another until the picture stands completed before our gaze.

All of this is to say that the imaginative *form* of Genesis 1 is itself part of the *meaning*, which is, of course, God's creation of the world. The meaning has been incarnated in the form. The artistry is not something added to the meaning, it is part of it. Nor does the writer step outside of his story to state his theme as a proposition. All of this, in turn, illustrates how the Bible contributes to aesthetic theory by its example, not simply by its doctrine. The most emphatic thing we can say along these lines is that the Bible does not distrust the imagination and artistic form as a means of expressing the truth.

When we begin to deduce doctrine from this story of creation we find a great deal that touches upon the arts. We begin with the great premise that God created the physical world and that he created it "very good." This means that earthly, human reality is good in principle. It is real because God made it. Human experience in the world is worthy of study and understanding and love.

All of the arts feed upon the physical world around us, including, of course, the social world of people. The storyteller and dramatist write about the dynamics of human behavior, both individually and communally. The poet is concerned with the world of physical sensations and the inner life of the human emotions. The musician uses physical objects to produce sounds, and in the process often touches powerfully on the world of human emotions. And the visual artist works with very tangible materials to produce images that we experience with our eyes.

How do we know that these preoccupations of the writer, musician, and painter are a legitimate Christian pursuit? For an answer we need turn no further than the first page of the Bible, where we find God creating the earthly order of things and pronouncing it good in principle.

Equally important is the precise kind of world that God created. We need use only our senses to know that God created a world that is beautiful as well as functional. From a purely utilitarian point of view, God did not have to make a world filled with beautiful colors and symmetrical forms and varied textures and harmonious sounds. What we find here is not a functional mind but an artistic imagination at work. The kinds of things that God made are a model for the kinds of things that artists and musicians and writers should make and that all people should delight in. The doctrine of creation affirms as good the artistic concern of both the creative artist and the audience with beauty, form, and artistry.

The key biblical text in this regard is Genesis 2:9, which tells us that when God created Paradise he "made to grow every tree that is pleasant to the sight and good for food." Mankind's perfect environment, in other words, satisfies a dual criterion, both aesthetic and utilitarian. The conditions for human well-being have never changed from that moment in Paradise. People live by beauty as well as truth.

The Image of God in People

The climax of the Bible's creation story is the creation of man. The crucial ingredient of this part of the story is that "God created man in his own image" (Gen. 1:27).

Exactly what does this mean? When we first read about the image of God in Genesis 1, we have as yet heard nothing about God as redeemer or the God of providence or the covenant God or the God of moral truth. The one thing that we know about God is that he is "maker of heaven and earth," as the Apostles' Creed puts it. In its immediate narrative context, then, the doctrine of the image of God in people emphasizes that people, like God, are creators.

The classic study of what the image of God in people means to aesthetic theory is Dorothy L. Sayers' book, *The Mind of the Maker.* Sayers writes,

> How then can [man] be said to resemble God? Is it his immortal soul, his rationality, his self-consciousness, his free will, or what, that gives him a claim to this rather startling distinction? A case may be argued for all these elements in the complex nature of man. But had the author of *Genesis* anything particular in his mind when he wrote? It is observable that in the passage leading up to the statement about man, he has given no detailed information about God. Looking at man, he sees in him something essentially divine, but when we turn back to see what he says about the original upon which the "image" of God was modeled, we find only the single assertion, "God created." The characteristic common to God and man is apparently that: the desire and the ability to make things.[1]

What does the image of God in people say about the artistic enterprise? It affirms human creativity as something good, since it is an imitation of one of God's acts and perfections. Abraham Kuyper has written, "As image-bearer of God, man possesses the possibility both to create something beautiful, and to delight in it. . . . The world of sounds, the world of forms, the world of tints, and the world of poetic ideas, can have no other source than God; and it is our privilege as bearers

1. Dorothy L. Sayers, *The Mind of the Maker* (Elnora, N.Y.: Meridian Press, 1956), p. 34.

of His image, to have a perception of this beautiful world, artistically to reproduce, and humanly to enjoy it."[2]

Can a student justify the time involved in taking a course in fiction writing or poetry writing? Can a person in good conscience spend hours painting a picture? Is it worthwhile to take two hours to attend something as non-utilitarian as a concert or an art gallery? The answer from Genesis 1 is clear: to be creative in the arts, and to enter into the creativity of others, is to exercise the image of God within oneself.

The doctrine of the image of God in people also provides a theological explanation for why people create. The creative impulse is an expression of human likeness to God. Laurence Perrine has said that "the primal artistic act was God's creation of the universe out of chaos, shaping the formless into form; and every artist since, on a lesser scale, has sought to imitate him—by selection and arrangement to reduce the chaotic in experience to a meaningful and pleasing order."[3]

When God made people in his image, he also conferred upon them a command to rule the earthly order in the name of God: "let them have dominion over the fish of the sea, and over the birds of the air, and over the cattle, and over all the earth . . ." (Gen. 1:26). This is popularly known as "the cultural mandate"—a command to subdue and control the entire earthly order for the glory of God. Applied to the arts, this doctrine affirms the artist's concern to bring human experience in the world under the purview of human understanding. Chad Walsh has written that the artist "can honestly see himself as a kind of earthly assistant to God (so can the carpenter), carrying on the delegated work of creation, making the fullness of creation fuller." The cultural mandate also renders legitimate the reader's or listener's or viewer's immersion in the world of art and human culture.

2. Abraham Kuyper, *Calvinism* (Grand Rapids: Eerdmans, 1943), pp. 142, 156-57.

3. Laurence Perrine, ed., *Sound and Sense: An Introduction to Poetry*, 3rd. ed., (New York: Harcourt, Brace & World, 1971), chap. 14.

The link between divine and human creativity also helps to define art. Throughout the history of Western art there have been two main theories of what art is. The classical theory that art is an imitation of reality dominated aesthetic theory from the time of Aristotle through the eighteenth century. The other theory is that art is a created artifact, to be explained not so much as a copy of real life but as a new imaginative world that the artist creates.

Christians have championed both views. C. S. Lewis came to the conclusion that "if I have read the New Testament aright, it leaves no room for 'creativeness' even in a modified or metaphorical sense. . . . An author should never conceive himself as bringing into existence beauty or wisdom which did not exist before, but simply and solely as trying to embody in terms of his own art some reflection of eternal Beauty and Wisdom. Our criticism would therefore from the beginning group itself with some existing theories of poetry against others."[4]

But such a theory of art fails to do justice to the importance of early Genesis. The Renaissance poet Sir Philip Sidney gave a classic expression to the theory of the poet as creator when he wrote that we should "give right honor to the heavenly Maker of that maker [i.e., the human artist], who, having made man to his own likeness, set him beyond and over all the works of that second nature [i.e., the world of the artistic imagination]."[5] Dorothy Sayers comments, "This word—this idea of Art as *creation* is, I believe, the one important contribution that Christianity has made to aesthetics."[6] The biblical doctrine of creation, coupled with the idea that people are made in the image of God, has allowed Christian artists and users of art to revel in the creation of a new thing for which there is no previously existing model that is adequate to explain the new thing.

4. C. S. Lewis, *Christian Reflections* (Grand Rapids: Eerdmans, 1967), p. 7.

5. Sir Philip Sidney, *Apology for Poetry*.

6. Dorothy L. Sayers, "Towards a Christian Aesthetic," in *Unpopular Opinions* (London: Victor Gollancz, 1946), p. 37.

There is even implicit in this doctrinal matrix a methodology for enjoying and using the arts. Traditionally Christians have defended their immersion in the arts on the basis of its didacticism (teaching ability) or its realism. I believe that the Christian doctrine of creativity suggests something else, namely, that works of art have value because they are imaginative and because they are the product of someone else's creativity and ultimately of God's image implanted in the artist.

The Christian doctrine of creation also justifies the artist's and writer's preoccupation with "images" of reality. Christians regard the created world as an expression or image of God's character and attributes, and they regard people as made in the image of God. This should lead us to question again the classical obsession with art as an imitation of external reality. In the words of Dorothy Sayers, ". . . let us take note of a new word that has crept into the argument by way of Christian theology—the word *Image*. Suppose, having rejected the words 'copy,' 'imitation' and 'representation' as inadequate, we substitute the word 'image' and say that what the artist is doing is *to image forth* something . . . which, by being an image, *expresses* that which it images."[7]

Recreation and Leisure

The last thing that God did when he created was to rest. The precise wording in the Genesis text is important here:

> And on the seventh day God finished his work which he had done, and he rested on the seventh day from all his work which he had done. So God blessed the seventh day and hallowed it, because on it God rested from all his work which he had done in creation (Gen. 2:2-3).

What is the meaning of God's rest? The Christian tradition has emphasized what is surely the main meaning: God's rest on

7. Sayers, "Christian Aesthetic."

the seventh day is the origin and model for a day of worship in every week.

But is this all that it means? What did God do on his day of rest? So far as we can understand the mystery of divine rest, we must conclude that God contemplated and delighted in the perfection of his creation. Abraham Kuyper comments, "After the Creation, God saw that all things were good. Imagine that every human eye were closed and every human ear stopped up, even then the beautiful remains, and God sees it and hears it."[8] In other words, God's rest after creation sanctified the aesthetic acts of celebration and enjoyment.

God's rest after creation suggests something of the nature of recreation for people. It is, to begin, a resting from work and acquisitiveness. Much of the restorative effect of recreation comes from the way in which a person is freed from utilitarian ends and can perform a pleasurable activity for its own sake. As God's rest after creation suggests, life is built on a rhythm in which work and rest or recreation alternate.

At its best, recreation is a quality of mind and soul. Its goal is human joy and satisfaction. As God contemplated the work of his creativity, he found it good; made in God's image, we, too, can be satisfied by the creative work of the artist and can find it good. If we are looking for an answer to the question, "How can I read literature or listen to music or look at art to the glory of God?" we can say on the basis of Genesis 2, "By enthusiastically enjoying the beauty of the arts, recognizing God as the ultimate source of all such creativity and beauty."

Josef Pieper has stated the Christian case for leisure thus:

> Leisure . . . is a mental and spiritual attitude—it is not simply the result of external factors, it is not the inevitable result of spare time, a holiday, a weekend or a vacation. It is, in the first place, an attitude of mind, a condition of soul. . . . Compared with the exclusive ideal of work as toil, leisure appears . . . as

8. Kuyper, *Calvinism*, p. 156.

an attitude of contemplative "celebration." . . . Leisure draws its vitality from affirmation. . . . We may read in the first chapter of Genesis that God "ended his work which he had made" and "behold, it was very good." In leisure, man too celebrates the end of his work by allowing his inner eye to dwell for a while upon the reality of the Creation. He looks and he affirms: it is good.[9]

Aristotle in the *Politics* says something curious about leisure. The Spartans, according to Aristotle, remained strong while they were at war, but they collapsed once they had acquired an empire. Their fatal flaw was that they did not know how to use the leisure that peace brought to them. Is our own culture really any different?

One of the great tragedies of our own day is that people do not know how to use their leisure time in enriching ways. In the Christian community the problem seems to be that we have no adequate theory of leisure and play. Regarding recreation as something frivolous or ignoble, Christians often sink to mediocrity by default. Paul Elmen, in his book *The Restoration of Meaning to Contemporary Life*,[10] analyzes the cultural malaise that is perhaps most evident in many people's leisure time: boredom, the search for distraction, the fear of spending time by oneself, sensuality, escape into comedy, violence, and the appeal of horror ("the fun of being frightened"). Pascal made a comment that I have seen verified again and again: "All the unhappiness of men arises from one single fact, that they cannot stay quietly in their own chamber."[11]

In such a context, surely, C. S. Lewis' comments about the moral significance of choosing good leisure pursuits have a particular relevance: "Our leisure, even our play, is a matter of serious concern. There is no neutral ground in the universe;

---

9. Josef Pieper, *Leisure: The Basis of Culture* (New York: New American Library, 1963), pp. 40-43.

10. (Garden City: Doubleday, 1958).

11. Blaise Pascal, *Pensées*, II, 139.

every square inch, every split second, is claimed by God and counterclaimed by Satan. . . . It is a serious matter to choose wholesome recreations."[12] Leisure, in other words, is unavoidably an arena of choice within which people exercise good or bad stewardship. Frank Gaebelein has said that "the very word 'leisure' implies responsibility. . . . Leisure and working time are equally to be accounted for to the Lord."

The key to the wise use of leisure is education, broadly defined. We do in our leisure time what we have learned to do. If left to ourselves, the law of mental laziness takes its course and our horizons remain rather narrow. Aristotle claimed that the goal of education was the wise use of leisure time. That may be an overstatement, but one of the best tests of whether a person is truly educated is what he does with his leisure time. According to Milton, a "complete and generous education" is one that equips a person to perform "all the offices, both private and public" that life affords.[13] In our economically oriented society we know how to perform our public roles, chiefly the one our job requires. But what about the private role of living an enriching life of the mind and imagination?

An education is adequate only if it equips a person to spend an evening doing something more than listening to the kind of music or watching the type of television program that most people in our culture are satisfied with. What I am saying here is particularly relevant to college students. Compared with the college years, no other phase of life is likely to provide quite the same luxury of opportunity to develop one's capacity for meaningful kinds of recreation. Our mind is a mansion; its furniture depends on us.

After the Fall

Thus far all that I have said about the arts has been positive. But unfortunately for the human race Genesis 1 and 2 are not

12. Lewis, *Christian Reflections*, pp. 33-34.
13. John Milton, *Of Education*.

self-contained; they are part of a triad of stories that includes Genesis 3, the story of the fall of mankind. The biblical doctrine of the fall introduces a whole further set of considerations into a Christian philosophy of the arts.

The fall drastically affected human nature. The New Testament commentary on the fall suggests that it was a fall from both knowledge or truth (Col. 3:10) and "true righteousness and holiness" (Eph. 4:24). This means, right away, that we cannot automatically assume that a work of created art is either truthful in its vision of life or moral in its impact on an audience. What Newman said about literature is true of all the arts in a fallen world: "It is a contradiction in terms to attempt a sinless Literature of sinful man."

The human imagination suffered from the fall as severely as the rest of human nature. Already in Genesis 6:5 we read that "The Lord saw that the wickedness of man was great in the earth, and that every imagination of the thoughts of his heart was only evil continually." Two chapters later we read that "the imagination of man's heart is evil from his youth" (Gen. 8:21).

To confirm this pessimistic assessment of the human imagination we need look no farther than the current movie offerings of any major city (fewer than five percent of the movies in recent years have been suitable for children) or the paperback novels of a typical department store. The English poet William Wordsworth, with his gift of prophecy, sounded this alarm over the debasement of art a century and a half before the appearance of X-rated movies and the popular music of our day:

For a multitude of causes, unknown to former times, are now acting with a combined force to blunt the discriminating power of the mind, and, unfitting it for all voluntary exertion, to reduce it to a state of almost savage torpor. . . . To this tendency of life and manners the literature and theatrical exhibitions of the country have conformed themselves. The invaluable works of our elder writers, I had almost said the works of Shakespeare and Milton, are driven into neglect by frantic novels . . . and deluges of idle and extravagant stories. . . . When I think upon this degrading thirst after outrageous stimulation, I am almost ashamed to have spoken of the feeble endeavour made in these volumes to counteract it.[14]

Wordsworth, of course, is describing the *abuse* of the arts, not the arts in principle; yet it is this very abuse that is the issue for a Christian viewer or reader or listener.

What exactly are the effects of the fall on the artistic enterprise? Essentially the fall imposes on the Christian artist and Christian consumer of art the task of aesthetically testing the spirits to see if they are of God. On the intellectual side this involves weighing the ideational content and world view of a work of art by the standard of biblical truth. Morally it involves assessing whether a work has a moral or immoral effect, as judged by a biblical standard of morality. For the Christian artist it imposes an obligation to express truth rather than falsehood, to add to the world's beauty and joy rather than its ugliness and despair, and to avoid the arrogance of assuming that every manifestation of his or her creativity is automatically either truthful or moral.

The fall is the ultimate theological explanation for the objections against the arts that have never been absent from Western civilization since Plato nor from the Christian church since the Church Fathers. Basically the objections can be summarized in six basic contentions:

1. The arts are either deficient in truth and knowledge, or they actually teach error.
2. The arts are merely pleasurable and serve no useful function.
3. The arts are a waste of time.
4. The arts are too emotional or appeal too much to the senses.

14. William Wordsworth, *Preface to Lyrical Ballads*.

5. The arts are only an imitation of reality, and therefore are unrelated to real life.
6. The arts have an immoral effect on people's behavior.

In a perfect world these objections to the arts would not have existed; in a fallen world they will always be problem areas for the arts.

Regarding a Christian approach to the arts we can truly say that it all started with Genesis. And the overall lesson that the first three chapters of the Bible teach is the need for a delicate balance between affirmation and negation, between enthusiasm for the arts and skepticism about them. The first three chapters of Genesis imply that such phenomena as the world, human experience, human creativity, and human delight in the arts are good in principle. Yet as practiced by sinful people in a fallen world they are capable of agonizing abuses. Early Genesis, in fact, lays the foundation for both the glory and the shame of the arts.

The Arts

A Bridge Between the Natural and Spiritual Realms

C. Nolan Huizenga

Great art has qualities that suggest something beyond the merely earthly and temporal. The permanence of art, for example, led poets such as Keats and Yeats to seek in art what Christians would call eternal life. The mystery of great art, combined with its ability to communicate meanings beyond the verbal and rational, gives art a quality akin to the religious. And the sheer magnificence that we sense in great art suggests transcendence.

It is small wonder, then, that sensitive people outside the Christian experience have found it attractive to equate art with religion and to make art their religion. The following essay proposes a Christian alternative: art is a bridge between the natural and supernatural, between the earthly and spiritual. Many of the things we associate with art — beauty, permanence, mystery, perfection —are qualities that are equally characteristic of God and heaven. In elaborating this concept, the essay touches upon the biblical doctrines that are especially relevant to a Christian philosophy of the arts.

The Artistic Implications of Creation and Incarnation

Art, beauty, aesthetic pleasure in a world of poverty, starvation, drug abuse, crime, the ecological crisis? Creation and enjoyment of beauty with a lost humanity on one hand and New Testament imperatives on the other? What do the arts mean for a believer in Jesus Christ faced with the Great Commission, the call to obedient discipleship, and the new life in Christ?

A Christian philosophy of the arts must be based upon the biblical view of God, man, and the world. Central to this view are the doctrines of creation, sin, and redemption. The Christian scholar who seeks a meaningful view of the whole range of human culture sooner or later wrestles with the crucial question of the relation of sin and redemption to God's original purpose in creation.

The major premise of a Christian world view, including a Christian aesthetic, is that God is the Creator. "In the beginning God created the heavens and the earth" (Gen. 1:1). Viewing nature and man, "God saw everything that he had made, and behold, it was very good" (Gen. 1:31). Here the infinite designer-artist takes pleasure in his creation. For the Christian the material order is neither intrinsically evil nor opposed to the spiritual order. It possesses the dignity and stamp of the Creator-God.

The New Testament word for the created order is *kosmos*, meaning arrangement, beauty, world. The verb form, *kosmeo*, means to set in order, to adorn, to beautify, to polish. These two Greek words convey two closely related concepts: beauty and order, both fundamental to a Christian aesthetic.

The cosmos reveals beauty and order not only in its original creation but also in its eternal purpose under a sovereign God. "For God so loved the world [the cosmos, the created order] that he gave his only begotten Son" (John 3:16). The key to the cosmos is Christ:

> He is the image of the invisible God, the firstborn of all creation; for in him all things were created, in heaven and on earth, visible and invisible, whether thrones or dominions or principalities or authorities—all things were created through him and

for him. He is before all things, and in him all things hold together. He is the head of the body, the church; he is the beginning, the first-born from the dead, that in everything he might be pre-eminent. For in him all the fulness of God was pleased to dwell, and through him to reconcile to himself all things, whether on earth or in heaven, making peace by the blood of his cross (Col. 1:15-20).

Jesus Christ is the creator, sustainer, and goal of all created reality. He is the source, medium, and consummation of all things.

For the Christian, the world of created phenomena, the world apprehended through the senses, reveals the glory of God. The psalmist finds this thought too sublime for prose so he utters it in the beautiful parallelism of Hebrew poetry:

The heavens are telling the glory of God;
    and the firmament proclaims his handiwork.
Day to day pours forth speech,
    and night to night declares knowledge.
There is no speech, nor are there words;
    their voice is not heard;
Yet their voice goes out through all the earth,
    and their words to the end of the world (Ps. 19:1-4).

The Apostle Paul states the same thought in writing to the Romans:

For what can be known about God is plain to them, because God has shown it to them. Ever since the creation of the world his invisible nature, namely, his eternal power and deity, has been clearly perceived in the things that have been made (Rom. 1:19, 20).

These passages teach that the visible world of nature reveals the invisible realm of supernature, God's eternal power and deity. That which we know through the senses and that which is spiritual are closely linked in God's creative purpose. Christianity, in contrast to all asceticism, whether religious or philosophical, places a high value on natural creation and rejects the world-denying dualism of matter and spirit, body and soul. Moreover, it proclaims a redemptive drama from creation to recreation, played out on a material-spiritual stage. Its Main Actor is the God-man, the "Word made flesh"; and the goal of the play is the restoration of man to his essential body-soul unity.

The crowning example of the dignity of matter and the intimate relation between flesh and spirit is the incarnation of Jesus Christ, God's own invasion of human history:

> In the beginning was the Word, and the Word was with God, and the Word was God. . . . And the Word became flesh and dwelt among us, full of grace and truth; we have beheld his glory, glory as of the only Son from the Father (John 1:1, 14).

The Apostle John saw grace and truth and glory as he looked upon Jesus in the flesh. A Christian artist sees in the incarnation God's glorious "self-portrait."

Further, he discovers in "God made flesh" the essential principle of the arts, the enfleshment of the spiritual in the sensuous. Every artistic creation or performance "from stone to tone" may become a little "incarnation" of spiritual reality in a sensuous medium. Finally, the artist finds that the incarnation of Christ authenticates and dignifies his humanity by redeeming his material-spiritual nature. This affirmation of man's body-soul unity becomes a major principle in the *modus operandi* of the Christian artist.

But what do these truths mean for the arts? In my view, the arts are a wonderful bridge between the two worlds into which God placed man by creation. The arts can lead to a mysterious synthesis of the material world of the senses and the spiritual realm. Firmly rooted in the here and now media of sights and sounds, they nevertheless convey not only the pleasure of the senses and emotions but also intellectual, moral, and spiritual insights. The Christian is free to enjoy beauty wholeheartedly on all these levels while at the same time insisting on the supremacy of moral and spiritual values.

A Christian view of the arts rests on the biblical revelation of a sovereign, personal God who himself is ultimate truth, beauty, and goodness. This fact alone commits the Christian to seeking excellence in the intellectual, aesthetic, and moral realms. Moreover, a Christian in the arts finds it impossible to divorce beauty from truth or morality. His respect for God and ultimate truth means that he believes the arts must be subject to reasonable evaluation and criticism. This task, though difficult, is perhaps easiest in the verbal arts, harder in the visual and plastic arts, and hardest in the non-verbal, non-visual art of music.

The Cultural Mandate

Man is able to apprehend truth, beauty, and goodness because he is a rational being created in the moral and spiritual image of God. The Christian artist is convinced that a significant aspect of God's image in man is his imagination, his mysterious and wonderful power to form new mental images. He believes that his urge to shape and create and his magnetic response to beauty derive directly from his Creator. He creates in full and humble recognition that his abilities are not self-generated but rather given by God for his greater glory. The Scriptures affirm, "We love him because he first loved us." To this we may add, "We create because he first created us in his image."

In the presence of nature, a Christian is awe-struck by its profuse variety and extravagance, its infinite detail, its intricate design. In his love God has showered his gifts upon people without reserve. The Christian artist is compelled to share his creative gifts with others. He creates not merely for self-expression or psychological catharsis but out of a loving desire to communicate his view of beauty and reality to others.

Because man was uniquely created in God's likeness, he was given a special commission as God's agent over the natural order:

> And God blessed them, and God said to them, "Be fruitful and multiply, and fill the earth and subdue it; and have dominion over the fish of the sea and over the birds of the air and over every living thing that moves upon the earth" (Gen. 1:28).

This command, sometimes called the cultural mandate, enjoins man to exercise his God-given power and dominion over the earth and nature. The psalmist expresses man's noble task in these lines:

> Yet thou hast made him little less than God,
>   and dost crown him with glory and honor.
> Thou hast given him dominion over the works of thy hands;
>   thou hast put all things under his feet. . . .
> O Lord, our Lord,
>   how majestic is thy name in all the earth! (Ps. 8:5, 6, 9).

Implicit in God's command to subdue the earth is the responsibility to develop the entire range of human culture for man's use under the sovereignty of God. Our English word "culture" derives from the Latin *colere*, to till or cultivate the ground. A comprehensive Christian definition of culture, in the words of Henry Van Til, is "the activity of man as image-bearer of his Creator in forming nature to his purposes"; or "any and all human effort and labor expended upon the cosmos to unearth its treasures and riches and bring them into the service of man for the enrichment of human existence unto the glory of God."[1]

---

1. Henry Van Til, *The Calvinistic Concept of Culture* (Grand Rapids: Baker Book House, 1959), pp. 27, 29–30.

The arts are as universal as man. They exist in every human culture, from the most primitive to the highly civilized. But how do they relate to the cultural mandate given man at his creation? It is easy to see how the sciences enable man to subdue and develop his environment, but what about the arts?

On one level the arts represent man's celebration of his natural environment through his senses. On another, they embody his emotional responses to human experience. On still another level, the arts reflect man's lifelong quest for meaning, for purpose, and his attempt through symbol and metaphor to bring unity to his fragmented existence. If the sciences represent man's dominion over his physical environment, the arts on their highest level represent one phase of man's cultural attempt to understand, control, and ennoble the psychological and spiritual areas of his life.

Artistic Implications of the Fall and Redemption

Thus far our consideration of the arts has centered on the biblical doctrine of God the Creator and man the image-bearer and cultural agent of God under the creation mandate. We have omitted a crucial factor—sin, man's rebellion against God, with the resulting defacement of God's image in man, the subjection of nature to decay and death, and the perversion of human culture.

When man sinned, he did not lose his creaturehood, his humanity. Nor did God release man from the original creation mandate to multiply, to have power over nature, to use nature for his purposes. Man retains his cultural urge, his instinct to rule, his love of power, his ability to shape matter after his will. But culture now becomes an end in itself rather than a means to the glory of God.

Man's culture becomes fragmented; the relation of the parts to the whole eludes him, and he worships and serves the creature (or creation) rather than the Creator. Under the power of sin and Satan, man develops a self-centered culture that Augustine called the *civitas terrena*, kingdom of this world. By contrast, believers in Christ are motivated by the Holy Spirit to express their faith culturally in ways consistent with divine revelation and, therefore, glorifying to God. This concept of a faith-oriented culture Augustine called the *civitas dei*, kingdom of God. The resulting division of mankind into two opposing cultures is called by some "the antithesis."

One of the toughest questions for a thoughtful Christian arises at this point. What attitude should he take toward this deep-seated antithesis in human culture, and what are his cultural responsibilities? He is called to be "in the world"; he remains a human being. Yet he is not to be "of the world" in the sense of sharing its sinful desires, practices, and goals.

The Christian, on the basis of divine revelation, is a convinced cultural optimist. He believes that God "desires all men to be saved and to come to the knowledge of the truth" (I Tim. 2:4) and that God's ultimate purpose for creation is redemption and restoration in Christ. The ruin of God's image in man is already in process of restoration by the Holy Spirit in the hearts of twiceborn people:

> And we all, with unveiled face, beholding the glory of the Lord, are being changed into his likeness from one degree of glory to another; for this comes from the Lord who is the Spirit (II Cor. 3:18).

More than this, the Christian is assured that this divine restoration will stop at nothing less than the complete transformation of his body into the likeness of Christ's glorious body: he "will change our lowly body to be like his glorious body, by the power which enables him even to subject all things to himself" (Phil. 3:21). In the resurrection, human personality, fragmented by sin, is restored to its body-soul unity and wholeness. And finally the believer is promised a fully restored environment, the redemption of all nature:

For the creation waits with eager longing for the revealing of the sons of God; for the creation was subjected to futility, not of its own will but by the will of him who subjected it in hope; because the creation itself will be set free from its bondage to decay and obtain the glorious liberty of the children of God (Rom. 8:19-21).

In the light of all this, the Christian's cultural stance is characterized by faith and hope. He lives his present life in the light of the comprehensive and pervasive nature of God's redemptive plan for creation. He rejects all ascetic withdrawal from the world, he scorns a convenient sacred-secular dualism, and he seeks to bring all of life under Christ's lordship, realizing that for him all things are his and he is Christ's.

In the believer's heart, that mysterious center of his being, God is transforming the defaced image of the first Adam into the image of Christ, the second Adam. As a member of the new humanity, Christ's man begins to fulfill, though partially and imperfectly, the original cultural mandate given the first Adam.

But how should a Christian view the artistic products of a culture antithetical to Christianity? Is human culture so depraved that it reflects no truth, beauty, or goodness? The Scriptures teach that one aspect of God's grace, sometimes called common grace, has to do with the restraint of sin, the maintenance of order, and the promotion of culture and civil righteousness in human life. Although the motivation and goal of human culture are sinful and selfish, unregenerate people are nevertheless enabled through common grace to produce works of relative truth, beauty, and goodness. God is the ultimate source of these qualities regardless of where they are found. For the Christian in the arts, the doctrine of common grace helps explain how unregenerate, even immoral people can produce artistic creations of enduring beauty and meaning. A Christian view of human culture must take seriously the antithesis between the kingdom of God and the kingdom of this world while at the same time recognizing the operation of common grace in worldly culture.

One of the greatest needs of contemporary evangelism is the development of a thoroughly biblical and Christian aesthetic and, in the case of the performing arts such as music, practical Christian criteria of performance. We have only begun to bring the arts into captivity to Christ. For this profound and exciting endeavor Paul has given us a grand incentive:

Finally, brethren, whatever is true, whatever is honorable, whatever is just, whatever is pure, whatever is lovely, whatever is gracious, if there is any excellence, if there is anything worthy of praise, think about these things (Phil. 4:8).

part 2

Christian Perspectives on the Arts

Introduction

All of the arts share a multitude of elements.

In music, a sonata follows a fixed pattern of three parts with an A-B-A structure (exposition, development, recapitulation); in literature, an English sonnet follows a fixed pattern of three quatrains (four-line units) and a concluding couplet. The colors in a painting are selected so that their tones work together rather than against each other; the sounds in a piece of music are brought together so that they harmonize. A painting is designed to bring the eye to a focal object or point; in a story the individual episodes all relate to one or more unifying themes.

It is obvious that much of what we say about one of the arts applies to others. In fact, the elements of artistic form can be found in all of the arts. They include unity, variation, balance, contrast, repetition, and rhythm. All of the arts have these ingredients; they differ in the medium by which they express them. Music uses sound, literature uses words, and painting uses color and texture.

The discipline that studies the arts as a group of related phenomena is called *aesthetics*. The essays in this section fall under that heading, and they discuss issues that are relevant to all of the arts.

Some Perspectives on Art

Francis A. Schaeffer

Christians who participate in the arts have returned again and again to the same questions. These issues arise whenever we try to relate the arts to the Christian faith. We might call them the "classic problems" of a Christian philosophy of the arts.

No essay articulates these classic problems more clearly than the following one by Francis Schaeffer, who has provided such stimulus for integrating the various disciplines with each other and with the Christian world view. This essay attempts to answer at least six basic questions:

1. *How important is sheer artistic form (apart from ideational content) in a work of art?*
2. *What is the relationship between form and content in a work of art?*
3. *What is the role of truth in art? How does an untruthful world view affect a Christian's response to a work of art?*
4. *What are the standards by which a Christian should evaluate works of art?*
5. *What subject matter and forms are appropriate for Christian artists?*
6. *What things should distinguish Christian "consumers" of art from non-Christian consumers?*

In what follows I wish to develop a Christian perspective on art in general. How should we as creators and enjoyers of beauty comprehend and evaluate it? There are, I believe, at least eleven distinct perspectives from which a Christian can consider and evaluate works of art. These perspectives do not exhaust the various aspects of art. The field of aesthetics is too rich for that. But they do cover a significant portion of what should be a Christian's understanding in this area.

1. The first is the most important: *A work of art has a value in itself*. For some this principle may seem too obvious to mention, but for many Christians it is unthinkable. And yet if we miss this point, we miss the very essence of art. Art is not something we merely analyze or value for its intellectual content. It is something to be enjoyed. The Bible says that the art work in the tabernacle and the temple was for beauty.

How should an artist begin to do his work as an artist? I would insist that he begin his work as an artist by setting out to make a work of art. What that would mean is different in sculpture and in poetry, for example, but in both cases the artist should be setting out to make a work of art.

Many modern artists, it seems to me, have forgotten the value that art has in itself. Much modern art is far too intellectual to be great art. I am thinking, for example, of artists such as Jasper Johns. Many modern artists seem not to see the distinction between man and non-man, and it is a part of lostness of modern man that they no longer see value in the work of art as a work of art.

I am afraid, however, that as evangelicals we have largely made the same mistake. Too often we think that a work of art has value only if we reduce it to a tract. This too is to view art solely as a message for the intellect.

There are, I believe, three basic possibilities concerning the nature of a work of art. The first view is the relatively recent theory of art for art's sake. This is the notion that art is just *there*, and that is all there is to it. You can't talk about it, you can't analyze it, it doesn't say anything. This view is, I think, quite misguided. No great artist functions on the level of art for art's sake alone.

The second possibility is that art is only an embodiment of a message, a vehicle for the propagation of a particular message about the world, or the artist, or man, or whatever. This view has been held by Christians as well as non-Christians, the difference between the two versions being the nature of the message which the art embodies. But, as I have said, this view reduces art to an intellectual statement and the work of art as a work of art disappears.

The third basic notion of the nature of art—the one I think is right, the one that really produces great art and the possibility of great art—is that the artist makes a body of work and this body of work shows his world view. No one, for example, who understands Michelangelo or Leonardo can look at their work without understanding something of their respective world views. Nonetheless, these artists began by making works of art, and then their world views showed through the body of their work. I emphasize the body of an artist's work because it is impossible for any single painting, for example, to reflect the totality of an artist's view of reality. But when we see a collection of an artist's paintings or a series of a poet's poems or a number of a novelist's novels, both the outline and some of the details of the artist's conception of life shine through.

How then should an artist begin to do his work? I would insist that he begin by setting out *to make a work of art*. He should say to himself, "I am going to make a work of art." Perspective number one is that a work of art is first of all a work of art.

2. *Art forms add strength to the world view which shows through, no matter what the world view is or whether the world view is true or false.* Think, for example, of a side of beef hanging in a butcher shop. It just hangs there. But if you go to the Louvre and look at Rembrandt's painting, "Side of Beef Hanging in a Butcher Shop," it's very different. It's startling to

come upon this particular work because it says a lot more than its title. Rembrandt's art causes us to see the side of beef in a concentrated way, and, speaking for myself, after looking and looking at his picture, I have never been able to look at a side of beef in a butcher shop with the superficiality I did before. How much stronger is Rembrandt's painting than merely the label, A Side of Beef.

In literature, there is a parallel. Good prose as an art form has something bad prose does not. Further, poetry has something good prose does not. We may have long discussions on what is added, but the fact that there are distinct differences is clear. Even in the Bible the poetry adds a dimension lacking in the prose. In fact, the effect of any proposition, whether true or false, can be heightened if it is expressed in poetry or in artistic prose rather than in bald, formulaic statement.

3. *In all forms of writing, both poetry and prose, it makes a tremendous difference whether there is a continuity or a discontinuity with the normal definitions of words in normal syntax*. Many modern writers make a concerted effort to disassociate the language of their works from the normal use of language in which there is a normal definition of words and a normal use of syntax. If there is no continuity with the way in which language is normally used, then there is no way for a reader or an audience to know what the author is saying.

What is true in literature is also true in painting and sculpture. The common symbolic vocabulary that belongs to all men (the artists and the viewers) is the world around us, namely God's world. That symbolic vocabulary in the representational arts stands parallel to normal grammar and normal syntax in the literary arts. When, therefore, there is no attempt on the part of an artist to use this symbolic vocabulary at all, then communication is impossible here, too. There is then no way for anyone to know what the artist is saying. My point is *not* that making this sort of art is immoral or anti-Christian but rather that a dimension is lost.

Totally abstract art stands in an undefined relationship with the viewer, for the viewer is completely alienated from the painter. There is a huge wall between them. The painter and the viewer stand separated from each other in a greater alienation than Giacometti could ever show in his alienated figures. There is a distinct limitation to totally abstract art.

4. *The fact that something is a work of art does not make it sacred*. Heidegger in *What Is Philosophy?*[1] came finally to the view that there are small beings, namely people, who verbalize, and therefore we can hope that Being has some meaning. His great cry at the end of this book is to listen to the poet. Heidegger is not saying that we should listen to the content of what the poets say, because one can find two different poets who give absolutely opposite content; this doesn't matter. The poet became Heidegger's upper-story optimistic hope.

As Christians, we must see that just because an artist—even a great artist—portrays a world view in writing or on canvas, it does not mean that we should automatically accept that world view. Art may heighten the impact of the world view (in fact, we can count on this), but it does not make something true. The truth of a world view presented by an artist must be judged on grounds other than artistic greatness.

5. What kind of judgment does one apply, then, to a work of art? *I believe that there are four basic standards: (a) technical excellence, (b) validity, (c) intellectual content, the world view which comes through, and (d) the integration of content and vehicle*.

I will discuss *technical excellence* in relationship to painting because it is easy to point out through this medium what I mean. Here one considers the use of color, form, balance, and texture of the paint, the handling of lines, the unity of the canvas, and so forth. In each of these there can be varying degrees of technical excellence. By recognizing technical excel-

---

1. Martin Heidegger, *What Is Philosophy?* (New Haven, Conn.: College & University Press, 1956).

lence as an aspect of an art work, we are often able to say that while we do not agree with such and such an artist's world view, he is nonetheless a great artist.

We are not being true to the artist as a man if we consider his art work junk simply because we differ with his outlook on life. Christian schools, Christian parents, and Christian pastors often have turned off young people at just this point. Because the schools, the pastors, and the parents did not make a distinction between technical excellence and content, the whole of much great art has been rejected with scorn and ridicule. Instead, if the artist's technical excellence is high, he is to be praised for this, even if we differ with his world view. Man must be treated fairly as man. Technical excellence is, therefore, an important criterion.

Validity is the second criterion. By validity I mean whether an artist is true to himself and to his world view or whether he makes his art only for money or for the sake of being accepted. If an artist makes an art work solely for a patron— whether that patron is the ancient noble, the modern art gallery to which the artist wants access, or the modern art critics of the moment—his work does not have validity. The modern forms of "the patron" are more destructive than even that of the old noble.

The third criterion for the judgment of a work of art is its *content*, that which reflects the world view of the artist. As far as a Christian is concerned, the world view that is shown through a body of art must be seen ultimately in terms of the Scripture. The artist's world view is not to be free from the judgment of the Word of God. In this the artist is like a scientist. The scientist may wear a white coat and be considered an "authority" by society, but where his statements impinge upon what God has given us in Scripture, they come under the ultimate authority of his Word. An artist may wear a painter's smock and be considered almost a holy man, yet where his work shows his world view, it must be judged by its relationship to the Christian world view.

I think we can now see how it is possible to make such judgments concerning the work of art. If we stand as Christians before a man's canvas and recognize that he is a great artist in technical excellence and validity—if in fact he is—and if we have been fair with him as a man and as an artist, then we can say that his world view is wrong. We can judge this view on the same basis as we judge the views of anybody else— philosopher, common man, laborer, businessman, or whatever.

Some artists may not know that they are revealing a world view. Nonetheless, a world view usually does show through. Even those works which were constructed under the principle of art for art's sake often imply a world view. Even the world view that there is no meaning is a message. In any case, whether the artist is conscious of the world view or not, to the extent that it is there it must come under the judgment of the Word of God.

There is a corollary to this third criterion. We should realize that if something untrue or immoral is stated in great art it can be far more destructive and devastating than if it is expressed in poor art or prosaic statement. Much of the crude art commonly produced by the underground press is laden with destructive messages, but the art is so poor that it does not have much force. But the greater the artistic expression, the more important it is to consciously bring it and its world view under the judgment of Christ and the Bible.

The common reaction among many, however, is just the opposite. Ordinarily, many seem to feel that the greater the art, the less we ought to be critical of its world view. This we must reverse.

There is a second corollary related to judging the content of an art work: It is possible for a non-Christian writer or painter to write and paint according to a Christian world view even though he himself is not a Christian. To understand this, we must distinguish between two meanings of the word *Christian*. The first and essential meaning is that a Christian is a person who has accepted Christ as his Savior and has thus passed from death to life, from the kingdom of darkness to the kingdom of God by being born again. But if a number of people really are Christians, then they bring forth a kind of consensus that exists apart from themselves, and sometimes non-Christians paint and write within the framework of that consensus even though they as individuals are not Christians.

The fourth criterion for judging a work of art involves how well the artist has *suited the vehicle to the message*. For those art works which are truly great, there is a correlation between the style and the content. The greatest art fits together the vehicle that is being used and the message that is being said.

A recent example is found in T. S. Eliot's "The Waste Land." When Eliot published this in 1922, he became a hero to the modern poets, because for the first time he dared to make the form of his poetry fit the nature of the world as he saw it, namely, broken, unrelated, ruptured. What was that form? A collection of shattered fragments of language and images and allusions drawn seemingly haphazardly from all manner of literature, philosophy, and religious writings from the ancients to the present. But modern poets were pleased, for they now had a poetic form to fit the modern world view of unrelatedness.

6. *Art forms can be used for any type of message from pure fantasy to detailed history*. Because a work of art is in the form of fantasy or epic or painting does not mean that there is no propositional content. Just as one can have propositional statements in prose, there can be propositional statements in poetry, in painting, in virtually any art form.

7. Many Christians, especially those unused to viewing the arts and thinking about them, reject contemporary painting and contemporary poetry not because of their world view but simply because they feel threatened by a new art form. It is perfectly legitimate for a Christian to reject a particular work of art intellectually, that is, because he knows what is being said by it. But it is another thing to reject the work of art simply because the style is different from that which we are used to.

In short: *Styles of art form change and there is nothing wrong with this*.

As a matter of fact, change is one difference between life and death. There is no living language which does not undergo constant change. The languages which do not change, Latin, for example, are dead. As long as one has a living art, its forms will change. The past art forms, therefore, are not necessarily the right ones for today or tomorrow. To demand the art forms of yesterday in either word systems or art is a bourgeois error. It cannot be assumed that if a Christian painter becomes "more Christian" he will necessarily become more and more like Rembrandt. This would be like saying that if the preacher really makes it next Sunday morning, he will preach to us in Chaucerian English. Then we'll really listen!

Not only will there be a change in art forms and language as time progresses, but there will be a difference in art forms coming from various geographical locations and from different cultures. Take, for example, Hebrew poetry. It has alliteration and parallelism and other such rhetorical forms, but it hardly ever rhymes. Does this mean it is not poetry? Or does it mean that English poetry is wrong when it rhymes? Surely not. Rather, each art form in each culture must find its own proper relationship between world view and style.

Then what about the Christian's art? Here three things should be stressed. First, Christian art today should be twentieth-century art. Art changes. Language changes. The preacher's preaching today must be twentieth-century language communication, or there will be an obstacle to being understood. And if a Christian's art is not twentieth-century art, it is an obstacle to his being heard. It makes him different where there is no necessity for difference. A Christian should not, therefore, strive to copy Rembrandt or Browning.

Second, Christian art should differ from country to country. Why did we ever force the Africans to use Gothic architecture? It's a meaningless exercise. All we succeeded in doing was making Christianity foreign to the African. If a Christian artist is Japanese, his paintings should be Japanese; if Indian, Indian.

Third, the body of a Christian artist's work should reflect the Christian world view. In short, if you are a young Christian artist, you should be working in the art forms of the twentieth century, showing the marks of the culture out of which you have come, reflecting your own country and your own contemporariness and embodying something of the nature of the world as seen from a Christian standpoint.

8. While a Christian artist should be modern in his art, he does face certain difficulties. First, we must distinguish carefully between style and message. Let me say firmly that *there is no such thing as a godly style or an ungodly style*. The more one tries to make such a distinction, the more confusing it becomes.

Yet while there is no such thing as a godly or ungodly style, we must not be misled or naive in thinking that various styles have no relation whatsoever to the content or the message of the work of art. Styles themselves are developed as symbol systems or vehicles for certain world views or messages. In the Renaissance, for example, one finds distinctively different styles from those which characterize art in the Middle Ages. It does not take much education in the history of art to recognize that what Filippo Lippi was saying about the nature of the Virgin Mary is different from what was being said in paintings done before the Renaissance. Art in the Renaissance became more natural and less iconographic. In our own day, men like Picasso and T. S. Eliot developed new styles in order to speak a new message.

Think, for example, of T. S. Eliot's form of poetry in "The Waste Land." The fragmented form matches the vision of fragmented man. But it is intriguing that after T. S. Eliot became a Christian, for example in "The Journey of the Magi," he did not use quite this same form. Rather, he adapted it for the message he was now giving—a message with a Christian character. But he didn't entirely give up the form; he didn't go back to Tennyson; rather, he adapted the form that he used in "The Waste Land," changing it to fit the message that he was now giving. In other words, T. S. Eliot the Christian wrote somewhat differently than T. S. Eliot the "modern man."

The form in which a world view is given can either weaken or strengthen the content, even if the viewer or reader does not in every case analyze this completely. In other words, depending upon the vehicle you use, though an audience may not notice, you will be moving either toward your world view or away from your world view.

In conclusion, therefore, often we will use twentieth-century art forms, but we must be careful to keep them from distorting the world view which is distinctively ours as Christians. In one way styles are completely neutral. But in another way they must not be used in an unthinking, naive way.

9. *The Christian world view can be divided into what I call a major and a minor theme.* (The terms *major* and *minor*, as I am using them, have no relationship to their use in music.) First, the *minor theme* is the abnormality of the revolting world. This falls into two parts: (a) Men who have revolted from God and not come back to Christ are eternally lost; they see their meaninglessness in the present and they are right from their own standpoint. (b) There is a defeated and sinful side to the Christian's life. If we are at all honest, we must admit that in this life there is no such thing as totally victorious living. In every one of us there are those things which are sinful and deceiving and, while we may see substantial healing, in this life we do not come to perfection.

The *major theme* is the opposite of the minor; it is the meaningfulness and purposefulness of life. From the Christian viewpoint, this falls into two headings, (a) metaphysics and (b) morals. In the area of metaphysics (of being, of existence, including the existence of every person) God is there, God exists. Therefore, all is not absurd. Furthermore, man is made in God's image and so man has significance. The major theme is an optimism in the area of being: everything is not absurd, there is meaning.

There is also a major theme in relation to morals. Christianity gives a moral solution on the basis of the fact that God exists and has a character which is the law of the universe. There is therefore an absolute in regard to morals. It is not that there is a moral law beyond God that binds both God and man, but that God himself has a character and this character is reflected in the moral law of the universe. Thus when a person realizes his inadequacy before God and feels guilty, he has a basis not simply for the feeling but for the reality of guilt. Man's dilemma is not just that he is finite and God is infinite, but that he is a sinner guilty before a holy God. But then he recognizes that God has given him a solution to this in the life, death, and resurrection of Christ. Man is fallen and flawed, but he is redeemable on the basis of Christ's work. This is beautiful. This is optimism. And this optimism has a sufficient base.

Notice that the Christian and his art have a place for the minor theme because man is lost and abnormal and the Christian has his own defeats. There is not only victory and song in my life. But the Christian and his art don't end there. He goes on to the major theme because there is an optimistic answer. This is important for the kind of art Christians are to produce. First of all, Christian art needs to recognize the minor theme, the defeated aspect to even the Christian life. If our Christian art only emphasizes the major theme, then it is not fully Christian but simply romantic art. And let us say with sorrow that for years our Sunday school literature has been romantic in its art and has had very little to do with genuine Christian art. Older Christians may wonder what is wrong with this art and wonder why their kids are turned off by it, but the answer is simple. It's romantic. It's based on the notion that Christianity has only an optimistic note.

On the other hand, it is possible for a Christian to so major on the minor theme, emphasizing the lostness of man and the abnormality of the universe, that he is equally unbiblical. There may be exceptions where a Christian artist feels it his calling to picture only the negative, but in general for the Christian, the major theme is to be dominant—though it must exist in relationship to the minor.

10. *Christian art is by no means always religious art, that is, art which deals with religious themes*. Consider God the Creator. Is God's creation totally involved with religious subjects? What about the universe? the birds? the trees? the mountains? What about the bird's song? and the sound of the wind in the trees? When God created out of nothing by his spoken word, he did not just create "religious" objects. And in the Bible, as we have seen, God commanded the artist, working within God's own creation, to fashion statues of oxen and lions and carvings of almond blossoms for the tabernacle and the temple.

We should remember that the Bible contains the Song of Solomon, the love song between a man and a woman, and it contains David's song to Israel's national heroes. Neither subject is religious. But God's creation—the mountains, the trees, the birds, and the birds' songs—are also non-religious art. Think about that. If God made the flowers, they are worth painting and writing about. If God made the birds, they are worth painting. If God made the sky, the sky is worth painting. If God made the ocean, indeed, it's worth writing poetry about. It is worth man's while to create works upon the basis of the great works God has already created.

This whole notion is rooted in the realization that Christianity is not just involved with "salvation" but with the total man in the total world. The Christian message begins with the existence of God forever and then with creation. It does not begin with salvation. We must be thankful for salvation, but the Christian message is more than that. Man has a value because he is made in the image of God and thus man as man is an important subject for Christian art. Man as man—with his emotions, his feelings, his body, his life—this is important subject matter for poetry and novels. I'm not talking here about man's lostness but about his humanness. In God's world the individual counts. Therefore, Christian art should deal with the individual.

Christian art is the expression of the whole life of the whole person who is a Christian. What a Christian portrays in his art is the totality of life. Art is not to be solely a vehicle for some sort of self-conscious evangelism.

If, therefore, Christianity has so much to say about the arts and to the artist, why is it that recently we have produced so little Christian art? I should think the answer would now be clear. We have not produced Christian art because we have forgotten most of what Christianity says about the arts.

Christians, for example, ought not to be threatened by fantasy and imagination. Great painting is not "photographic"; think of the Old Testament art commanded by God. There were blue pomegranates on the robes of the priest who went into the Holy of Holies. In nature there are no blue pomegranates. Christian artists do not need to be threatened by fantasy and imagination, for they have a basis for knowing the difference between them and the real world "out there." The Christian is the really free person—he is free to have imagination. This too is our heritage. The Christian is the one whose imagination should fly beyond the stars.

A Christian artist does not need to concentrate on religious subjects. After all, religious themes may be completely non-Christian. Religious subjects are no guarantee that a work of art is Christian. On the other hand, the art of an artist who never paints the head of Christ, never once paints an open tomb, may be magnificent Christian art. For some artists there is a place for religious themes, but an artist does not need to be conscience-stricken if he does not paint in this area. Some Christian artists will never use religious themes. This is a freedom the artist has in Christ under the leadership of the Holy Spirit.

11. *Every artist has the problem of making an individual work of art and, as well, building up a total body of work*. No artist can say everything he might want to say or build everything he might want to build into a single work. It is true that some art forms, such as the epic and the novel, lend themselves to larger conceptions and more complex treatments, but even there not everything that an artist wants to do can be done in one piece. Therefore, we cannot judge an artist's work from one piece. No art critic or art historian can do that. We must judge an artist's performance and an artist's world view on the basis of as much of that artist's work as we can.

If you are a Christian artist, therefore, you must not freeze up just because you can't do everything at once. Don't be afraid to write a love poem simply because you cannot put into it everything of the Christian message. Yet, if a man is to be an artist, his goal should be in a lifetime to produce a wide and deep body of work.

What Is Truth in Art?

Frank E. Gaebelein

At its best, human art can give us contact with greatness. The French novelist Flaubert has written, "I remember how violently my heart leapt at the sight of one wall of the Acropolis." And then he adds, "I wonder whether a book . . . may not produce the same effect. Is not there an intrinsic virtue, a kind of divine impulse in the precision of the grouping, the perfection of the parts, the surface polish, the total harmony?"

Made in the image of a God who is great, the human spirit in its best moments longs for an encounter with greatness. This capacity, moreover, is something that grows with exercise. That is why Alfred North Whitehead lists as one of the ingredients of true education "the habitual vision of greatness."

In the following essay, Dr. Gaebelein explores the elements of truth (which in this context is synonymous with greatness or excellence or highest quality) that are common to all of the arts.

The Importance of Truth in Art

What is truth in art? What does a symphony or novel, a painting or a play, have to do with truth? Aesthetics has few more difficult questions than this. Yet the difficulty gives no

99

excuse for not thinking about it, for the arts in one form or another pervade our environment and influence us all.

Genius and talent come from God. He gives some men and women the ability to make or perform works of art. To think of literature, painting, music, and the other arts as merely peripheral to the main business of life does no honor to the Giver of every good and perfect gift. Man's aesthetic faculty reflects the image of the God who created him. While only a minority write, compose, paint, or design, everyone has some capacity for responding to art. As Abraham Kuyper said, "As image-bearer of God, man possesses the possibility both to create something beautiful and to delight in it."

All truth is of God. Every facet of it is related to the Father, who is the God of truth; the Son, who is the truth; and the Spirit, who is the Spirit of truth. Moreover, truth is related to Scripture, the written word of truth. All the arts must be judged by Christians in relation to truth. They are, as Calvin Seerveld has said, not to be "excluded from the test of truth as if they were simply a collected insight in a realm outside of verifiability."

My purpose in this essay is to propose several marks of truth in art—not to attempt to give a complete answer to the question of truthfulness in art but simply to shed some light on it.

Durability

A good place to begin is with durability. Truth is not transient. It never wears out. If something is true, it keeps on being true. One of the early works in aesthetics, the Greek treatise *Longinus on the Sublime*, expresses this insight: "That is really great which bears a repeated examination, and which is difficult or rather impossible to withstand, and the memory of which is strong and hard to efface. . . . For when men of different pursuits, lives, ambitions, ages, languages, hold identical views on one and the same subject, then the verdict which results, so to speak, from a concert of discordant elements makes our faith in the object of admiration strong and unassailable." So art that is deeply true stands up to the passage of the years.

We must distinguish between durability in artistic works and the unique changelessness of God. "Jesus Christ is the same yesterday, today, and forever"—that is eternally durable truth. So are the other great truths about God and man revealed in Scripture. These constitute Truth, as distinct from truth in art and other fields of human endeavor. In the latter, truth has durability but on the finite rather than eternal level.

But the principle of durability does not help us with what is newer in art. However much we love the great aesthetic achievements of the past, to confine our attention to them alone is parochial. Durability must not be pressed so far as to rule out contemporary art from any claim to lasting truth. Nor does the application of it always require many years: occasionally contemporary judgment quickly recognizes a masterpiece and is proved right by posterity. More commonly, however, great works do not come into their own till years after their creation. For example, Melville's *Moby Dick*, now a secure masterpiece, was practically forgotten for decades. And Bach's *St. Matthew Passion* lay dormant for nearly a hundred years till Mendelssohn's revival of it revealed its towering greatness.

Unity

Consider next unity as a mark of truth in art. Truth has its own inner coherence. The criterion is very old. Biblically it is rooted in the oneness of the Triune God. Outside the Bible it found classic expression in Aristotle's *Poetics*. It has been well said that form is the cup of art. When one finds that a book or symphony lacks unity, he does not have to know the *Poetics* to say, "It doesn't hold together."

The concept of order, which is related to that of unity, is implicit in the cultural mandate in Genesis. When God created man, he was placed in a garden and told to cultivate and keep it. Order is implicit in this idea of cultivating a garden. The creative process in man is not innately disorderly.

At its truest, art tends toward unity and order. The reason for this relates to the incarnational nature of art. As Goethe said, "The spirit tends to take to itself a body." In the arts, the concept or idea is given definite form; it is "embodied" in sound, color, or words; in wood or stone; in action or movement, as in drama or ballet. But embodiment requires unity and order; a body cannot function effectively in a state of disorganization.

Certain aspects of contemporary art show a centrifugal and even schizophrenic trend. This stems from the sense of lostness and rebellion so prevalent today. Contemporary art does serve as a barometer of the times. But is this enough? Surely art that is ultimately true can do more than reflect what *is*. It can also have its prophetic function. The history of literature, music, and the other arts contains notable examples of genius that not only spoke to the present situation but went beyond it to break new trails for aesthetic advance.

Integrity

Closely linked to unity as a mark of truth in art is integrity. Although both terms have to do with basic form or structure, integrity is more comprehensive, having to do with the matter of wholeness. A novel may be structurally unified, yet fall short of integrity if the characters or dialogue are unconvincing. Integrity refers to the overall truthfulness of a work of art. When we say that a person has integrity, we mean his entire personality is morally sound. So it is with integrity in art.

In the arts, integrity demands that anything contrived merely for the sake of effect and not organically related to the purpose of the work must be ruled out. Regrettably, there is much in evangelical literature, music, and art that lacks integrity. Sentimental pictures of Christ are widely promoted, records dress up hymn tunes in commonplace variations, and fiction written by evangelicals rarely rises even to the level of competent literary craftsmanship. It is evident that many Christians have much to learn about integrity in their use of the arts. In contrast, think of the art with which our Lord used words. He told the parables of the Prodigal Son, the Good Samaritan, and the Pharisee and the Publican without moralizing, and with an integrity that has never been surpassed. As St. Paul said of him, "He is before all things, and in him all things hold together" (Col. 1:17).

The Christian writer has the advantage of being in a position to tell the whole story. Because he is a Christian he can present the full picture of not only man's alienation and lostness but also the possibility of his redemption through Christ. This added dimension has characterized the work of great Christian writers from Dante through Milton and Bunyan to Dostoevsky, T. S. Eliot, Graham Greene, François Mauriac, and Flannery O'Conner. In a letter written about ten years after his conversion, C. S. Lewis said, "One of the minor rewards of conversion is to be able at last to see the real point of all the literature we were brought up to read with the point left out."

Inevitability

Still another mark of truth in art is inevitability. Some works of art seem to be the final and inevitable expression of an aesthetic idea. Here a kind of paradox we may call "the familiarity of the unfamiliar" is involved. We may experience this when we hear an unfamiliar work by a composer like Beethoven, in which the inevitability of certain phrases or modulations gives the impression of something already known. In painting, one recognizes that a picture by a master like Raphael is completely right and could have been done in no other way. In great poetry we have the same sense of inevitability. In such cases we say, "This is right; this is the way it has to be."

In a letter to his publisher, Keats pointed to this quality in describing the kind of writing he hoped to achieve: "I think poetry should . . . strike the reader as a wording of his own highest thoughts and appear almost a remembrance." And one of Haydn's contemporaries, the critic Ernst Ludwig Gerber, said of that great composer, "He possesses the great art of making his music oftentimes seem familiar." To be sure, this recognition of inevitability of expression does not always come at once. It may be delayed till one knows the work more thoroughly, because art does not always wear its heart on its sleeve.

These four criteria—durability, unity, integrity, and inevitability—give us some insight into the nature of aesthetic truth. They are not the whole answer to the question "What is truth in art?" but they are components of it. And they are closely interrelated principles; each contains something of the others.

Truth in Christian Art

To these four marks of truth in art let us add two examples from art that is Christian. For here the criterion is the reflection of the reality of God himself.

The musically sensitive Christian who listens to a performance of Bach's B-Minor Mass experiences a supreme example of truth-telling in sound. Truth may be defined as correspondence with reality. The ultimate reality is God, and the Christian knows this reality in Jesus Christ, God manifest in human form. Anything in art that sheds light on this reality has truth at the highest level.

So consider a Christian hearing the B-Minor Mass. As he listens to the hushed sound of the "Crucifixus" with its mysterious downward progressions, he hears a tonal portrayal of the atonement that goes straight to the heart. Then, at the end of the "Crucifixus," there is the sudden outburst of joy in the "Resurrexit," as choir and orchestra acclaim the risen Lord Jesus Christ with a power few if any written commentaries ever attain. This presentation of the truth transcends barriers of language as it speaks to all Christian hearers. Aristotle spoke of art as *mimesis* or "imitation." Here is *mimesis* in the highest sense, as Bach puts into music the profound truths of Christ's passion and victory over death.

To turn to another field, consider Rembrandt's great portrayal of the supper at Emmaus. Here is truth in form and color. Unlike Salvador Dali, who painted a blond Christ on a cross suspended between heaven and earth, Rembrandt portrayed Christ with integrity. His pictures show us our Lord as he was—Jewish, a real human being here on earth. Yet when this great artist paints the supper at Emmaus, he gives us the very moment of truth when the disciples' eyes are opened and they see the risen Lord. The person they see is indeed human. We recognize him as the Christ, but Rembrandt shows us at the same time his glory. Here again we have truth in art, *mimesis* in its highest Christian sense.

But what about truth in lesser works of art and literature? Truth in art cannot be limited to the works of supreme genius. Wherever there is integrity, honest craftsmanship, and devoted cultivation of talent, there something of truth may break through. Literature has its minor classics and painting its primitives. Folk music can speak as authentically as a sonata. Honest craftsmanship, as in functionally beautiful furniture or pottery, enriches culture. And though these may not receive universal renown, they can attain a measure of truth.

Beauty and Truth in Art

No discussion of truth in art can be considered complete without some reference to the relation of beauty to truth. After contemplating an ancient vase, John Keats wrote his "Ode on a Grecian Urn." The final lines of the poem—" 'Beauty is truth, truth beauty,'—that is all/Ye know on earth, and all ye need to know"—seem to provide a definitive answer to the question.

Yet this identification of beauty with truth, so often taken for granted, needs scrutiny. Writers and other artists correctly reject the tendency to put moralizing into art. But do they have no moral responsibility whatever? Is art devoid of any ethical dimension?

The great biblical phrase "the beauty of holiness" answers with a qualified negative. Even if one were to grant autonomy to the beauty found in works of art, there still remains the artist himself. Like every human being, he stands under the ethical judgment of God. What he creates may be beautiful and aesthetically true. Yet it may tell a lie. The French writer Jean Genet writes beautiful prose, but his work is decadent. Picasso's erotic drawings are beautiful but corrupt. For the basic analogy, however, we need to go back to what Scripture says about Satan. There is a depth of meaning in Paul's statement that Satan himself is transformed into an angel of light. Beauty itself can become the vehicle for a lie.

To this possibility two kinds of beauty stand as exceptions—the chaste intellectual beauty encountered in such things as pure mathematics or scientific equations, and that beauty which Ernest Lee Tuveson has called "the aesthetics of the infinite." The latter is the beauty reflected in God's work in creation. The Scottish mountaineer W. H. Murray tells of seeing the Buachaille Etive More, the great peak in Glencoe, in brilliant winter moonlight: "Let us speak of the unspeakable, for there is no speech so profitable. [Its] face was washed by intense light so searching that no shade was cast by ridge or buttress. All detail merged in the darkness of one arrowy wall, pale as shadowed milk, impregnably erect. At the remote apex, a white crest broke spume on the high seas of infinity. . . . To my unaccustomed eye the scene at first bore an appearance of unreality; yet the more I gazed, the more surely I knew that I saw not an illusion greater than is usual, but truth made manifest."[1] This was one of what Murray called those "fleeting glimpses of that beauty which all men who have known it have been compelled to call truth." Such beauty is incorruptible.

---

1. W. H. Murray, *Mountaineering in Scotland* (London: Denton, 1947), p. 222.

And what of the purely intellectual beauty of higher mathematics or scientific equations? The physicist Dirac maintained that the truth of an equation is evidenced by its beauty. So those who are trained to think in these realms recognize beauty in the balance and symmetry of conceptual thought and in the disciplined simplicity of symbolic logic. Just as a chess master speaks of a beautiful series of moves, so a mathematician sees beauty in numbers and symbols. On this level, beauty, while manifest through the mind of man, has a certain incorruptibility, even though it may be put to debased uses, just as the pristine beauty of nature may be despoiled by man.

But for most of the beauty man attains, Keats's identification of it with truth must always be qualified by the Christian artist. Nor can he accept the finality of the poet's conclusion, "—that is all/Ye know on earth, and all ye need to know."

The Christian artist has to know more than this. He must know his responsibility to God who gave him his talent, and he must also know the misuses to which beauty is prone. Beauty is not exempt from the consequences of the fall. Like money or power, art may become an idol. Apostasy may assume angelic forms. This is why the Christian artist stands so in need of humility. Like Bach, who appended to his compositions the words "Soli Deo Gloria," he must never depart from the priority of seeking to glorify God in all he does.

To identify beauty with what is immediately pleasing or captivating is to have a superficial view of beauty. The difference between a Rembrandt portrayal of Christ and one by Sallman is the difference between depth and superficiality.

Moreover, to identify beauty exclusively with harmony and orderliness does scant justice to the power and truth the arts are capable of. Rouault's paintings of Christ are not conventionally beautiful, but they have the inner beauty of truth. Merely to look at Grünewald's Isenheim altarpiece with its agonizing crucifixion scene is to be confronted with the most terrible yet true picture ever painted of Christ's suffering for the sin of the world. Dissonance in music, stark realism in literature, and the "ugly" in visual art all have an indispensable relation to beauty. The concept of beauty in art must be large enough to include the aesthetic astringencies. For beauty wears different faces. There is the unclouded serenity of Raphael in his Alba Madonna or the seraphic slow movement of Mozart's last piano concerto. In contrast, we have the thorny beauty of Browning in *The Ring and the Book* or the rugged beauty of Béla Bartók's music.

To turn again to "the aesthetics of the infinite," the incorruptible beauty of God's handiwork in nature has its terrible as well as its pleasing aspect. The bleak wastes of the Sahara are beautiful in a different way from the smiling loveliness of a Hawaiian landscape. Moreover, our apprehension of beauty changes as we develop our aesthetic faculties. Only comparatively recently have some of the greater aspects of natural beauty been appreciated. In the eighteenth century, majestic mountain scenery was often avoided rather than recognized as sublime evidence of God's creative power. Fashions in art and literature change. But elusive and difficult to define though it is, true beauty continues. Just as God has yet more light to shine forth from his Word, he has greater dimensions of beauty for us to comprehend in his creation and in man's making of art.

Therefore, besides being aware of the perils of the misuse of beauty, we must recognize that beauty has profound theological implications. Among the great theologians and Christian philosophers, no one saw this more clearly than Jonathan Edwards. He spoke of God as "the foundation and fountain of all being and all beauty . . . of whom, and through whom, and to whom is all being and all perfection; and whose being and beauty are, as it were, the sum and comprehension of all existence and excellence."

The relation of beauty to God, so profoundly developed by Edwards, means that we cannot downgrade the arts as side issues to the serious business of life and service, as some Christians do. When we make and enjoy the arts in faithful stewardship and integrity, they can reflect something of God's own beauty and glory. Through them we can celebrate and glorify the God "in whom we live, and move, and have our being."

On Evil in Art

Thomas Howard

Christians have probably agonized over the problem of how to portray evil in art more than any other single aesthetic problem. We know from the example of the Bible that we should not try to avoid the realistic depiction of evil in art. The Bible itself gives us many "images of evil" — deceit, lust, sexual perversion, violence, cruelty, abuse of power, hypocrisy, and a dozen other sins.

When we pass from the realism of the Bible to that of modern literature and art, however, we move into quite a different world. The images of evil in many modern works of realism differ in both technique and content from biblical realism.

Christians (especially artists and writers) who see nothing objectionable in modern realism tend to defend such art on the principle of verisimilitude, or lifelikeness. Art merely reflects what is in the world, the argument runs, and there is nothing wrong with the artist portraying evil as it really exists in the world. Yet can verisimilitude by itself ever be an adequate criterion for a Christian? To claim that the mere fact that something degrading exists in the world is sufficient warrant for Christian artists and audiences to immerse themselves in it disregards much that the Bible says about purity of thought and personal holiness.

111

The following essay explores some key differences in the ways by which various artists portray evil in art. The discussion eventually comes to focus on the quality of aesthetic distance in art.

The Problem of Portraying Evil in Art

On the recommendation of a friend I went to see the film *The Devils*. It is about an outbreak of supposed demon possession in a convent in Loudun, France, in the seventeenth century. Before the depicted situation gets sorted out, everyone has been embroiled in political intrigue, carnal chaos, emotional havoc, inquisition, cruelty, and the most bizarre forms of voluptuous decadence imaginable.

The makers of this film chose to handle their subject matter as vividly as they could. The opening scene whisks one straight into a perfumed moral bog, with Louis XIV participating in a dionysian frolic in front of a bored and elegant Mazarin. From then until he leaves the theater, the viewer is up to his neck in blood, incense, silk, tinsel, grapes, powder, wine, and flesh.

The film exhibits rather vividly a matter that is worth our attention. It is a matter we encounter in one form and another again and again in our own epoch. It has to do with the *Zeitgeist,* and with public imagination, and with the discussion and portrayal of moral issues, and, eventually, with the whole aesthetic question.

Perhaps what I am referring to ought to be cast as a question: Does there come a point at which the artistic portrayal of evil crosses a certain line and itself begins to participate in the very evil it is portraying?

All the red flags are up and aflutter as soon as anyone embarks on a line of thought like this. Censorship! Tyranny! The Index! Didacticism! Inquisition! Prudery! Victoria! Mrs. Grundy! But perhaps if we back off a bit and look at what is entailed, it will not appear so outrageous.

The Portrayal of Evil in Great Art

We would have to back all the way off to the question of what art *is* if we were really to get the discussion on a firm footing, but what with Aristotle and the Renaissance Florentines and Elizabethans and Goethe and Shelley and a thousand others, we would never get to the matter at hand. It may be enough here to say that art, whatever else it does, represents the effort of the human imagination to get hold of its experience of life by giving some concrete *shape* to it all. That shape may appear in stone or syntax or oils or melody, but the whole enterprise of poetry and sculpture and drama (and hence cinema) does bespeak that effort.

Parenthetically, the question of entertainment might arise here. Isn't all this appeal to heady aesthetic doctrine likely to dignify and elevate something that isn't half so weighty? What about mere enjoyment? What about the books that have been written and the plays that have been produced simply to divert people for a couple of hours? Let's not read Armageddon in every playroom scuffle, or the Beatific Vision in wallpaper.

It is not easy to find the border between "art" and "entertainment," if indeed there is one. By its very nature, art aims at furnishing pleasure, and we are entertained by pleasure. But the word *entertainment* with its suggestion of diversion and lightness doesn't serve very well when we speak of Dante or Vermeer, say, since the pleasure we get from what these artists have done seems to partake rather of sublimity than of mere diversion. Perhaps entertainment is a subdivision of pleasure— or a low rung on the ladder whose top reaches to Paradise.

It is a fact, of course, that a great deal of what we call "great art" came into being for rather utilitarian reasons—a rich man's commission, a new cantata for next Sunday, a play for the Globe theater; and on that level it is hard to untangle the occasional from the sublime. What happens is that an occasional piece may turn out to be sublime because the man who made it is a genius. His sonnet about the Piedmont massacre or the death of the Countess, unabashedly occasional, somehow participates in the sublime because he has a great and noble imagination. On the other hand, we can get planning committees together and decide to have a breathtaking spectacle and hire all the necessary professionals and work out all the logistics and blow all the trumpets—and succeed only in bringing forth appalling bathos (viz. Radio City Music Hall Christmas and Easter productions, or the cinematic biblical extravaganzas that started with *The Ten Commandments*).

Let us say, then, that authentic art emerges from a noble imagination whatever the occasion is that has asked for it. And, further, that if a noble imagination is at work, authentic art appears, whether the subject matter happens to be "high" or "low." It is not very difficult, on the one hand, to see how great feats of courage, skill, or strength (as in Beowulf, Achilles, Hercules) can give rise to noble treatment. By the same token, the longings, perplexities, or doubts that beset the human mind have been fruitful sources of high utterance (for Shelley, Browning, and Wordsworth, for example). Or the soul's experience of God often furnishes the matter for genuine poetry (Donne, Herbert, Eliot). These are easy enough to cite in connection with a theory of good art.

But what about evil—real evil—as subject matter? How do we work this in?

Dante, for instance, writes about hell, which is as low as you can get. And he writes explicitly and at great length. Here are all the damned, pictured vividly, with discussions of what it was that landed them there and of what their particular torment is. There are explicit notations of sin—lechery, gluttony, wrath, avarice, sloth, and so on.

Or take Shakespeare. What, after all, is *Macbeth* about? Foul murder. We watch Lady Macbeth turning herself into a monster. Or what about Chaucer? One of his most mature poems, the *Troilus and Criseyda*, is about illicit love. Then there is one of the most towering figures in all of English poetry—Milton's Satan.

It will be obvious here that a distinction needs to be made between "good and evil" on the one hand, and "high and low" on the other. Clearly, great evil can furnish "high" subject matter (as in Dante and Milton). The *Inferno* and Satan are "low" only on some cosmic hierarchical accounting. They are "high" in the sense that they embody the biggest issues conceivable by the human imagination.

Similarly, really "low" stuff can afford the matter for genuine art. Take Fielding, with his tumble of hilarious but scurrilous situations in eighteenth-century England or Evelyn Waugh's brilliantly funny novels about upper-class decadence in early twentieth-century England (or, for that matter, Faulkner's wholly serious handling of American decadence).

What seems to emerge from this line of observation is that it is entirely the *treatment* that decides the worth (and hence the goodness or badness) of a piece of art. There can be good art about bad things, and bad art about good things (a discussion of this last would embarrass us all, alas).

Preserving Aesthetic Distance and Privacy

Which brings us back to the question about *The Devils*. It is, to use the favorite word of blurbs and critics now, "frank." Isn't that a point in its favor? It treats demonism (or bogus demonism—that is never really decided), and all the carnality and terror and horror that follow in its wake, colorfully and explicitly. What's wrong with this? Can't we be bold? Can't we call a spade a spade? Haven't we done well to shake off our nineteenth-century humbug and timorousness (and by this time, we all know we can be talking about only one possible topic—sex)?

No. We have not done well. In its frenetic disavowal of sexual reticence, the twentieth century has torn the veil and blundered into the Holy of Holies, as it were—and you can't do that with impunity. It is in the nature of the case that the Ark be secluded: you can't use it for a sawhorse. It is in the nature of the case that the shewbread be reserved—David didn't eat it for lunch every day. And by the same token, it is in the nature of the case that human sexuality be shrouded. It is not a public matter. (Someone will bring up the *Canticles* here: that is a great poem of carnal love; perhaps it is not a *public* poem?) Not only is nothing gained by the louder, shriller, more frequent and explicit discussion and portrayal of sexuality, but there is every reason to suppose that something is being lost—something good, along with the humbug and prudery.

And this is not necessarily to take a huggermugger or sanctimonious view of sexuality. Anyone who misses the fun—even the funny—in sex is missing part of it. But, like a tiresome three-year-old's pun, the human cloys when it is insisted upon too loud and long.

But sex isn't really the center of the matter. The guilt of *The Devils* (and of a hundred novels, plays, revues, and films one could trot out) is broader than that. It is that it fails to preserve *distance*. It not only points to the stew. It stirs it. It jumps in.

To isolate and articulate the difference between Dante's handling of hell and this film's handling of Loudun is difficult. Perhaps it has to do with a leer. If anything is leering from Dante's pit, it is leering at the poet as well as the reader, whereas you get the uneasy feeling in *The Devils* that not only Louis XIV leers at you from the screen but the filmmaker does as well.

We cannot say, of course, that *all* filmmakers (and novelists and poets) whose work fails because of this failure of distance are leering. That would be to pass a dangerous judgment on a great many people. Perhaps there is a prior fault in the era that the artists, because they live and work in the era, can escape only with difficulty. The fault would have something to do with the erosion in the modern world of such categories as absolute truth, and glory, and the holy, and thence of such responses as awe, humility, and reticence.

Finally, one has the unhappy feeling that in a great deal of contemporary art, literature, and cinema, inadequate imaginations are attempting very high summits. Scriptwriters, directors, producers, agents, and the rest, whose interest must be, above all, commercial, are addressing themselves quite blithely to imponderables that would give pause to the most sublime imaginations of history. The result is a proliferation of peepshows in Vanity Fair.

part 3

Christian Perspectives on Literature

Introduction

The reason why literature held the central place in educational programs until this century is not hard to see. Literature is perhaps the most comprehensive of all disciplines. It is a hybrid. Like music and painting, it is itself an artistic object and a source of aesthetic beauty. And because literature is made out of words and expresses ideas, it belongs with the "thought" disciplines, especially philosophy and theology. Literature, in short, is both a fine art and a humane art.

Briefly defined, literature is an interpretive presentation of human experience in an artistic form. Its subject matter is human experience. Its approach to human experience, moreover, is not abstract or propositional but concrete and incarnational. Literature does not tell *about* an experience but instead *presents* it as a living reality. Literature is also interpretive, inasmuch as writers select and mold their subject matter according to their own view of the world. And the content of literature, of course, always comes to us in a distinctively literary *form*—a story or poem or play, for example, each with its own further elements of artistic form.

121

In any literary situation, there are four ingredients present, as the following diagram shows:

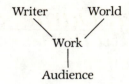

You can use this scheme as an organizing framework when reading the essays in this section, noting which ingredients and relationships each author discusses.

Homer, Dante, and All That

Thomas Howard

"Art," said G. K. Chesterton, "is the signature of man." That is, art identifies man as man, different from the rest of God's visible creation. It is small wonder, therefore, that defenses of literature and the arts repeatedly stress the human element in art.

Literature puts us in touch with what is elemental and enduring and universal in human experience. That is why Aristotle, in the earliest extant work of literary criticism, The Poetics, said that literature imitates "the universal," in contrast to history, which records "the particular." Wordsworth echoed the claim when he said that the poet pictures "the primary laws of our nature" and sings "a song in which all human beings join with him." According to Shelley, "a poem is the very image of life expressed in its eternal truth." More recently, Northrop Frye has stated, "The poet's job is not to tell you what happened, but what happens: not what did take place, but the kind of thing that always does take place."

The subject of literature is human experience. Its effects, as the essay below suggests, are to make us feel our own humanness, to expand our understanding of human experience, to enlarge our human com-

123

passion. The writer reaches into common human experience and finds the words to express that experience with power. The reader receives it with what has been called "the shock of recognition." Literature, in short, gives us forms for our feelings and our experiences of life.

Affirming Our Humanity as Christians

An essay on the reading of literature by Christians (that is, the reading by Christians of literature) is odd in that there are certainly no reasons for reading literature peculiar to a Christian's case. Furthermore, the thing that Christians see to be supremely important about life does not attach itself to culture.

If there are reasons why any human being ought to trouble himself with literature (and by literature I mean humane letters—serious poetry, drama, fiction, essay—and not philosophy, panegyric, tracts, journalism, and rubbish), they apply neither more nor less to a Christian than to anyone else. A Christian is, first of all, a human being. This sounds like heterodoxy at first, perhaps, in that we incline to feel that the call of God to us is *away* from human existence to a spiritual realm where we will be free of these old evil selves. But that is exactly the point: redemption is the redemption of *human* nature. It is not God's will to make us seraphim, or rainbows, or titans. It is *men* he seeks. Human beings. Beings who will exhibit what he had in mind to begin with—this particular kind of creature, neither angelic nor animal, this excellent thing whose glory would be to choose to love him, and to serve him under the special mode of flesh and blood. Indeed, his supreme unveiling of himself was under that mode. And there is to be no shuffling off of these dragging bodies in the end. The biblical description of the Last Things is of a *resurrection*—a reunion of flesh and spirit (form and content) from that grotesquery we call death, that obscene disjuncture of flesh and spirit that spoils God's creature man, and into whose bailiwick the Son of Man ventured, and whose spoliation he spoiled. So that a Christian is wrong to suppose that grace calls him away from human existence. It is precisely *to* authentic human existence (the kind announced and embodied in Jesus Christ) that he is called, so that he may embody for men and angels the special glory of his species. He is called away from *evil*, not human existence. It is evil—disobedience, pride, greed, gluttony, perfidy, cynicism, cowardice, niggardliness, and so on—that wrecks human nature, and God calls men to return to the glory first seen in one Adam, then lost, then restored by another Adam.

A Christian, then, is a human being, subject to all the laws (physical, political, moral, psychological) of that species, so that what is good for any man (vitamins, protection, fidelity, calmness) is good for him. The reading of serious literature is good for a man; hence it is good for a Christian.

Culture Is Not Christianity

This raises the other point mentioned in the opening paragraph—that the thing Christians see to be supremely important about life does not attach itself to culture (I mean culture in the humanistic, not the anthropological, sense—a man's intellectual cultivation, not his tribe). That is, a Christian sees the great and only issue in human life to be man's movement toward the perfection of love—what St. Paul called being sanctified, or transformed into the image of Christ. This is the only thing that really matters finally, so that a Christian sees every single thing in life—success, pain, fame, loss, education—as secondary to that. Why, then, it will be asked, are you talking as though *literature* were something important for a Christian? We've got our hands full with this business of sanctification and serving the Lord. We've no time for *cultchah*. We're people of one Book, and it's a book that contains all we need to know about life. Don't siphon us off to primrose byways of poetry and novels. Nobody ever needed that sort of thing to make him holy. You're not suggesting, are you, that an educated man has a better chance to be holy than an uneducated man? Whom did Jesus call? The philosophers? You have a rather sticky wicket to defend.

It is sticky indeed. These objections are convincing, and there is truth in them—namely, that it *is*, in the end, irrelevant whether a man is a scholar or a sailor. The City of God will be populated by men who, whatever else they happened to be doing on earth, learned the way of *caritas*. The credentials asked at the gate will not be books written, kingdoms conquered, or research accomplished. They will be obedience, purity, humility, faith, love. The shepherd, the duke, the housemaid, the tycoon, and the professor will stand, unshod, side by side, clad either in soiled rags or in the one garment of righteousness.

Why, then, an essay crying up the merits of literature? Haven't you just destroyed your own case? Isn't it, in fact, irrelevant and maybe even dangerous?

No connection, it seems to me, can be established between culture and holiness. The following comments do not tend toward that idea. Certain rewards come to the man who will read serious literature. If those rewards commend themselves to the Christian's imagination, good. They are certainly no *less* applicable to him than to any other man, and they may, like any other equipment (muscle, money, brains), be brought to the service of either altar, God's or Satan's.

Literature: Orator of the Imagination

In the first place we need to be clear about the nature of literature. Literature addresses the imagination, which is the faculty in us that enables us to organize the random tumble of experience into some sort of form and hence to manage it and savor it. Imagination is the source of all ritual. We shake hands, or set the table for breakfast, or lower our voices in a museum, or stand up to honor a dignitary: these are ritual formalizings of experience. Imagination is the image-making capacity in us, so that we speak of feeling like a wrung-out dishrag, or of a man's brow as looking like a thundercloud, or of the Kingdom of Heaven as being like a man planting seeds. And imagination is what makes art possible, because art is the transfiguration of the abstracts of experience (perception, emotion, ideas, and so on) into special forms (marble, melody, words), the idea being not only that it is legitimate to handle human experience in this way, but, oddly, that in this way something emerges about human experience that is hidden from all the discursive analysis in the world.

There is a sense in which the imagination works in an opposite direction from the analytic faculty in us: it tends always toward concretion (the image), while analysis tends toward abstraction (the dismantling of the thing in question—blood, granite, neurosis). A Christian, of course, would see this tendency as enormously appropriate in a universe whose tendency is also toward concretion. The original creative energy, the Word, uttered itself in rock and soil and water, not in equations. And again, the ultimate utterance of that Word was in the shape of a man. Even the book given by that Word was not mainly expository and analytic but narrative and poetic and parabolic. Indeed, one suspects that the whole post-Baconian methodology (the sort of thing that leads us to think we are saying something *more true* about the solar system when we speak of gravity and centrifugal force than when we speak of Atlas holding the earth on his shoulders) may be leading us, ironically, *away from* the way things are. For its tendency is toward depersonalization and abstraction, whereas the Christian understands the original creative energy as moving always toward personhood and concretion.

In any case, literature addresses this imagination in us. It hails us with vivid cases in point of otherwise blurred and cluttered experience. Homer's heroic handling of jealousy, rage, bravery, cynicism, love, and endurance in the figures of Achilles, Agamemnon, Hector, Paris, Ulysses; Dante's cosmic geography of hell, purgatory, and paradise—what modern categories would reduce to abstractions like alienation, discipline, bliss; Shakespeare's probing of overweening pride in *Macbeth*, or of jealousy in *Othello*; Milton's shaping of the human experience of evil and loss into *Paradise Lost*. These are familiar to us. We read them in school. And perhaps we remember a stirring in us, or a brief glimpse of something that arrested us, or even a tidal wave of new awareness of what was at stake in human existence.

The world is full of such works of the imagination, all of them trying to see and utter and shape the human experience. There is Boethius's lovely *De Consolatione*, in which philosophy as a lady visits the discouraged man in his prison (Boethius was, in fact, thrown into prison). There are the dark and simple and noble Anglo-Saxon poems from the huge *Beowulf* to the winsome *Dream of the Rood* (spoken by the Cross about its own experience of Christ's crucifixion), to the sad *Deor's Lament* (about the passing of everything dear), to the fragmentary *Battle of Maldon*. The Middle Ages are full of magnificent dreams and allegories, giving us powerful images of beauty and sin: *The Pearl*, about a man who lost his little girl and found her in paradise; *The Vision of William Concerning Piers Plowman*, one of the most overpowering allegorical descriptions of society, evil, virtue, and nearly everything else, written in the fourteenth century about that century but true in every point about our own. The sixteenth century produced the greatest drama our language knows (Shakespeare and his contemporaries), as well as unsurpassed lyric beauty in the work of Spenser, Sidney, and again Shakespeare. For someone who is looking for specifically Christian experience in his literature, the seventeenth century is the pot of gold. Virtually every major poet was Christian, and made it his entire poetic business to shape his religious experience into verse: Donne, Herbert, Crashaw, Vaughan, and of course Milton. There were some naughty "cavalier poets" whose amorous verse is really very good, too.

The Goal of Literature: Heightened Awareness

The list could go on, of course, but it would be just that— a list—and would do little good. The point is that our language is full of works of the imagination, each of them uttering something of the human experience of life, each of them throwing some light onto experience, each giving some shape to it all. And for the person who will allow himself the austere luxury of reading it, there is that high guerdon of art, the heightening of consciousness.

By participating in the noble fictions of the human imagination, we enlarge our capacity to apprehend experience. There comes a sense both of the oneness of human experience and of its individuality. The figures of myth and fiction—Ulysses, Beowulf, Roland, Don Quixote—are not cards in a computer, but their experience is a paradigm of all human experience. As a man becomes familiar with the follies, sins, and troubles of the great characters in fiction and drama—Tom Jones, Henry V, Jane Austen's Emma, George Eliot's Dorothea, Hardy's Tess, James's Isabel, Tolstoy's Anna—he realizes that here are profound probings by noble minds of the ambiguities of human experience, and his own appreciation of these ambiguities is sharpened.

Along with this heightened consciousness of human experience there comes an awareness of what was at stake in redemption. Minds that have been schooled in humane letters have been those that have often spoken eloquently to us of God: St. Paul, Sir Thomas More, Erasmus, Melanchthon, Pascal, Newman, Mauriac, T. S. Eliot, J. R. R. Tolkien, C. S. Lewis. There is in them none of the stridence or flatulence that often marks the biblical exposition of men who have brought only their own myopia to the Word of God. (The point here is not that the Holy Ghost does not at his pleasure pick out someone whom scholars would call an ignoramus and through his mouth bring to nothing the wisdom of men. He does. But his freedom to do this has led altogether too many ignoramuses to assume that divine mantle and bleat their foolishness abroad in the name of the Lord; it will not do.)

The reading of serious literature, then, may increase our sense of participating in the human experience. It may enrich our sympathies, sharpen our focus, broaden our awareness, mellow our minds, and ennoble our vision. And it may energize that faculty in us by which we apprehend the world as image (which it is), the imagination.

Literature and the Greatness of Man

Roland M. Frye

People do not need the arts to exist physically. Our capacity for the arts is something that we indulge after our basic needs for food and clothing and shelter have been met. In that sense the arts are a luxury.

Yet no culture in the entire history of the world has been wholly without art. Such universality suggests that, although the arts may not be a physical necessity, they are a necessity for the human spirit.

A century ago, Matthew Arnold analyzed why the hold of the arts upon the human race has been so compelling. "When we set ourselves to enumerate the powers which go to the building up of human life," theorized Arnold, "they are the power of conduct, the power of intellect and knowledge, the power of beauty, and the power of social life and manners. . . . Human nature is built up by these powers; we have the need for them all." And therein, claimed Arnold, lies the strength of literature and the arts, for they deal with all four areas and their interrelationships.

The following essay develops a thesis similar to Arnold's. While concerned with literature specifically, the author's comments apply to other

This selection is excerpted from chapter 2 (pp. 57-79) of Roland M. Frye's book, Perspective on Man: Literature and the Christian Tradition.

arts as well. The arts, claims the author, nurture the human capacity for beauty, understanding, and compassion.

The Clarification of Life

Man is inescapably engaged in the evaluation of his life and of the alternatives which his life presents to him. Apart from evaluation he cannot live, for life consists of a series of choices apart from which action is impossible. He may, of course, choose superficially, or naïvely, or unwisely, but choose he must and every choice has at its base an evaluation. By literature man may be assisted in relating his evaluations to the general conditions of human existence in terms of beauty, understanding, and compassion. In this way literature both undergirds and increases the greatness of man.

Sir Philip Sidney followed and summarized the perennial classical view of literature when he defined poetry as "an art of imitation . . . with this end, to teach and delight."[1] In our own time Robert Frost puts it in a slightly different way, but to the same purpose when he writes that poetry "begins in delight and ends in wisdom," or in "a clarification of life." This literary clarification may be a small one, but nonetheless valuable, such as we can so often find in the poetry of Frost himself, or it may be a great clarification such as is found in the writings of Shakespeare and Sophocles, or it may even be an ultimate clarification, such as is found in the Christian Scriptures, but genuine literature always offers some new and clearer vision of reality. This is its greatest value to the generality of men, for as Frost says, "we are always hurling experience ahead of us

1. Sir Philip Sidney, *An Apology for Poetry*, in *The Prelude to Poetry: The English Poets in Defense and Praise of Their Own Art* (New York: Everyman's Library, Dutton, 1927), p. 16; and Robert Frost, from "The Figure a Poem Makes," in *Writers on Writing*, ed. Walter Allen (London: Phoenix House, 1948), p. 22. The two anthologies from which these quotations are taken constitute excellent collections of the views expressed by literary men on the art of literature, and both will reward serious reading.

to pave the future with against the day when we may want to strike a line of purpose across it for somewhere."[2]

This much is so even when the writer is focusing our attention upon inanimate nature, for the result here as elsewhere must be a clarification of life. As Walt Whitman put it, people "expect of the poet to indicate more than the beauty and dignity which always attach to dumb real objects—they expect him to indicate the path between reality and their souls."[3] Literature, then, even when it is regarded as a mirror held up to nature, is a mirror with a difference; it is not a mere replica reproduction of something external and objective. George Bernard Shaw described the mirror of art in this way: "You use a glass mirror to see your face; you use works of art to see your soul."[4]

The result is not just the expression of the writer's individualistic view, but is the communication of something relevant to the entire human situation. "The efforts of the best poets and esthetic writers," Goethe wrote, "have been directed toward the universally human."[5] William Faulkner made the same point when he declared that all genuine writers belong to one universal school of man, treating in a mutual language "much older than any intellectual tongue because it is the simple language of humanity," "a very old story . . . the story of human beings in conflict with their nature, their character, their souls, with others, or with their environment."[6]

The clarification of life, a deeper understanding of the human situation, the charting of pathways between reality and the human soul, the treatment of the universally human in the simple language of humanity—these are characteristics of great literature. So understood, literature provides insights into the

2. Frost, in *Writers on Writing*, p. 23.

3. Walt Whitman, preface to *Leaves of Grass*, in *Writers on Writing*, p. 51.

4. G. B. Shaw, *Back to Methuselah*, in *Selected Plays* (New York: Dodd, Mead and Company, 1949), vol. 2, p. 250.

5. Goethe, "World Literature," in *Seven Arts*, vol. 3, ed. Fernando Puma (New York: Falcon's Wing Press, 1955), p. 225.

6. William Faulkner, *Faulkner at Nagano*, ed. Robert A. Jelliffe (Tokyo: Kenkyusha, Ltd., 1956), pp. 95, 156, 177, 205.

human situation which we ignore only to our peril and to the foreshortening of our understanding. In this sense Abelard raised a very foolish question when he asked: "What has Horace to do with the Psalter, Virgil with the Gospel, Cicero with the Apostle?"[7] The answer is simply that Horace, Virgil, and Cicero clarify the human situation to which the salvation of God is addressed through Psalter, Gospel, and Apostle. Christianity cannot deny the value of Horace, Virgil, and Cicero without denying the value of man, which it cannot do and remain Christian. Concerned as it is with man in his greatness and misery, Christian faith addresses itself to the very situation which literature clarifies, examines, and makes in some limited measure manageable.

And yet the question of relevance has been repeatedly raised, whether with Abelard as we have seen, or with Tertullian's "What has Athens to do with Jerusalem," or Alcuin's "What has Ingeld to do with Christ," or Erasmus's "What has Aristotle to do with Christ." A highly intelligent answer to these questions was proposed some four centuries ago by John Calvin. Now Calvin was surely not one to overestimate man apart from the grace of God, but neither was he willing to underestimate him. Of the value of secular, and even pagan, literature, Calvin wrote:

> So oft therefore as we light upon profane writers, let us be put in mind by that marvelous light of truth that shineth in them, that the mind of man, how much so ever it be perverted and fallen from the first integrity, is yet still clothed and garnished with excellent gifts of God. If we consider that the spirit of God is the only fountain of truth, we will neither refuse nor despise the truth itself, wheresoever it shall appear, except we will dishonorably use the Spirit of God: for the gifts of the Holy Ghost cannot be set light by, without contempt and reproach of Himself.[8]

7. Peter Abelard, quoted in Harbison's *The Christian Scholar in the Age of Reformation* (New York: Charles Scribner's Sons, 1956), p. 37.

8. John Calvin, *Institutes of the Christian Religion*, trans. Thomas Norton (London: John Norton, 1611), II.ii.15.

It is indisputable, of course, that great literature not only may serve but often has served as a bearer of Christian truth, as in the works of Dante and Milton, for example. . . . For the present, however, we are concerned with literature as bearing general human truth. . . . Let us return now to Faulkner and his statement that literature concerns "the old universal truths" of human anguish and triumph. . . . These old universal truths Mr. C. S. Lewis in his *Abolition of Man* calls the *Tao*, the conception of human values, of character, understanding, pity, honor, and virtue which run through all the lasting forms of humane thought, "Platonic, Aristotelian, Stoic, Christian and Oriental alike."[9] There can be no living of man together with man in any civilized way apart from these ancient values, for apart from them there never has been and never can be any civilization. They are the *given* upon which all human value and humane life rests, the *Tao* or way upon which all men and societies must walk if any human dignity and worth is to be maintained. Lewis, as a Christian, knows that the *Tao* is not the equivalent of Christian faith and cannot be substituted for it, but he is also, like Calvin, too profound and too literate a Christian thinker ever to assume that these universal truths can be ignored by Christians "except we will dishonorably use the Spirit of God."[10]

This universal truth to the human situation, this *Tao*, may be memorably treated by men who are in their own lifes mean, little, and even wicked. Two eminent Christian writers, Milton and Tolstoi, both held that the poet must be a good man, and their opinion is sometimes falsely taken to be the Christian position. It is not. Augustine wrote that, in order that God's good gift of beauty not be made an idol, "God dispenses it even to the wicked,"[11] while Thomas Aquinas held that "the test of the artist does not lie in the will with which he goes to work,

9. C. S. Lewis, *The Abolition of Man* (New York: Macmillan, 1947), p. 12.
10. Calvin, *Institutes*, II.ii.15.
11. Augustine, *City of God*, 15.22.

but in the excellence of the work he produces."[12] John Calvin elaborated the same position when he discussed the attribution in Genesis of arts and skills to the wicked line of Cain, through Jabal, Jubal, and Tubal-cain. "The invention of arts and such other like things which serve for the common use and benefit of life," Calvin wrote, "is the gift of God, not to be despised, and a virtue worthy to be praised. . . ."[13] . . . The common caricature of the poet as an amoral eccentric, a caricature which is so popularly accepted in our time, is decidedly unfair to most *great* poets, but even where it applies it does not invalidate works of literature which carry value in their own right, quite apart from the lives of the men who produced them.

Literature and the Nurture of Beauty

[From great] literature, I would like to suggest, we can gain sustenance for our own basic humanity through the nurture of beauty, the nurture of understanding, and the nurture of compassion. In each of these ways literature both points toward and contributes to human greatness.

First, there is the nurture of beauty. We go far astray if we regard beauty as mere ornament or decoration, as a filigree attached to the surface of life. Yet it is too often regarded in this way, and in America especially the general appreciation of beauty is on a very low plane indeed. Walk into a typical American house and you find all the utility which credit can afford, but an appalling poverty of beauty. When you do find a few individual objects of some beauty they too often fail to harmonize either with each other or with the rest of the room in which they are placed. This pervasive Philistinism of American taste is sometimes rather glibly attributed to our Puritan

---

12. Thomas Aquinas, *Summa Theologica* I-II, Q. 57, Art. 3.
13. Quoted in Arnold Williams, *The Common Expositor* (Chapel Hill: University of North Carolina Press, 1948), p. 145.

heritage, but the attribution is false, as you can readily discover if you study the planning, architecture, and interiors of New England villages. One of the most striking ironies in the history of taste is that the creators of the lovely Puritan houses, village greens, and churches should be called tasteless by twentieth-century people who are themselves submerged in the most appalling mass of ugliness and vulgarity which the Western world has perhaps ever known.

. . . Beauty is not excrescent to the general well-being of man, but essential to it. Beauty brings order out of anarchy, harmony out of cacophony. Beauty, at base, is the result of the creative activity of God, and artistic beauty is, if I may strain the terms, a humanly created revelation. Thus Shelley declared of poetry that it "lifts the veil from the hidden beauty of the world."[14] Art reveals beauty to us, makes us conscious of what we ignore. When we read in *Hamlet* that "the morn, in russet mantle clad, Walks o'er the dew of yon high eastward hill,"[15] we have had a veil lifted from the world's hidden beauty and we see that beauty afresh both *in* Shakespeare's words and *through* those words.

To paraphrase Coleridge we may say that the sense of beauty consists in the intuition of the proportioned relations of parts to each other and to a whole, the melody of the parts being united in the harmony of the whole.[16] Beauty comes to us as we perceive an ordered and harmoniously proportioned creation. . . . That is what Christopher Fry has called the logic of beauty, and of it he says: "What part this logic plays in our life here on earth is beyond calculation. If it awakens harmony, modulation, and the resolving of discord in us, we are nearer to our true natures."[17] When beauty is understood in that

14. Percy Bysshe Shelley, *A Defense of Poetry*, in *The Prelude to Poetry*, p. 216.

15. Shakespeare, *Hamlet*, I. 1. 166-67.

16. Samuel Taylor Coleridge, *On the Principles of Genial Criticism Concerning the Fine Arts: Essay Third*, in *Biographia Literaria*, vol. 2, ed. J. Shawcross (London: Oxford University Press, 1954).

17. Christopher Fry, "Why Verse?" *World Theatre* (1955), 4:59.

sense—and it has been so understood by the great Christian humanists—it becomes clear why beauty is an essential to the health of individuals and of societies.

Art must thus be seen as indispensable to human wellbeing, and beauty is very closely allied to goodness. But beauty is *not* goodness. . . . [It] is comparable to courage, in that both are neutral values which may be applied toward the ends of evil as well as the ends of goodness. Aldous Huxley has made this point with great force, by considering the "beauties of unholiness" as well as the "beauties of holiness." He writes that the

"beauties of holiness" strengthen faith where it already exists and, where there is no faith, contribute to conversion. Appealing, as they do, only to the aesthetic sense, they guarantee neither the truth nor the ethical value of the doctrines with which they have been, quite arbitrarily, associated. As a matter of plain historical fact, the beauties of holiness have often been matched and indeed surpassed by the beauties of unholiness. Under Hitler, for example, the yearly Nuremberg rallies were masterpieces of ritual and theatrical art. "I had spent six years in St. Petersburg before the war in the best days of the old Russian ballet," writes Sir Nevile Henderson, the British ambassador to Hitler's Germany, "but for grandiose beauty I have never seen any ballet to compare with the Nuremberg rally." One thinks of Keats— "beauty is truth, truth beauty." Alas, the identity exists only on some ultimate, supramundane level. On the levels of politics and theology, beauty is perfectly compatible with nonsense and tyranny.[18]

The point which Mr. Huxley makes is a very important one indeed, and should be kept in mind in any discussion of beauty. Basically, however, the function of beauty when it expresses itself without perversion to false goals is to nurture a higher and more harmonious life for man.

18. Aldous Huxley, *Brave New World Revisited* (New York: Harper and Brothers, 1958), pp. 64–65.

Literature and the Nurture of
Understanding and Compassion

In addition to the nurture of beauty, literature also provides for the nurture of understanding, a broadening of horizons and a deepening of awareness, which may come in many ways. It may come through a brief phrase which clarifies for us some particular human personality, or even in a seemingly chance witticism which illuminates the entire human landscape, like a momentary flash in the darkness. . . . [This] increment of understanding may bring with it an increment of compassion. . . .

The nurture of compassion comes only through the focus upon a common humanity. Shut up as most of us are within the narrow compass of our own lives, we do not naturally break out from ourselves either into the larger world which surrounds us or into the other small worlds of individuals whose lives impinge upon our own. Although it is true that man cannot ultimately and finally free himself from bondage to himself by his own efforts—as there is a sort of law of psychodynamics operating here according to which we cannot lift ourselves by our own bootstraps—it is equally true that there may be some proximate breaking down of barriers between man and man. Upon this proximate and limited breakthrough of man to meet man all worthy human society is based, and to it art contributes by the enlargement of understanding but even more by the expansion of sympathy. This is what Tolstoi meant when he wrote that "art should cause violence to be set aside,"[19] and Shelley got at it even more explicitly when he wrote that literature provides, through the imagination, the means by which one man may put himself in the place of other men:

19. Leo Tolstoi, in *Seven Arts*, vol. 2, ed. Fernando Puma (New York: Permabooks, 1954), p. 48.

The great secret of morals is love, or a going out of our nature, and an identification of ourselves with the beautiful which exists in thought, action or person, not our own. A man, to be greatly good, must imagine intensely and comprehensively; he must put himself in the place of another and of many others; the pains and pleasures of his species must become his own. The great instrument of moral good is the imagination; and poetry administers to the effect by acting upon the cause.[20]

. . . If ever an age needed compassion it is our own age, and yet the very brutality of our era seems to inoculate us against compassion, for we do not hear of murders and persecutions of single men and women but of mass slaughter, of the deportation and oppression of thousands and even millions. The numbers are so staggering that we soon lose a sense of proportion and hide ourselves from human suffering by a barrier of statistics. But literature breaks through that barrier for us, and brings us into feeling relationship with all human suffering by exposing us to it in critical instances. . . .

Literature, then, serves to deepen and to extend human greatness through the nurture of beauty, understanding, and compassion. In none of these ways, of course, can literature, unless it be the literature of Christian faith, lead us to the City of God, but it may make our life in the city of man far more a thing of joy and meaning and humanity, and that in itself is no small achievement. Great literature may not be a Jacob's ladder by which we can climb to heaven, but it provides an invaluable staff with which to walk the earth.

---

20. Shelley, *The Defense of Poetry*, in *The Prelude to Poetry*, pp. 216-17.

Religion and Literature

T. S. Eliot

No essay on the topic of the relationship between literature and Christianity has been more influential in the world of literary scholarship than this one by T. S. Eliot. Written by one of the towering figures of modern literature, it lays out with prophetic conviction a core of assumptions that are at the very heart of a Christian approach to literature.

As you read the essay, you will find that the following five premises permeate the discussion:

1. Christians should apply their own Christian standards (ethical and theological) to the literature they read.
2. Christians should apply such standards to all literature, not only to Christian literature.
3. Christians should know how to read non-Christian literature without being swept into acquiescence as they read.
4. Literature really does influence our thought and behavior.
5. The influence of modern literature is often harmful because of its secular bias.

The division of the essay into sections with headings has been done by the editor with the publisher's permission.

These five principles constitute Eliot's main argument, but the entire essay is filled with insight. Though the essay is not easy reading, it is a work that the serious student of literature should mine often for its varied ore.

The Relevance of Religion to Literature

What I have to say is largely in support of the following propositions: Literary criticism should be completed by criticism from a definite ethical and theological standpoint. In so far as in any age there is common agreement on ethical and theological matters, so far can literary criticism be substantive. In ages like our own, in which there is no such common agreement, it is the more necessary for Christian readers to scrutinize their reading, especially of works of imagination, with explicit ethical and theological standards. The "greatness" of literature cannot be determined solely by literary standards; though we must remember that whether it is literature or not can be determined only by literary standards.[1]

We have tacitly assumed, for some centuries past, that there is *no* relation between literature and theology. This is not to deny that literature—I mean, again, primarily works of imagination—has been, is, and probably always will be judged by some moral standards. But moral judgments of literary works are made only according to the moral code accepted by each generation, whether it lives according to that code or not. In an age which accepts some precise Christian theology, the common code may be fairly orthodox: though even in such periods the common code may exalt such concepts as "honour," "glory" or "revenge" to a position quite intolerable to Christianity. The dramatic ethics of the Elizabethan Age offers an interesting study. But when the common code is detached from its theological background, and is consequently more and more merely

---

1. As an example of literary criticism given greater significance by theological interests, I would call attention to Theodor Haecker: *Virgil* (Sheed and Ward).

a matter of habit, it is exposed both to prejudice and to change. At such times morals are open to being altered *by* literature; so that we find in practice that what is "objectionable" in literature is merely what the present age is not used to. It is a commonplace that what shocks one generation is accepted quite calmly by the next. This adaptability to change of moral standards is sometimes greeted with satisfaction as an evidence of human perfectibility: whereas it is only evidence of what unsubstantial foundations people's moral judgments have.

Three Types of Religious Literature

I am not concerned here with religious literature but with the application of our religion to the criticism of any literature. It may be as well, however, to distinguish first what I consider to be the three senses in which we can speak of "religious literature." The first is that of which we say that it is "religious literature" in the same way that we speak of "historical literature" or of "scientific literature." I mean that we can treat the Authorized translation of the Bible, or the works of Jeremy Taylor, as literature, in the same way that we treat the historical writing of Clarendon or of Gibbon—our two great English historians—as literature; or Bradley's *Logic*, or Buffon's *Natural History*. All of these writers were men who, incidentally to their religious, or historical, or philosophic purpose, had a gift of language which makes them delightful to read to all those who can enjoy language well written, even if they are unconcerned with the objects which the writers had in view. And I would add that though a scientific, or historical, or theological, or philosophic work which is also "literature," may become super-annuated as anything but literature, yet it is not likely to be "literature" unless it had its scientific or other value for its own time. While I acknowledge the legitimacy of this enjoyment, I am more acutely aware of its abuse. The persons who enjoy these writings solely because of their literary merit are essentially parasites; and we know that parasites, when they become too numerous, are pests. I could fulminate against the men of letters who have gone into ecstasies over "the Bible as literature," the Bible as "the noblest monument of English prose." Those who talk of the Bible as a "monument of English prose" are merely admiring it as a monument over the grave of Christianity. I must try to avoid the by-paths of my discourse: it is enough to suggest that just as the work of Clarendon, or Gibbon, or Buffon, or Bradley would be of inferior literary value if it were insignificant as history, science and philosophy respectively, so the Bible has had a *literary* influence upon English literature *not* because it has been considered as literature, but because it has been considered as the report of the Word of God. And the fact that men of letters now discuss it as "literature" probably indicates the *end* of its "literary" influence.

The second kind of relation of religion to literature is that which is found in what is called "religious" or "devotional" poetry. Now what is the usual attitude of the lover of poetry—and I mean the person who is a genuine and first-hand enjoyer and appreciator of poetry, not the person who follows the admirations of others—towards this department of poetry? I believe, all that may be implied in his calling it a *department*. He believes, not always explicitly, that when you qualify poetry as "religious" you are indicating very clear limitations. For the great majority of people who love poetry, "*religious* poetry" is a variety of *minor* poetry: the religious poet is not a poet who is treating the whole subject matter of poetry in a religious spirit, but a poet who is dealing with a confined part of this subject matter: who is leaving out what men consider their major passions, and thereby confessing his ignorance of them. I think that this is the real attitude of most poetry lovers towards such poets as Vaughan, or Southwell, or Crashaw, or George Herbert, or Gerard Hopkins.

But what is more, I am ready to admit that up to a point these critics are right. For there is a kind of poetry, such as most of the work of the authors I have mentioned, which is the product of a special religious awareness, which may exist without the general awareness which we expect of the major poet. In some poets, or in some of their works, this general awareness may have existed; but the preliminary steps which represent it may have been suppressed, and only the end-product presented. Between these, and those in which the religious or devotional genius represents the *special* and limited awareness, it may be very difficult to discriminate. I do not pretend to offer Vaughan, or Southwell, or George Herbert, or Hopkins as major poets:[2] I feel sure that the first three, at least, are poets of this limited awareness. They are not great religious poets in the sense in which Dante, or Corneille, or Racine, even in those of their plays which do not touch upon Christian themes, are great Christian religious poets. Or even in the sense in which Villon and Baudelaire, with all their imperfections and delinquencies, are Christian poets. Since the time of Chaucer, Christian poetry (in the sense in which I shall mean it) has been limited in England almost exclusively to minor poetry.

I repeat that when I am considering Religion and Literature, I speak of these things only to make clear that I am not concerned primarily with Religious Literature. I am concerned with what should be the relation between Religion and all Literature. Therefore the third type of "religious literature" may be more quickly passed over. I mean the literary works of men who are sincerely desirous of forwarding the cause of religion: that which may come under the heading of Propaganda. I am thinking, of course, of such delightful fiction as Mr. Chesterton's *Man Who Was Thursday*, or his *Father Brown*. No one admires and enjoys these things more than I do; I would only remark that when the same effect is aimed at by zealous persons of less talent than Mr. Chesterton the effect is negative. But my point is that such writings do not enter into any serious consideration of the relation of Religion and Literature: because

2. I note that in an address delivered in Swansea some years later (subsequently published in *The Welsh Review* under the title of "What Is Minor Poetry?") I stated with some emphasis my opinion that Herbert is a major, not a minor poet. I agree with my later opinion. [1949]

they are conscious operations in a world in which it is assumed that Religion and Literature are not related. It is a conscious and limited relating. What I want is a literature which should be *un*consciously, rather than deliberately and defiantly, Christian: because the work of Mr. Chesterton has its point from appearing in a world which is definitely not Christian.

The Need to Scrutinize What We Read

I am convinced that we fail to realize how completely, and yet how irrationally, we separate our literary from our religious judgements. If there could be a complete separation, perhaps it might not matter: but the separation is not, and never can be, complete. If we exemplify literature by the novel—for the novel is the form in which literature affects the greatest number—we may remark this gradual secularization of literature during at least the last three hundred years. Bunyan, and to some extent Defoe, had moral purposes: the former is beyond suspicion, the latter may be suspect. But since Defoe the secularization of the novel has been continuous. There have been three chief phases. In the first, the novel took the Faith, in its contemporary version, for granted, and omitted it from its picture of life. Fielding, Dickens and Thackeray belong to this phase. In the second, it doubted, worried about, or contested the Faith. To this phase belong George Eliot, George Meredith and Thomas Hardy. To the third phase, in which we are living, belong nearly all contemporary novelists except Mr. James Joyce. It is the phase of those who have never heard the Christian Faith spoken of as anything but an anachronism.

Now, do people in general hold a definite opinion, that is to say religious or anti-religious; and do they read novels, or poetry for that matter, with a separate compartment of their minds? The common ground between religion and fiction is behaviour. Our religion imposes our ethics, our judgment and criticism of ourselves, and our behaviour toward our fellow men. The fiction that we read affects our behaviour towards our fellow men, affects our patterns of ourselves. When we read of human beings behaving in certain ways, with the approval of the author, who gives his benediction to this behaviour by his attitude toward the result of the behaviour arranged by himself, we can be influenced towards behaving in the same way.[3] When the contemporary novelist is an individual thinking for himself in isolation, he may have something important to offer to those who are able to receive it. He who is alone may speak to the individual. But the majority of novelists are persons drifting in the stream, only a little faster. They have some sensitiveness, but little intellect.

We are expected to be broadminded about literature, to put aside prejudice or conviction, and to look at fiction as fiction and at drama as drama. With what is inaccurately called "censorship" in this country—with what is much more difficult to cope with than an official censorship, because it represents the opinions of individuals in an irresponsible democracy, I have very little sympathy; partly because it so often suppresses the wrong books, and partly because it is little more effective than Prohibition of Liquor; partly because it is one manifestation of the desire that state control should take the place of decent domestic influence; and wholly because it acts only from custom and habit, not from decided theological and moral principles. Incidentally, it gives people a false sense of security in leading them to believe that books which are *not* suppressed are harmless. Whether there *is* such a thing as a harmless book I am not sure: but there very likely are books so utterly unreadable as to be incapable of injuring anybody. But it is certain that a book is not harmless merely because no one is consciously offended by it. And if we, as readers, keep our religious and moral convictions in one compartment, and take our reading merely for entertainment, or on a higher plane, for aesthetic pleasure, I would point out that the author, whatever his

---

3. Here and later I am indebted to Montgomery Belgion, *The Human Parrot* (chapter on The Irresponsible Propagandist).

conscious intentions in writing, in practice recognizes no such distinctions. The author of a work of imagination is trying to affect us wholly, as human beings, whether he knows it or not; and we are affected by it, as human beings, whether we intend to be or not. I suppose that everything we eat has some other effect upon us than merely the pleasure of taste and mastication; it affects us during the process of assimilation and digestion; and I believe that exactly the same is true of anything we read.

The fact that what we read does not concern merely something called our *literary taste*, but that it affects directly, though only amongst many other influences, the whole of what we are, is best elicited, I think, by a conscientious examination of the history of our individual literary education. Consider the adolescent reading of any person with some literary sensibility. Everyone, I believe, who is at all sensible to the seductions of poetry, can remember some moment in youth when he or she was completely carried away by the work of one poet. Very likely he was carried away by several poets, one after the other. The reason for this passing infatuation is not merely that our sensibility to poetry is keener in adolescence than in maturity. What happens is a kind of inundation, of invasion of the undeveloped personality by the stronger personality of the poet. The same thing may happen at a later age to persons who have not done much reading. One author takes complete possession of us for a time; then another; and finally they begin to affect each other in our mind. We weigh one against another; we see that each has qualities absent from others, and qualities incompatible with the qualities of others: we begin to be, in fact, critical; and it is our growing critical power which protects us from excessive possession by any one literary personality. The good critic—and we should all try to be critics, and not leave criticism to the fellows who write reviews in the papers—is the man who, to a keen and abiding sensibility, joins wide and increasingly discriminating reading. Wide reading is not valuable as a kind of hoarding, an accumulation of knowledge, or what sometimes is meant by the term "a well-stocked mind." It is valuable because in the process of being affected by one powerful personality after another, we cease to be dominated by any one, or by any small number. The very different views of life, cohabiting in our minds, affect each other, and our own personality asserts itself and gives each a place in some arrangement peculiar to ourself.

It is simply not true that works of fiction, prose or verse, that is to say works depicting the actions, thoughts and words and passions of imaginary human beings, *directly* extend our knowledge of life. Direct knowledge of life is knowledge directly in relation to ourselves, it is our knowledge of *how* people behave in general, of *what* they are like in general, in so far as that part of life in which we ourselves have participated gives us material for generalization. Knowledge of life obtained through fiction is only possible by another stage of self-consciousness. That is to say, it can only be a knowledge of other people's knowledge of life, not of life itself. So far as we are taken up with the happenings in any novel in the same way in which we are taken up with what happens under our eyes, we are acquiring at least as much falsehood as truth. But when we are developed enough to say: "This is the view of life of a person who was a good observer within his limits, Dickens, or Thackeray, or George Eliot, or Balzac; but he looked at it in a different way from me, because he was a different man; he even selected rather different things to look at, or the same things in a different order of importance, because he was a different man; so what I am looking at is the world as seen by a particular mind"—then we are in a position to gain something from reading fiction. We are learning *something* about life from these authors direct, just as we learn something from the reading of history direct; but these authors are only really helping us when we can see, and allow for, their differences from ourselves.

Now what we get, as we gradually grow up and read more and more, and read a greater diversity of authors, is a variety of views of life. But what people commonly assume, I suspect, is that we gain this experience of other men's views of life only by "improving reading." This, it is supposed, is a reward we get by applying ourselves to Shakespeare, and Dante, and Goethe, and Emerson, and Carlyle, and dozens of other respectable writers. The rest of our reading for amusement is merely killing time. But I incline to come to the alarming conclusion that it is just the literature that we read for "amusement," or "purely for pleasure" that may have the greatest and least suspected influence upon us. It is the literature which we read with the least effort that can have the easiest and most insidious influence upon us. Hence it is that the influence of popular novelists, and of popular plays of contemporary life, requires to be scrutinized most closely. And it is chiefly *contemporary* literature that the majority of people ever read in this attitude of "purely for pleasure," of pure passivity.

The Christian and Modern Literature

The relation to my subject of what I have been saying should now be a little more apparent. Though we may read literature merely for pleasure, of "entertainment" or of "aesthetic enjoyment," this reading never affects simply a sort of special sense: it affects our moral and religious existence. And I say that while individual modern writers of eminence can be improving, contemporary literature as a whole tends to be degrading. And that even the effect of the better writers, in an age like ours, may be degrading to some readers; for we must remember that what a writer does to people is not necessarily what he indends to do. It may be only what people are capable of having done to them. People exercise an unconscious selection in being influenced. A writer like D. H. Lawrence may be in his effect either beneficial or pernicious. I am not sure that I have not had some pernicious influence myself.

At this point I anticipate a rejoinder from the liberal-minded, from all those who are convinced that if everybody says what he thinks, and does what he likes, things will somehow, by some automatic compensation and adjustment, come right in the end. "Let everything be tried," they say, "and if it is a mistake, then we shall learn by experience." This argument might have some value, if we were always the same generation upon earth; or if, as we know to be not the case, people ever learned much from the experience of their elders. These liberals are convinced that only by what is called unrestrained individualism will truth ever emerge. Ideas, views of life, they think, issue distinct from independent heads, and in consequence of their knocking violently against each other, the fittest survive, and truth rises triumphant. Anyone who dissents from this view must be either a mediaevalist, wishful only to set back the clock, or else a fascist, and probably both.

If the mass of contemporary authors were really individualists, every one of them inspired Blakes, each with his separate vision, and if the mass of the contemporary public were really a mass of *individuals* there might be something to be said for this attitude. But this is not, and never has been, and never will be. It is not only that the reading individual today (or at any day) is not enough an individual to be able to absorb all the "views of life" of all the authors pressed upon us by the publishers' advertisements and the reviewers, and to be able to arrive at wisdom by considering one against another. It is that the contemporary authors are not individuals enough either. It is not that the world of separate individuals of the liberal democrat is undesirable; it is simply that this world does not exist. For the reader of contemporary literature is not, like the reader of the established great literature of all time, exposing himself to the influence of divers and contradictory personalities; he is exposing himself to a mass movement of writers who, each of them, think that they have something individually to offer, but are really all working together in the same direction. And there never was a time, I believe, when the reading public was so large, or so helplessly exposed to the influences of its own time. There never was a time, I believe, when those who read at all, read so many more books by living authors than books by dead authors; there never was a time so completely parochial, so shut off from the past. There may be too many publishers; there are certainly too many books published; and the journals ever incite the reader to "keep up" with what is being published. Individualistic democracy has come to high tide: and it is more difficult today to be an individual than it ever was before.

Within itself, modern literature has perfectly valid distinctions of good and bad, better and worse; and I do not wish to suggest that I confound Mr. Bernard Shaw with Mr. Noel Coward, Mrs. Woolf with Miss Mannin. On the other hand, I should like it to be clear that I am not defending a "high"-brow against a "low"-brow literature. What I do wish to affirm is that the whole of modern literature is corrupted by what I call Secularism, that it is simply unaware of, simply cannot understand the meaning of, the primacy of the supernatural over the natural life: of something which I assume to be our primary concern.

I do not want to give the impression that I have delivered a mere fretful jeremiad against contemporary literature. Assuming a common attitude between my readers, or some of my readers, and myself, the question is not so much, what is to be done about it? as, how should we behave towards it?

I have suggested that the liberal attitude towards literature will not work. Even if the writers who make their attempt to impose their "view of life" upon us were really distinct individuals, even if we as readers were distinct individuals, what would be the result? It would be, surely, that each reader would be impressed, in his reading, merely by what he was previously prepared to be impressed by; he would follow the "line of least resistance," and there would be no assurance that he would be made a better man. For literary judgment we need to be acutely aware of two things at once: of "what we like," and of "what we *ought* to like." Few people are honest enough to know either. The first means knowing what we really feel: very few know that. The second involves understanding our short-comings; for we do not really know what we ought to like unless we also know why we ought to like it, which involves knowing why we don't yet like it. It is not enough to understand what we ought to be, unless we know what we are; and we do not understand what we are, unless we know what we ought to be. The two forms of self-consciousness, knowing what we are and what we ought to be, must go together.

It is our business, as readers of literature, to know what we like. It is our business, as Christians, *as well as* readers of literature, to know what we ought to like. It is our business as honest men, not to assume that whatever we like is what we ought to like. And the last thing I would wish for would be the existence of two literatures, one for Christian consumption and the other for the pagan world. What I believe to be incumbent upon all Christians is the duty of maintaining consciously certain standards and criteria of criticism over and above those applied by the rest of the world; and that by these criteria and standards everything that we read must be tested. We must remember that the greater part of our current reading matter is written for us by people who have no real belief in a super-natural order, though some of it may be written by people with individual notions of a supernatural order which are not ours. And the greater part of our reading matter is coming to be written by people who not only have no such belief, but are even ignorant of the fact that there are still people in the world so "backward" or so "eccentric" as to continue to believe. So long as we are conscious of the gulf fixed between ourselves and the greater part of contemporary literature, we are more or less protected from being harmed by it, and are in a position to extract from it what good it has to offer us.

There are a very large number of people in the world today who believe that all ills are fundamentally economic. Some believe that various specific economic changes alone would be enough to set the world right; others demand more or less drastic changes in the social as well, changes chiefly of two opposed types. These changes demanded, and in some places carried out, are alike in one respect, that they hold the assumptions of what I call Secularism: they concern themselves only with changes of a temporal, material, and external nature; they concern themselves with morals only of a collective nature. In an exposition of one such new faith I read the following words:

"In our morality the one single test of any moral question is whether it impedes or destroys in any way the power of the individual to serve the State. [The individual] must answer the questions: 'Does this action injure the nation? Does it injure other members of the nation? Does it injure my ability to serve the nation?' And if the answer is clear on all those questions, the individual has absolute liberty to do as he will."

Now I do not deny that this is a kind of morality, and that it is capable of great good within limits; but I think that we should all repudiate a morality which had no higher ideal to set before us than that. It represents, of course, one of the violent reactions we are witnessing, against the view that the community is solely for the benefit of the individual; but it is equally a gospel of this world, and of this world alone. My complaint against modern literature is of the same kind. It is not that modern literature is in the ordinary sense "immoral" or even "amoral"; and in any case to prefer that charge would not be enough. It is simply that it repudiates, or is wholly ignorant of, our most fundamental and important beliefs; and that in consequence its tendency is to encourage its readers to get what they can out of life while it lasts, to miss no "experience" that presents itself, and to sacrifice themselves, if they make any sacrifice at all, only for the sake of tangible benefits to others in this world either now or in the future. We shall certainly continue to read the best of its kind, of what our time provides; but we must tirelessly criticize it according to our own principles, and not merely according to the principles admitted by the writers and by the critics who discuss it in the public press.

The Christian Reader

Nancy M. Tischler

Literary theorists have historically had a great deal more to say about writers and writing than about readers and reading. This fascination with how works of literature come into being, while understandable, is a little unbalanced, since the overwhelming majority of people experience literature as readers rather than writers.

Why do people read literature or attend plays? The reasons are varied and interrelated. We read literature for enjoyment or entertainment; because literature gives shape or expression to our own feelings; for intellectual stimulation; as a necessary retreat from real life; as a way of working through the problems of real life; as a way of celebrating our joys; in order to discover ourselves; as a way of organizing our understanding of life; in order to enter a world more interesting than our own; because we relish the beauty of literary form.

As is true of other topics treated in this book, the issues involved in reading literature take on an added dimension whenever Christians consciously begin to place their reading of literature into the context of their Christian faith. The following essay lays out the basic issues that face a Christian reader. These include (a) determining what constitutes good literature and therefore good reading material for a Christian, (b) discovering where the boundary lies between freedom and license in our reading habits, (c) deciding what a Christian reader can legiti-mately expect from a writer (especially a Christian writer), and (d) developing a methodology for gaining the maximum benefit from reading literature that is less than totally Christian in its viewpoint.

The Need for Christian Evaluation

Read any good books lately? This time-honored conversation-starter leads to a discussion of the latest novel on the coffee table. It can even lead to an aesthetic or philosophic debate over values.

But behind this simple question is an implied premise—that we know how to identify a good book. For the usual reader or critic, this is a matter of aesthetic judgment. In a well-written book, certain accumulated standards in such areas as language, characterization, point of view, and probability, are presupposed. (In actuality, even in an age of "rules criticism" such as the eighteenth century there has been precious little agreement on such standards in particular cases, so we can expect even less in our libertarian era.)

For the Christian reader or critic, "good" involves more than an aesthetic judgment. It is an ethical and religious term, implying standards of another sort. For most of us, standards for goodness are even less clearly perceived than those for beauty. This perhaps accounts for the increasing array of criticism in which Christians analyze literature without evaluating it. Although we eagerly identify Christ figures or discuss religious imagery, we hesitate to posit a standard for good (moral or beautiful) literature.

On the other hand, we are often quite clear about what is bad: it is the book that is poorly conceived and clumsily written, thematically debasing, shallow, and false. Most books written in any age are not art. They may be propaganda, uplifting or downgrading tracts; they may serve a moral or spiritual function; but they are not art. Few works of Christian literature have enough beauty or intellectual content to be judged in the same category with the real touchstones of Christian literature: *The Divine Comedy*, *Pilgrim's Progress*, *Paradise Lost*, *Ash Wednesday*. These pieces all have a grandeur in scope, a precision in expression, a reality in detail, a psychological truth, and an enduring appeal. The writers love words and form. They are craftsmen as well as impressive thinkers, who know how to transform individual experience into objects of beauty that communicate to man regardless of differences in country or period. Thus, we must first establish that a work is art; then we can explore the next question—is it Christian?

Issues in the Christian's Assessment of Literature

Is there a formula for Christian literature? One might be tempted to generalize about characteristics that must be present, such as: God must be a part of the story as an active force; man must be presented in a balanced, serious, and responsible way; actions must be seen to have significance and consequences; there can be no dishonest endings to reward the innocent and punish the guilty; the style must call attention to the idea rather than to the artist; the plot must reflect a universe with order and meaning. But such rules begin to sound suspiciously constricting. They ominously echo those precise regulations of the medieval church that perverted so much of art for so many years—the significance of colors, the proper subject matter, and the appropriate expression, composition, and presentation were all carefully dictated by the clergy. Even in the Renaissance we are repelled by orthodoxy's infringement on the artist: putting loincloths on Michelangelo's glorious nudes and whitewashing the rainbow colors of the cathedrals. And the eighteenth century with its precise criticism seems equally unenlightened.

While the Protestant may be somewhat less likely than the medieval or modern Catholic to restrict the artist in a programmed manner (except perhaps in his response to pornography), he is likely to have a deep-seated suspicion of beauty and a proclivity toward iconoclasm. Like the Old Testament Jew, he is distrustful of the graven image. Our capacity to create—to be makers—is but a dim reflection of that ultimate Creator's genius; yet it tempts man to feel pride and to worship. The image of God looks at the products of his own creativity and worships both the golden calf he forms and the hands that formed it. Thus, we see that the golden calf is neither better nor worse than the cherubim of the temple; both are lifeless matter formed by man and surprisingly capable of eliciting a response in man. Yet one was created for the glorification of man and the other for the greater glory of God.

The difference lies not only in the motivating force behind the artist (which is always difficult to discern) but also in the response of the viewer. Do we marvel at the beauty of the work, at the genius of the artist, or at the magnificence of the God who gave man such capabilities? The Hebrew, living under the law, revered that beauty which pointed toward God—the temple, the paean of faith, the poetry of vision. But the Christian, inheritor of pagan as well as Hebrew traditions, has found his path more complex. Paul tells us we are obliged to walk with the Spirit as free men. This liberty has proven a blessing and a burden to the artist.

Although there was little temptation to use pagan narrative forms in the early centuries of the Church—the narratives of the apostles (except for John's) were simple catalogues of events with minimal stylistic interference—the early Christians did assimilate pagan architecture and art. In addition, Paul knew all the techniques of epistle writing, and John knew how to unite history with imagery for maximum effect.

After the theatres were condemned and closed, pagan drama moved over into the Church; and the medieval Christian writers drew heavily on such poets as Virgil for their technical inspiration. Gradually, as Christians grew willing to agree that fiction is not untruth, they incorporated this form into their culture as well. Thus, though the early Christian would have frowned on the frivolous and decadent forms of pagan prose fiction, drama, and poetry, later Christians gradually learned to use these art forms as tools for their faith. The medieval mystery plays, the poetry of Dante, the narrative of Bunyan's Pilgrim all owe clear debts to pagan ancestors.

That early reluctance to embrace pagan beauty has reversed itself in the twentieth century. The Christian increasingly looks at the art world as territory to be colonized. Scholars are busily discovering the religious implications in Vonnegut's latest novel, or the ritual structure of Albee's plays. It reminds one of the days when Christians strove to find redeeming elements in Virgil so they could be justified in reading and copying him.

The growing zeal for religious content has resulted in (or perhaps resulted from) a growing tendency among artists to play with religious themes and ideas. It is natural that art would return to such central concerns of man. Art and religion both center on man's deepest needs: for truth and beauty and meaning. Serious artists in the contemporary world frequently explore the nature of man, of innocence, of guilt, of freedom, of love, of death, and of God. The critic-scholars often see their obligation to help us understand our artists, and perhaps even to evaluate them.

Reading from a Christian Perspective

This brings us back to our original problem: When the Christian reader or critic explores a novel, poem, or play, how does he judge? Does he analyze the ideas, hold them up against standards of orthodoxy (his, or the artist's, or some church's), and then evaluate the work as good or bad according to its "correctness"? Does he have in mind a model of the good play, novel, or poem? Does he believe there is such a thing as "Christian" literature?

Most critics refuse to deal with this final question. Certainly a novel cannot be Christian any more than a golden calf can be pagan. It is the artist and the viewer who must bear the brunt of such judgment, not the work itself. Some works are more likely to provide orthodox responses than others. For example, Robert Penn Warren's *All the King's Men* provides rich materials for contemplating the Fall and the nature of man; the novel carries the reader along a path of thought that most Christians would approve. But this novel is more often read as a statement about the nature of American politics. The pagan reader can enjoy the social commentary and the romantic adventure, skipping hastily over the theological sections. Graham Green's *The Power and the Glory* makes a very powerful statement about God and his priests in a most effective form. But again many readers enjoy the novel for its degrading portrayal of the whiskey priest who fathered an illegitimate child, missing the central point altogether.

We do not posit an ideal novel, poem, or play, because we cannot. We can cite touchstones of Christian expression (Milton's or Dante's) that grew out of those ages and those men and those audiences that once in a great while come together to produce greatness, but more than that we cannot do. Like Aristotle, who could tell us only what his favorite tragedy looked like, not what all good tragedy must be, most of us can point out novels or plays we have liked or disliked but cannot say what novels or plays must be. We can be analytic and descriptive, but not proscriptive and prescriptive.

Art is, after all, an exploration often beyond the limits of rational thought. It is frequently wiser than the artist; under the inspiration of the Muses or the Holy Spirit, he may have recorded more than he knew. Man cannot limit art without destroying it. Even in an individual artist this is obvious. *War and Peace*, growing out of the troubled, confused mind of Tolstoy, is aesthetically superior to the clear, doctrinaire products of his conversion to Christianity. The Communist world has found that its neat rules destroy art and breed rebellion. Ireland has found its artists leave when it seeks to legislate their art. We who have freedom in Christ are obliged to remember that this responsible freedom must extend to the writer and reader as well.

Not all writers respond responsibly to their freedom. Milton commented on the license that so often replaces liberty. The plethora of pornography today is evidence that man is all too eager to sell his soul and his pen for a price. The chaotic content and form of so much modern literature shows man's willingness to reflect his meaningless world rather than to strive for meaning and order. The delight in depravity and sniggering at morality should not surprise those of us accustomed to viewing man as fallen. We live, after all, east of Eden, where the world, man, and his art are all fallen and in need of redemption.

Even Christian writers lapse from time to time, substituting license for their liberty. In their day, all our heroes of Christian art have had their critics who pointed with horror to the feet of clay. The Church was shocked at Dante's divine poetry; the orthodox were appalled by Milton's view of creation and temptation, not to mention his defense of divorce; and many moderns doubt Eliot's sincerity and artistry. We have no examples of perfect Christian artists, but then we have only one example of the perfect Christian. We should know better than to expect perfection. We should know better than to expect we shall ever see an artist who can satisfy Christians for his orthodoxy and critics for his excellence.

Finding Pieces of the Truth

I am therefore inclined to accept Milton's view that we must learn to piece together bits of perfection. Truth, he said, is like the body of Osiris, fragmented and scattered. Our job is to collect, to judge, and to select those pieces that truly belong to God. Thus we must learn to make use of those scattered insights that the artist captures and communicates.

Regardless of Solzhenitsyn's religious stance, we can gain from his understanding of the nature of evil. He need not call man "fallen" to show that he is. Nor need he call those occasional flashes of beauty in human nature the "image of God." Those moments of heroism, of generosity, of personal integrity, and of compassion in the cancer ward or prison camp portray man transcending his hellish surroundings. They make mockery of Pavlovian psychology and Marxian materialism.

Faulkner, in *The Sound and the Fury*, as he portrays the simple faith of Dilsey, who so willingly bears another's burdens, also reflects something of the true experience of the Christian. The ageless black heroine takes the idiot offspring of the white "aristocrats" to her black church, where she staunchly faces the furious congregation. Her love for Benjy has nothing to do with race, class, sex, or mentality. But this does not mean Faulkner's whole book is built on the Christian world-view. I would reject his central vision that life is a tale told by an idiot, full of sound and fury, signifying nothing. On the contrary, I am convinced that we are part of a great plan and that each human life signifies a great deal.

But this is what I mean by our need to take bits and pieces out of our reading to enrich our life and our faith. God can speak to us through secular literature in a manner parallel to his speaking in sacred literature. A phrase, an idea, or a situation will suddenly catch our attention and magically illumine our lives. A really good novel or poem or play—by either a Christian or a non-Christian writer—generally includes a host of such moments.

We might wish for a day like Dante's when the creative imagination was aflame with Christian doctrine; but even in Dante's day, Boccaccio and Chaucer were inspired by other materials. We are indeed lucky that the twentieth century has given us such Christian literary giants as Eliot and Auden, whom we should appreciate without growing uncritical in our love. God obviously intends us to find random flowers among the briars, testing us by our choices here as elsewhere in life. Literature allows us to experience people and situations out of our ken, to enlarge our ideas as well as our experience. It is as full of temptations as the life it mirrors; it is as full of vitality and peril as Adam and the Garden he inhabited. And we are as free as Adam was to choose which fruits we select to eat.

A free man now, as then, is judged by his strength in the face of temptation.

Trusting the majesty and power of God, we need fear no words or ideas. We can devote the whole man to living the Christian life, using the mind to understand what is written, the eye and the heart to appreciate it emotionally and aesthetically. We should also bring to the analysis and appreciation of culture our wonder, responding to art as a mystery and a miracle, testimony to God's creative power. The Christian's response to art is parallel to his response to nature, joy in the created world, and worship of the Creator reflected in it.

Shakespeare and Christianity

Steve J. Van Der Weele

The aim of criticism, said Matthew Arnold, is "to see the object as in itself it really is." Just as the aim of the botanist is to see the plant as it really is, and the sociologist wishes to see society as it really is, the aim of the critic of art or music or literature is to see the work of art as it really is.

What, then, is distinctive about the process that a Christian critic undertakes? Christian readers, too, wish to see the work of literature as it really is. But they carry the process a step further than other readers may wish to do. Having described the work as it is in itself, Christian readers desire to see the work in relationship to Christian belief and biblical doctrine. In effect, Christian readers conduct a dialogue between the ethical or intellectual vision of the work and the teaching of the Bible. In the words of T. S. Eliot, for a Christian "literary criticism should be completed by a criticism from a definite ethical and theological standpoint."

The following essay is a model for this type of Christian literary criticism. Focusing on a single sonnet by Shakespeare, Professor Van Der Weele first looks closely at the text itself and then places the results into the context of Christian doctrine.

Was Shakespeare a Christian?

It is always tantalizing for a Christian interested in literature to speculate about the question of whether Shakespeare was a Christian. The materials for such speculation are, obviously, first, what little we know about his life (and among that, several incidents—perhaps apocryphal—which give little evidence of piety), and second, the corpus of his writings. Even though it is commonly assumed that he was at least a nominal member of the Church of England, an adherent of the *Via Media* of the Elizabethan Settlement, neither of the above sources answers the question with any finality. As for the first, it needs only to be pointed out that there was no Boswell for Shakespeare, and that the gall required for interviewing and the patience to pursue the minutiae of people's lives are of fairly recent origin.

And as for attempting to deduce Shakespeare's personal response towards the Christian faith from his writings, we are confronted with an almost impossible task. It is commonly observed that Shakespeare is no systematic philosopher or theologian, that his plays are woven from many strands—the Christian among them—and that it is dangerous at any point to equate the speech of this or that character with Shakespeare's own position. Thus Hiram Haydn, after examining thoroughly the various winds of doctrine which constituted Shakespeare's intellectual climate, concludes:

> Finally, then, I am admitting the traditional defeat. I can establish Shakespeare's awareness of the intellectual conflicts of his time, his use of Counter-Renaissance ideas and themes. And I can indicate the consistent elements in his point of view as he expressed it in the major tragedies. Yet, when that is done, it is little enough. The man escapes me, as he escapes every one else. There are all the other plays to contradict me; other scholars' material findings to suggest other influences than those I have cited, and other directions. Most of all, there is the man's

insistent interest in life as spectacle, rather than argument, and the incredible range of his creative sympathies.[1]

Reflections on Sonnet 129

I should like to discuss one of Shakespeare's sonnets against the background of the above preface outlining the difficulty of any attempt to ascertain Shakespeare's religion. This sonnet, number 129, seems to me to reflect in a rather pointed way Shakespeare's acquaintance with the Christian tradition of life and thought.

First, let me give a few comments about the sonnet sequence in which this sonnet appears. Shakespeare wrote 154 sonnets in all. Of these, 152 are usually regarded as a sequential unit; the other two fall outside the sequence. The group of 152 sonnets tells of Shakespeare's relations with especially two persons: a male friend, whose excellence and virtue he never tires of recounting, and Shakespeare's mistress, a married woman, "the Dark Lady," who alternately attracts and repels the poet. Sonnet 129 falls within the group which deals with Shakespeare's illicit liaison, and indicates the tension he experiences when confronted with the moral law on the one hand, and the beauty, grace, and charm of the woman on the other. In the well-known 129 he comments on the nausea, the bitter delusion which inevitably sets in upon moral dereliction. It will be helpful to have the sonnet before us:

> The expense of spirit in a waste of shame
> Is lust in action; and till action, lust
> Is perjur'd, murd'rous, bloody, full of blame,
> Savage, extreme, rude, cruel, not to trust:
> Enjoy'd no sooner but despised straight,
> Past reason hunted, and no sooner had,
> Past reason hated, as a swallowed bait
> On purpose laid to make the taker mad;

1. Hiram Haydn, *The Counter-Renaissance* (New York: Scribner's, 1950), p. 667.

Mad in pursuit and in possession so;
Had, having, and in quest to have, extreme;
A bliss in proof, and prov'd, a very woe;
Before, a joy propos'd; behind a dream.
All this the world well knows; yet none knows well
To shun the heaven that leads men to this hell.

I should like to comment first of all on the interesting use of the words *heaven* and *hell* in the last line of the sonnet. Shakespeare has obviously derived these words from historic, medieval Christianity. Nevertheless, he has poured a new meaning into them, and has thus participated in a practice common to Renaissance writers, namely, the secularization of Christian terms. When he uses the word *heaven* he means, clearly, the anticipated realization of one's sinful desires; by the word *hell* he means the remorse he subsequently suffers. Similarly, he employs in other sonnets such words as *eternity, love, transgression, angel, bliss, damnation, judgment, hope, faith, grace, penance* and *hymn* in ways foreign to their origin. He even adapts a line from the Lord's prayer and applies it to his friend: "Even as when first I hallowed thy fair name . . ." (Sonnet 108). Thus, Shakespeare has contributed to that history of word changes which enables us now to speak blithely about angel food cake, devil's-food squares, and divinity strips.

But despite Shakespeare's practice of transvaluating terms, the sonnet is permeated with a Christian sensibility. Let us examine it closer, and although we may not solve the problem with which this essay began, we can at least note an important tenet of Christian morality which Shakespeare exhibits for us.

In the first twelve lines Shakespeare makes three assertions about a sinful act—primarily adultery, we must suppose, although other sins are not precluded: (1) The act is essentially one, although it exists in three stages in time: anticipation, realization, and retrospect. (2) Each stage is characterized by irrationality, madness, perversity. (3) Sin is shameful, enervating, and deceptive. Then comes the couplet: "All this the world well knows; yet none knows well / To shun the heaven that leads men to this hell."

The Spirit of Western Humanism

My contention is that Shakespeare, in the words "All this the world well knows," is refuting a major premise of humanism—the principle that the good man will not knowingly do wrong, that enlightenment and understanding are so powerful that they must perforce flow into virtuous action, that right conduct and knowledge are two sides of the same coin. This premise was advanced first by Socrates, and continues to the very present. It is an intuition, which, despite numerous qualifications and occasional denials from past and present sources, has persisted as an article of faith with which man seemingly cannot do without, whatever be the metaphysics adduced in its support. One may at least say that no generation has been without those who could subscribe to Pope's couplet:

> Vice is a monster of so frightful mien,
> As to be hated needs but to be seen. . . .

This equation of the identity of knowledge and virtue represents a resilient and, in many ways, noble tradition. Its advocates include the intellectual giants of the West. To be sure, not all thought about ethics has adhered to Plato's insistence that virtue stems from a knowledge of an ideal world which exerts a divine attraction upon the good man, nor have all idealistic philosophers put matters in the same way that Plato did. Nevertheless, the spirit of this premise has been woven into the very fabric of Western humanism. It underlies the traditional importance placed on education in Western thought (cf. the designation *reform school*). It was reflected by Richard Nixon when, as vice-president, he asked while being pelted and insulted during a South American tour, "Don't you people want to hear any facts?" It underlies an observation made by a prisoner in a letter which appeared in an issue of the *Atlantic:* "Education and crime are incompatible." And this assumption has been a key principle in the democratic venture.

The Christian Alternative

Christianity has frequently found the equation of knowledge and virtue attractive, for it has experienced much misery from ignorance and from zeal unballasted by learning. It has been compelled to agree with humanism that neither hedonism nor experience are adequate substitutes for knowledge in the attainment of moral wisdom. However, it has taken issue with humanism on a crucial point, namely that enlightenment and knowledge are sufficient to deter one from evil. For one thing, Christian thought, generically speaking, has said that the inner law, man's conscience, is sufficient to deprive man of the excuse of ignorance. Moreover, Christianity has had to recognize the existence of "presumptuous" sin (Ps. 19:13), sin which is committed in the face of better knowledge. And it has been able to present a staggering amount of evidence from history, past and present, to show that mere knowledge is insufficient to contain the perversity and irrationality of man.

John Calvin's pronouncements on this subject can be regarded as typical of Christian thought. He discusses the matter at some length in his *Institutes*, Book II, ii, *passim*. In these pages he ascribes to man the faculty—imperfect though it is— of discriminating in a general way between good and evil, and he rejects as an extreme position the insistence of those who maintain that all sins arise from *deliberate* perversity and malice. Nevertheless, he takes issue with Plato for "imputing all sins to ignorance," and observes further that "sometimes the turpitude of the crime so oppresses the conscience of the sinner, that, no longer imposing on himself under the false image of virtue, he rushes into evil with the knowledge of his mind and the consent of his will."

How much of the Christian idea is Shakespeare expressing in his merely negative "none knows well?" It is hard to say. He does not go as far as Roger Ascham, an early contemporary, who in his *The Scholemaster* first juxtaposes and interrelates the classical and the Christian views on this subject, but then concludes, "Let God's grace be the bit. . . . Let God's grace be the bridle. . . ." But if Shakespeare is less than explicitly Christian, he is at least taking issue with the ethical tenet just discussed, namely, that virtue, though it requires moral heroism and strenuous effort, can be realized through one's own resources. Shakespeare seems to anticipate Cardinal Newman, who points out the limitations of knowledge and even of a liberal education in these words:

> Quarry the granite rock with razors, or moor the vessel with a thread of silk; then may you hope with such keen and delicate instruments as human knowledge and human reason to contend against those giants, the passion and the pride of man.[2]

How Christian Was Shakespeare?

Was Shakespeare a Christian? The answer, again, is that it is difficult to say with final certainty. But the sonnet just considered is one of any number of instances where it is obvious that Shakespeare had encountered the full impact of historic Christianity. Sonnet 146, for example, where the soul chides the body for neglecting the interior life, is reminiscent of many medieval poems on this subject.

There are still other data which indicate clearly that Shakespeare was aware of the Christian option of life and thought. For one thing, there is the strong moral concern, the ethical stimulation, universally acknowledged in his plays. Moreover, such a speech as Portia's mercy speech has no antecedent in

2. John Henry Cardinal Newman, "Knowledge Its Own End," Discourse V in *The Idea of a University* (1852).

Shakespeare's sources and comes gratuitously—strong evidence that Shakespeare's consciousness was suffused with the Christian habit of thought. Again, references to the Bible and biblical overtones are frequent. And consider, finally, such lines as these, written without obvious dramatic necessity, written also without inhibition or self-consciousness:

> . . . All the souls that were were forfeit once;
> And He that might the vantage best have took
> Found out the remedy.
> > (*Measure for Measure*, II, ii, 73ff.)

> . . . King Pharamond, . . .
> Who died within the year of our redemption
> Four hundred twenty-six. . . .
> > (*Henry the Fifth*, I, ii, 58ff.)

> Forthwith a power of English shall we levy;
> . . . To chase these pagans in those holy fields
> Which fourteen hundred years ago were nail'd
> For our advantage on the bitter cross.
> > (*Henry IV, Part I*, I, i, 22ff.)

There is a true beauty about these lines. It is difficult, or at least distressing, to suppose that the author of such lines as these should have spurned the resources of God's better beauty, grace.

The Bible as Literature

Leland Ryken

The Bible is central to any attempt to integrate Christianity and the arts. For one thing, the Bible has been the single greatest source and influence for literature, painting, and music in the history of the world. Then, too, biblical doctrine is the necessary foundation for a Christian approach to the arts.

In addition to the Bible as a source for art and a repository of doctrine about art, the very form of the Bible is full of implications for the arts. The Bible is not primarily an expository book. It is much more thoroughly a book of stories, poems, and letters. Its approach to truth is many-sided — through the intellect or reason, the emotions, the will, and the imagination. And the Bible is concerned with beauty as well as truth.

As Clyde Kilby writes in Christianity and Aesthetics, "The Bible comes to us in an artistic form which is often sublime, rather than as a document of practical, expository prose, strict in outline like a text-book, and carefully unfigurative and unsymbolic. The Bible is, in the finest sense, the most imaginative book ever written. . . . Is it not equally wrong to handle the Scripture unaesthetically as to handle it untruthfully?"

Some Misconceptions

There has long been a latent, half-articulate resistance among evangelical Christians to the idea of the Bible as literature. One

173

of the most frequently quoted statements on the subject is this one by C. S. Lewis:

> [The Bible is] not merely a sacred book but a book so remorselessly and continuously sacred that it does not invite, it excludes or repels, the merely aesthetic approach. You can read it as literature only by a *tour de force*. You are cutting the wood against the grain, using the tool for a purpose it was not intended to serve.[1]

People who cite this against the practice of reading the Bible as literature overlook the fact that Lewis intended his stricture against reading the Bible *only* as literature, that is, without believing its doctrinal content. That Lewis recognized the need for a literary approach to the Bible is evident from his introductory remarks in *Reflections on the Psalms*, where he writes, "There is a . . . sense in which the Bible, since it is after all literature, cannot properly be read except as literature; and the different parts of it as the different sorts of literature they are."

Christians who resist the idea of reading the Bible as literature do so for two chief reasons. First, belief in the Bible as the inspired Word of God has led Christians to place it in a different category from other books; some are wary of applying ordinary literary terms to the Bible on the assumption that to do this would put it on a level with the works of uninspired and even unchristian writers. Second, to speak of the Bible as literature implies to many people that it is being treated "only" as literature and that its religious content is ignored. At best this is frivolous, some have concluded, and at worst it destroys the real purpose of reading the Bible, namely, attaining belief in God and his truth.

These objections are quite unwarranted. They arise mainly from a misunderstanding of what reading the Bible as litera-

---

1. C. S. Lewis, *The Literary Impact of the Authorized Version* (Philadelphia: Fortress Press, 1963).

ture means. Thus any defense of reading the Bible as literature might profitably begin with an explanation of what is *not* meant by the phrase.

To say that much of the Bible is literary in no way detracts from its truth content. Nor does it imply that the Bible is fictional rather than historical or factual; literature can be either. Even where it is fictional, this does not detract from its truthfulness, as is evident in the parables of Scripture, for example. To say that the Bible must be approached as literature does not imply a preoccupation with matters of style. It does not even have to imply a disregard for theological analysis or practical application.

What, then, *does* it mean to read the Bible as literature?

Literary Form in the Bible

First of all, reading the Bible as literature means approaching a given passage by asking the questions that are appropriate to its literary form. The Bible is filled with conventional literary forms or genres, including narrative or story, epic, tragedy, satire, lyric poetry, epithalamion, elegy, encomium, proverb, parable, pastoral, prophecy, gospel, epistle, oratory, and apocalypse. Every literary form has its conventions or principles. To read the Bible as literature is to ask the questions that are appropriate to its literary forms.

Take the story, for example, a literary form that is particularly important in biblical literature. If every part of the Bible were an expository essay, the right question to ask about any passage would be, What is the writer's thesis and how does he develop his argument? This is how many people read the entire Bible, including the stories. But a storyteller has no thesis to develop—he has a story to tell. The appropriate questions to ask of a story are different from those we ask of an essay or sermon. The right questions to ask of a story include:

1. How is the story as a whole structured and unified?
2. What are the plot conflicts, and how are they resolved?
3. How do the individual episodes relate to the overriding framework of the story?
4. What are the important traits of the characters in the story?
5. How (if at all) do the characters in the story change and develop as the story progresses?
6. What tests (physical, mental, moral, or spiritual) does the protagonist of the story undergo?
7. What use does the storyteller make of such standard story devices as dramatic irony, foreshadowing, foils, archetypes, symbolism, allusion, suspense, reversal, and poetic justice?

Eventually a literary analysis of a story will ask what themes are embodied in the story. It is important to realize, however, that the thematic question, What is the writer's message? can be answered only if we first answer the narrative question, What happens to the characters in the story? Until we scrutinize the story as a series of events involving characters in a setting, we cannot make propositional statements about the content. Flannery O'Connor has said it all when she writes that a storyteller speaks "*with* character and action, not *about* character and action."[2]

Satires, such as the Book of Jonah and Christ's parable of the Pharisee and publican, should be approached with a different set of questions: What is the object of attack? What historical particulars occasioned the attack? What literary ingredients (such as character, action, setting, imagery) make up the vehicle by which the satire is presented? Is the satiric tone laughing or bitter? What is the satiric norm, that is, the standard of goodness or normalcy by which vice or folly is attacked in the work?

2. Flannery O'Connor, *Mystery and Manners* (New York: Farrar, Straus & Giroux, 1957), p. 76.

The literary conventions of a tragedy such as the Old Testament story of Saul lead to yet another set of questions: How is the tragic hero characterized? What is the hero's dilemma? What is the nature of the hero's tragic choice? Is there a flaw of character evident in his tragic choice? What form does his catastrophe and suffering take? Does the hero attain perception?

When we come to lyric poetry, the narrative questions outlined above will not help us, because a lyric poet does not tell a story. His intention is to express the reflective and emotional side of human experience. The important questions here are: What is the emotional or reflective experience that is presented in the poem and that unifies it? What elements of pattern and structure and artistic design does the poem have? What meanings are embodied in the images and figures of speech? In particular, what does the poem communicate through its hyperboles, allusions, metaphors, personifications, and rhetorical questions?

Reading the Bible as literature means first of all paying close attention to the characteristics inherent in the various literary forms. This is simply a way of saying that to read the Bible as literature we must learn to ask the right questions of the biblical text. The usual theological categories are not the only ones necessary for understanding the Bible. Good preachers have always realized this, but professional theologians seem bent on ignoring it.

Literature: The Voice of Human Experience

Reading the Bible as literature also means reading it with a keen awareness of the experiential, as distinct from abstract reasoning or ideas or propositional discourse. There is no necessary quarrel between the literary and propositional modes of discourse. The Bible contains an abundance of both forms, and all literature, no matter how concrete, embodies themes and ultimately a world view. It remains true, however, that literature tends to avoid the propositional in favor of immediate, concrete experience. Literature *presents* human experience.

The New Testament writer Paul gives us a theological explanation of the Fall when he writes that "the wages of sin is death"; the writer of Genesis 3, by contrast, incarnates that theology in a story about human characters and does not even use words such as "sin" or "disobedience" or "the Fall." A theological definition of providence is "that work of God by which He preserves all His creatures and directs all things to their appointed end." The same doctrine is expressed in a poetic metaphor in Psalm 23: "The Lord is my shepherd, I shall not want." The eighth commandment states propositionally, "You shall not murder." The story of Cain's murder of Abel in Genesis 4 leaves out the abstraction and presents the same truth as a story.

The usual way of reading and discussing the Bible leans decidedly toward theological abstraction. The basic vocabulary consists of such terms as creation, providence, sin, salvation, faith, love, and obedience. Yet such abstract concepts never do justice to the realities that they name. Reading the Bible as literature is necessary to balance the picture toward the experiential.

If the stories of the Bible are about providence, redemption, and judgment, they are also full of adventure, mystery, rescue, suspense, pageantry, celebration, courageous heroes, beautiful heroines, and villains who get their comeuppance. Similarly, the Psalms are, on the one side, theological in content; yet they are also about the weather, trees, crops, lions, hunters' traps, rocks of refuge, and human feelings such as terror and trust and joy. The Book of Job may be theologically about the philosophical problem of why the righteous suffer, but on another level it is about an ash heap, boils that itch, psychological alienation and despair and anger, snow, hail, mountain goats, the ostrich and the horse.

Perhaps we might say that to read the Bible as literature we must recover our ability to respond to biblical literature with a child's sense of wonder, a child's sensitivity to the concrete facts of everyday experience, and a child's imagination. Reading the Bible as literature certainly requires a greater responsiveness to the immediate, experiential aspect of biblical literature than our theological bent has traditionally encouraged. Reading the Bible as literature may require that we unlearn much of what we have had forced upon us in Bible courses and seminary training, and it will, in any event, require that we add a great deal to what we have learned there.

Christian preaching in our century has tended to take the style of Paul rather than Jesus as its model. Paul, of course, was theological, abstract, and propositional, while Jesus was concrete, narrative, and even poetic. There is a lesson that preachers and biblical expositors should have learned long ago from the impact and memorability of Jesus' parables and the Old Testament stories and the poetry of the Psalms and Proverbs. The stories of the Bible belong to children in a way that the Sunday morning sermon does not; is it *only* the children of whom this can be said?

Why Is a Literary Approach to the Bible Necessary?

Why do we need a literary approach to the Bible, especially since we seem to have gotten along without it for so long? The truth is, of course, that we have not gotten along without it. People who love to read the Bible have always been responsive to its literary qualities, whether or not they have had the literary terms to express that fact. And the tremendous impact of the Bible through the centuries has been due partly to its literary and imaginative qualities.

One reason why we need a literary approach to the Bible is that such an approach will help us to understand the Bible's message. Any piece of writing must be read in terms of what it is. A reader of Scripture is opening the door to misunderstanding whenever he or she ignores the literary principles of various literary forms. When we fail to ask literary questions we go astray, interpreting figurative expressions as if they were intended literally, looking for theological propositions in a lyric poem that contains mainly an outpouring of human emotion or in a story that is mainly a record of events, allegorizing the Song of Solomon because we do not know how to respond to pastoral love poetry, turning the character of Jonah into a model prophet because we fail to understand how satire works, regarding Ecclesiastes as wholly pessimistic because we overlook the pattern of contrast and the quest motif in the work, and so forth. Belief in the authority of the Bible will not by itself be sufficient for understanding it if the reader ignores the literary principles that underlie the Bible and determine much of its meaning.

A second reason why we should read the Bible as literature is that this is how we appreciate its artistic beauty. Not much can be said to commend biblical scholars and preachers on this score. They have taught us a great deal about the Bible as a repository of truth and a guide to righteous conduct, but where do we learn about the Bible as a source of beauty and artistic enrichment? Any consciously artistic work of literature has an aesthetic dimension that exists quite apart from the content. This artistic dimension, made up of the usual elements of artistic form such as unity, progression, design, balance, contrast, repetition, and variation, is part of the beauty that every writer of literature communicates through his form, whatever his subject matter may be. Why else would a biblical poet labor to make his statements fall into parallel form or to give his poem a carefully designed structure? It is this beauty and artistry that get shortchanged in the usual treatments of the Bible.

I get the impression that some Christians hope that if they ignore the artistic dimension of the Bible the artistry will somehow go away; but of course it won't. If the aesthetic side of the Bible strikes you as unimportant or perhaps even offensive, you need to ask yourself some questions. Why did God give us a Bible that includes so much craftsmanship and beauty if these things are unimportant? If holy men of God wrote the Bible as they were carried along by the Holy Spirit (II Peter 1:21), is it not likely that God inspired some of them to write in the artistic manner that we find in the Bible? If the Bible is the book that reveals God to us, is it possible that the artistic beauty and craftsmanship tell us something important about the character of God? If so, why should we want to slight that part of his revelation and his character? Why would God have created a world that is beautiful if functionality is the one thing needful? Why is heaven a place of beauty if truth is all that matters? If God did not neglect beauty in trees (Genesis 2:9), why would he have neglected it in words? If it is true that the beauty of nature can become, for the Christian, a way of knowing and loving and adoring God, can a Christian not experience God also in the beauty of his Word? Does it make any difference to us that the book that we regard as sacred is not a dull book but an interesting one? Is it not possible that the way in which the book is written (replete with artistic form and craftsmanship) is one of the reasons why it is so interesting?

The parts of the Bible that are the most artistically wrought are sometimes relatively short on theological material or homiletic potential. The story of Ruth, for example, lends itself to abundant literary analysis, while commentaries on the book are short and sermons rare. The story of David and Goliath is full of narrative technique but by itself light in theological material. Psalm 23 possesses a wealth of poetic technique and artistry all out of proportion to what it says theologically about providence, and exploring its images and metaphors takes much longer than stating its theological content. If we continue to think only in theological categories we will slight works that are both important and high in their human appeal. What is needed is a set of literary terms and expectations and responses that will do justice to the artistic beauty of these works.

Reading the Bible as literature offers yet another benefit: the possibility of recovering and sustaining the wonder and delight of Bible reading. Our tendency has been to bury the Bible under too much abstract theology and historical background, failing to respond to its wealth of stories and characters and poems. Reading the Bible as literature can revitalize one's experience of the Bible. And this is true not only for readers but for ministers, Sunday school teachers, and discussion leaders as well.

The literary approach to the Bible has immense implications for biblical scholarship. For one thing, it is one of the best correctives to some of the abuses of liberal biblical scholarship. In particular, a genuinely literary approach to the Bible can counteract the tendency to reduce the biblical text to a series of fragments, the obsession with sources (real and imagined), the speculation about how many redactors worked on a text, an overemphasis on historical and linguistic background, and a disparagement of the supernatural element in biblical literature. On the other side, conservative biblical scholarship has neglected questions of literary form almost entirely. It, too, has been absorbed with questions of historicity, authorship, and theology to the neglect of biblical works as finished literary products and as embodiments of actual human experience.

The time has come for biblical scholars to realize how specialized and esoteric some of their habitual preoccupations are to the general reader of the Bible. Speaking as a layman, I must confess how little I find that is useful to me in a typical survey of the Old or New Testament written by a biblical scholar. Such topics as authorship, historicity, chronology of composition, and cultural background are of course necessary for apologetics and can have a direct bearing on the study of the reliability of the Bible. Yet I must admit how difficult I find it to make any practical use of much of this material. To this day I do not know what to do, for example, with a fifteen-minute discourse on four theories of the authorship of the Book of Ruth or Jonah. Biblical scholars need to acknowledge how unequipped laymen are to assess the truth or falseness of their generalizations in these areas, and how much more useful they would often find material that gives tools for interacting with the text itself, or that shows the overall patterns of a story or poem, or that enhances a reader's response to the actual human experiences that are being presented in the Bible. All of these activities are simply what I mean by a literary approach to the Bible.

The Bible as Literature in the Classroom

With a suddenness that no one could have predicted, courses in the Bible as literature became common in high schools and colleges during the 1970s. The impetus for studying the Bible in public schools came with the Supreme Court's Schempp decision in 1963. Part of the majority opinion in that case asserted, "it certainly may be said that the Bible is worthy of study for its literary and historic qualities. Nothing we have said here indicates that such study of the Bible or of religion, when presented objectively as part of a secular program of education, may not be effected consistent with the First Amendment."

How should Christians view the literary study of the Bible in the school classroom? I think that Christians should affirm such study of the Bible in principle, while being critical of most forms that the movement has taken to date. Although courses in the literature of the Bible are good in theory, in practice they often fail both academically and religiously.

The chief problem is that the approach has not been genuinely literary. Sensing a lack of helpful literary criticism, teachers have taken liberal biblical scholarship as their model instead of relying on their own knowledge of literature and literary criticism. Instead of asking literary questions of the text, many teachers have talked instead about sources, the documentary hypothesis, and historical background. This procedure has erred academically because the theories of the prevailing biblical scholarship have been presented as facts rather than interpretations, and because courses labeled as literary in nature have not been such.

The solution to the problem is to insist that courses in the Bible be truly literary in nature. If the biblical text is approached as a work of literature, people of all religious persuasions can meet on a common ground in studying it.

Recovering a Christian Heritage

Reading the Bible is not simply a modern fad. It is a heritage from the Reformation and Renaissance, with its roots going back even further. Renaissance poets and rhetoricians showed a high regard for the literary dimension of the Bible. Such major English poets as Wyatt, Surrey, Sidney, and Milton paraphrased the Psalms in English, partly as a poetic apprenticeship. This practice attests the acceptance of biblical poetry as a model of poetic form and style. The noblest monument of Renaissance literary theory, Sir Philip Sidney's *Apology for Poetry*, repeatedly draws upon the Bible for illustrations of literary forms. Petrarch wrote that "to call Christ now a lion, now a lamb, now a worm, what pray is that if not poetical? And you will find thousands of such things in the Scriptures, so very many that I cannot attempt to enumerate them."

During the Renaissance, moreover, English grammar schools gave considerable attention to the rhetorical style of the Bible, and at least five books of rhetoric were based mainly or solely on biblical examples. The author of one of these manuals wrote regarding the Bible, "The Figurative . . . Elegancies of that blessed Book . . . abound with the most excellent and divinest eloquence."

Most instructive of all is the example of Milton. When writing his poems, Milton used biblical as well as classical models as guides. He speaks of the Book of Job as a brief epic, the Song of Solomon as a pastoral drama, Revelation as a "tragedy" (by which he meant serious drama), and biblical lyrics as songs. It is obvious that Milton was accustomed to looking at the Bible in terms of literary forms. An early biographer of Milton tells us that when the blind poet was working on *Paradise Lost* he would daily listen to readings from the Bible as well as other literature. "David's Psalms," writes the biographer, "were in esteem with him above all poetry." That this esteem was literary and artistic as well as doctrinal is evident from Milton's own statement that the lyric poems of the Bible, "not in their divine argument alone, but in the very . . . art of composition, may be easily made appear over all the kinds of lyric poesy to be incomparable."

Milton was right. The Bible is a literary work *par excellence*. A notorious disparager of Christianity in our century called the King James Bible "unquestionably the most beautiful book in the world."[3] Should a person who believes the content of the Bible be less enthusiastic than the cultured unbeliever about the literary artistry of the Bible?

---

3. Quoted in *Literary Style of the Old Bible and the New*, ed. D. G. Kehl (Indianapolis: Bobbs-Merrill, 1970), p. 7.

A Christian Approach to Modern Literature

A Christian Approach to Modern Literature

Virginia Ramey Mollenkott

Modern literature poses special problems for the Christian reader. Ours is an era of realism, and the realistic portrayal of evil, violence, profanity, sex, and sacrilege, especially without the restraints that earlier centuries expected, is inherently problematical for Christians. The prevailingly non-Christian or anti-Christian bias of most modern literature is also a barrier. And the complexity and obscurity of much modern literature has tended to make it seem remote from the interests of most people.

Yet no Christian can afford to be out of touch with the culture to which he is called to minister. The question for the Christian is not whether to read modern literature but how to read it.

The Christian and Modern Literature

The question of moral values in modern literature is one which confronts many earnest Christians who wish to keep abreast of contemporary art. All too often such people are left with furtive, semi-apologetic feelings about their reading interests. That there is some value in contemporary fiction, poetry, or drama they may not doubt; but often the values remain only half-formulated or completely hazy. The problem, then, of a Christian approach to modern literature is worthy of consideration.

For example, suppose a Christian woman, knowing that William Faulkner is considered one of America's greatest literary artists, desires to read, say, *The Sound and the Fury*. Beginning the book, she notices first of all a rather difficult style (this alone, unfortunately, is enough to stop many would-be readers of the modern authors). Persevering, she discovers coarse words and themes of sex, incest and lust. Often the result is either that she throws the book aside in disgust, or that she goes on reading because she is fascinated in spite of herself. Either result is lamentable. The usual remark heard sometimes in academic, highly cultured Christian circles, runs something like this: "Faulkner certainly is brilliant stylistically; it's just too bad he chose these poor subjects."

Such readers obviously forget that the distinction between style and content is largely an artificial one; form and content are in essence inseparable.

If form *is* content, the position of praising the style of Faulkner and other moderns, particularly the naturalists, while deprecating their content, seems to need rethinking.

What, then, are some principles that should guide a Christian reader in his or her approach to modern literature?

Respecting the Author's Intention

In the first place, every book, poem, or play deserves to be judged on the basis of its author's purpose. This is of prime importance in distinguishing the worthy and the unworthy in recent literature—or in any literature, for that matter. Potboilers, written for immediate sale and often catering to the lower nature simply to attract hosts of buyers, are ordinarily almost worthless. But often a writer of integrity must picture human violence and depravity to carry out a theme, to express his or her ideas. This concept should not be foreign to the Christian who is familiar with the Old Testament stories of violence, told not for the sake of violence but to illustrate sinful alienation from God's righteousness.

To return to the case of William Faulkner, a large part of his purpose in *The Sound and the Fury* and other novels is to reveal the degradation of the Old South—and of modern society— through materialism. Furthermore, according to Faulkner's 1949 Stockholm Address, all his writing is an attempt to show "the human heart in conflict with itself . . . to help man endure by lifting his heart, by reminding him of the courage and honor and hope and pride and compassion and pity and sacrifice which have been the glory of his past." In the view of many critical readers, these purposes could not be achieved without the inclusion of much sordid material. In fact, Faulkner believes that mature persons must learn to accept evil as well as good in the harmony of the world—and this part of his religious perception should not be too strange to one who realizes that without a knowledge of sin there can be no salvation.

We should not, therefore, be too quick to accuse an author of "wallowing in filth." Although this charge is brought most often against recent writers, it is actually connected with literature of any age; the same charge has been leveled at Jonathan Swift of the eighteenth century and Geoffrey Chaucer of the fourteenth. The only solution is to learn to judge literary works by their authors' purposes and motives, and by how well the authors achieve their goals with the materials they use.

The Value of Reading Modern Literature

Second, it is wise to approach a work of modern literature seeking actively for the values it can impart. And, as in the case of true art in any period, these are many—but they are rendered possibly more immediate because they are the contribution of great minds living in our own century, our own world climate.

For one thing, modern literature can bring an awareness of world views that oppose our own. This is valuable for obvious reasons; we need to break out of our insularity, to understand the concepts which large minds are thinking beyond the boundaries of our own ideological environment, however excellent that environment may be (cf. Acts 7:22: "And Moses was learned in all the wisdom of the Egyptians . . ."). This is not to say, however, that we should *accept* these opposing world views—or that we should become dulled in our rejection of the low moral standards we may read about. As T. S. Eliot points out in *Religion and Literature,* "So long as we are conscious of the gulf fixed between ourselves and the greater part of contemporary literature [i.e., that which does not admit of a Christian supernatural order] we are more or less protected from being harmed by it, and are in a position to extract from it what good it has to offer us."

Another value one may well seek in recent literature is a widening of one's human sympathies. In *The Sound and the Fury,* for instance, Faulkner gives the stream of consciousness of Benjy, an idiot. Whether or not Faulkner is completely correct in his surmises about what goes on in an undeveloped mind, certainly this sympathetic insight tends to soften one's attitude toward such members of the human race. There is also the confused stream of consciousness of a man about to commit suicide. In other words, life in other emotional climates is opened up. Certainly this deepening of human sympathy, the extension of our ability to "feel in" with others, is a part of maturation.

This heightened perception of human emotions often leads, furthermore, to the solution of one's own personal problems and to a better self-understanding.

Another result of the intelligent reading of contemporary literature is a sharpening of the analytical powers. One reason for Faulkner's difficult style—run-together sentences, abrupt gaps and jumps in the chronology—is to force the reader to participate in the story, to keep wrestling with the ideas until they come clear. This is true also in the symbolism of novelists like Ernest Hemingway and poets like T. S. Eliot. The same techniques of intensive, thoughtful reading are extremely valuable in Bible study, leading us to become aware of allusions and subtle shades of meaning.

All these values will, however, be received only through reading books commonly recognized as works of art. How can one tell, before investing time and money in a book, whether it is worthwhile? One can certainly not tell a book by its cover, and even dependence on the author's reputation may at times be deceiving. The best answer is probably reliance on the critic. Although twentieth-century "classics" are still fluid and it is dangerous to foretell which works will stand the test of time— we lack the perspective for that—the critics and reviewers in reputable newspapers or magazines are usually well enough trained and widely enough read to guide us through the deluge of printed matter to that which is of particular interest to us, and that which is worth our while.

Reality in
Modern Literature

Addison H. Leitch

To be significant, literature must adhere at some level to the reality principle; that is, it must touch on some aspect of our experience in the world. Great literature, moreover, looks upon life steadily and whole (to use Matthew Arnold's phrase).

With this criterion in mind, the following essay suggests, Christians have some problems when they turn to modern literature. Believing that reality includes God, heaven, and hell, the Christian naturally concludes that secular literature has looked at only half of reality. There is also the problem posed by the concentration of modern literature on the ugly, depraved, and bizarre aspects of life. A Christian believes that there is a realism of grace as well as a realism of carnality. Or, to use one of Addison Leitch's aphorisms, the rose bush in front of the house is as real as the garbage can behind the house.

The Problem of Deciding What Is "Real"

The chief difficulty in the Christian arts seems to center around what is called Reality. The question is posed over and over again. The consensus seems to be that in a "Christian" novel or film, there are certain things that have to happen to satisfy the Christian reader or viewer. A bad man is saved by the love of a good woman and after that their children don't even need braces on their teeth. Or a man's business is falling apart, but after he is saved everything goes well and even his partner sees the light. Or a man begins to tithe and soon he becomes a millionaire. So it goes.

But Christian writers and artists just don't believe that this is Reality. In terms of Reality, a Jeremiah can end up in a pit; a saint named John can end up in a lonely exile on Patmos. How things worked out for Hosea are quite unclear, and why the Holy God told his man to marry a harlot raises all kinds of questions. The fact that Job had many good things at the end of his life hardly erases the excruciating loss of loved ones along the way.

Artists generally believe that a non-Christian like Camus, for example, because of his integrity and his freedom from special pleading, is more likely to "tell it like it is." Right there is the hang-up: how does a Christian tell it like it is and still make it sound Christian? That men and women everywhere are saved by grace cannot be denied, but such bliss as may follow this event may well have its fulfillment in the next world rather than in this.

There is also the hard question of "timing." That a man is justified in 1966 does not mean that he is sanctified in 1976. The Old Adam, not to mention "that Ancient Foe," is not downed in the first round. Even when the victory is assured, the battle is not over, and the mopping-up operations can be very painful indeed. Should a Christian artist portray saints or sinners? If he portrays saints only, he finds that saints are in very short supply for close study. A "bad" Christian on the way up is essentially in better shape than a "good" pagan on the way down. Just how does one rightly portray either man?

This leaves the artist with the problem of how to deal with sinful, fallen humanity and still make his writing sound "decent." What shall be done with ugliness, brutality, vice, and plain meanness? Is it art to have a sand hog speak King James

English, and if he was saved just last night has he quit swearing today? There are many broken-hearted alcoholics who continue to have troubling times, and reformed gamblers who slip now and then, and that all-time favorite, the golden-hearted harlot who supports her invalid mother and who worries nice Christians when she appears in print.

All these are a part of Reality. The artist has the seeing eye and the understanding heart and the talent to enable us to see almost what he sees and hear almost what he hears. But what does he really see and hear? We must allow him his integrity.

The Challenge for Christian Artists

Another concern is the battle Christian artists constantly wage against the trivial and cheap. They simply cannot stomach the portrayal of the sublimity of their faith in tawdry forms. The pursuit of excellence in many other fields has somehow bypassed much of Christianity, so that often there is the quiet assumption that Christianity must make allowances for unworthy media because at least the wonder of the subject is somehow being portrayed. Poor writing, poor music, and poor pictures may be bad means, but since they serve good ends, all may be forgiven. One expects the film to break at a church movie. A cheap window can be forgiven because the people who donated it are so nice. All these sorts of things bleed out eventually in a general sloppiness of dress, table manners, and housekeeping. That there is essential blasphemy in this is a deep concern of Christian artists.

Meanwhile I have a concern or two myself about Christians in the arts. When they tell it like it is, they seem to be too plain (or maybe too anxious) in depicting sin and entirely too vague (or maybe too apologetic) in depicting redemption. For example, that peerless observer of humanity, Flannery O'Connor, whose Christian and Roman Catholic devotion no one can doubt, insists that there is grace at work at some crucial point in all her studies. I must confess that the grace is sometimes very hard to find.

Meanwhile one gets the impression that in order to make our total depravity plain, O'Connor makes too many of her characters bizarre. For example, in one of her great stories a woman with a wooden leg and a Ph.D. is seduced by a Bible salesman. That is not the sort of Reality I run into with any great frequency, which makes me wonder if that's the way it really is. I know there are subtleties that I miss in every art form; there are deeps in the parables of Jesus, for example, that I never plumb. But it seems to me that sometimes, just sometimes, artists should tell it like it is on the side of the angels.

Maybe the Christian artists are running just a little behind in the sin business these days. That things are just plain bad all over is no great discovery since the depression and Hitler; everyone is aware of the Reality of the Mafia. To those who have never known Christ, the total picture is absurd, of course. What I need desperately is for someone who knows the Lord to make vivid for me, as only an artist can, that there really is truth and light and especially hope. I think the Prodigal's Father can be portrayed just as well as the Prodigal Son. Let's have a little more Paradise Regained.

part 4

Christian Perspectives on Eight Literary Forms

Introduction

No one will read this book without sensing how important is the idea of artistic forms or types to the various arts. In order to respond fully to any individual work of literature, painting, or music, we need to know what to expect and look for. The whole artistic enterprise, in fact, could be seen as a matter of the artist's presenting, and the audience's responding to, the features that are appropriate to a given artistic form.

There are four basic forms in literature—so basic that they can occur in any of the literary genres (such as poem, story, or play). Because these four forms exist independent of, or prior to, the literary genres, they are sometimes called "pregeneric" forms. These forms are romance (portraying experience as we wish it to happen), anti-romance, also called satire and irony (presenting a world of total bondage and frustration), tragedy (a fall from bliss to bondage), and comedy (an ascent from bondage to bliss). When put together, these four types of literary material make up a single circular story, as the following diagram illustrates:

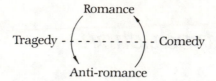

This circle of stories is called the "monomyth"—the "one story" of literature. It is the composite story of literature as a whole. Any work of literature that you will ever read can be plotted somewhere on the monomyth. The first four essays in this section of the book deal, in order, with the four basic forms of literature, viewing each one within a Christian framework.

The multitude of other literary forms are called literary *genres*. The three biggest literary genres are story, play, and poem. In this section there are essays on each of these, plus one on the hybrid that is so important in our own culture, the movie.

Myth:
A Flight to Reality

Thomas Howard

Myth is a type of literature that includes unrealistic or marvelous elements. Myth takes us to a world of the imagination filled with gods, monsters, bigger-than-life heroes, floating islands, and talking trees. On a superficial view, we are inclined to look upon such stories as an escape from reality.

We would do well to consider the matter more closely, however. To paraphrase a comment made by Oscar Wilde about utopian literature, a map of the world that does not include the country of myth is not even worth glancing at, for it leaves out the one place at which the human race is always landing.

The crucial question is, What realities do the unlifelike conventions or details of myth express? They include deity, transcendence, glory, heroism, courage, goodness, beauty, and a dozen others. Are these things real? If so, myth is not a flight from reality but to reality. Paradoxically, modern realistic literature, which has exiled the gods and heroes from its world, represents the real flight from reality.

The following essay was a landmark in my own thinking about literature. In particular, one should note the theory of literature that underlies the remarks about myth: literature is a world of the imagination; it gives us images of our own experience in the real world; the images with which we fill our imaginations have an impact on us for good or ill; the images that we encounter in some kinds of literature *are more redemptive and worthy than the images we encounter in other kinds of literature; our excursions into the world of the literary imagination send us back to real life with a renewed zest and understanding of it.*

Toward a Definition of Myth

Let me begin with the premise that when we speak of "myth" we don't mean something that is untrue. The important thing about myth is not that it involves an event that never occurred on this planet, or out of it, for that matter. The stories of Zeus and Odysseus are not myths by virtue of the fact that they didn't happen. On the contrary, they are myths at least partly because they occurred in a realm that is beyond the reach of the geographers' and historians' tools.

The question whether or not they occurred somewhere around a place we know geographically as the Aegean or the Baltic, or so many years before Pericles, is irrelevant. The question about myth is not whether the tales it tells have happened in our history or prehistory. There is probably no one alive today who would insist that they have occurred in that way.

But on the other hand, the people (nearly everybody, in effect) who blithely assume that of course these things didn't happen may be whistling in the dark. How do *they* know? Unless you are a doctrinaire materialist and live in a tiny universe whose limits are determined by microscopes, telescopes, and measurements like 186,000 miles a second, you will always wonder what's going on just outside your lens frame. A Christian, especially, living as he does in a huge universe all ringing with the footfalls of hurrying seraphim, cherubim, archangels, angels, men, and devils, will never be too peremptory concerning what creatures aren't in on the traffic. He can only demur and say, "Elves? I don't know much about them. I've never come across one (worse luck)."

The question about the myths is, rather, How true do they ring? Does such and such a tale or set of tales suppose a world that convinces us by its own integrity, that is, its fidelity to its own laws? Is the fabric of that world whole and tough? Or is it tattered? Does it hold together by some binding energy that is really at work in it? Or must it be basted together by pins and threads borrowed from some other world?

Perhaps it's here that we come upon the rather elusive clues to what makes myth different from other kinds of tales. We can say that myth represents a world created by the imagination. For one thing, there is a sense in which real myth must be large. You can't have a myth with only one incident, or one or two characters in it. The individual episodes form part of a whole landscape. Myth, moreover, has to do with a whole world, not necessarily a world of any particular geography or chronology. You can have an imagined geography (utopia or Lilliput) and not have what we call real myth. Or you can have our geography (Parnassus or Olympus) and yet have real myth.

What seems to be required is that there be a world, a whole world, that is remote from us and at the same time rooted in our world. We don't want our myths taking place in 1929, or even 1066, nor do we want them to occur in East Lansing or Gary, Indiana. If they did, they would have a distressing tendency to keep draining into the dry sand of history or contemporaneity. But on the other hand, remote and entire in themselves as they must be, we do want them to be in some sense rooted in our world, that is, in our understanding of experience. We don't want them to be crowded or spoiled by the immediate world, but we do want them to ring bells that our ears can hear.

The Meaning of Myth

The whole poetic or artistic or mythic phenomenon that we find when we look at the history of human imagination represents, I think, the search for perfection. Now you can give this perfection a hundred names—truth, beauty, goodness, wholeness, bliss, repose, order, form, the eternal, and so on—

depending on what you want to stress at the moment. There's no word in human language that will name it adequately. Let's call it *perfection* here. We all have imaginings of it (some poets would urge that we have memories of it). Perfection hounds us remorselessly. It is what stands over against every experience we have of nostalgia, frustration, and desire. We find sooner or later all the data of our experience to be faulted—our bodies, our minds, our wills, our relationships, our landscapes, our states, our institutions, our programs.

Politics, medicine, ecology, and jurisprudence are our efforts to repair the damage. Most of what we do, starting with brushing our teeth in the morning, would be seen by the angels as a waste of time, since they don't know what it is to be almost wholly occupied with shoring things up. When we've been allowed to take time from our plowing and fighting and brushing our teeth, we have tried to say something about perfection and our experience of the discrepancy that we feel between ourselves and perfection. We want tranquility and we find tumult. We want permanence and we find decay. We want order and we find havoc. We want health and we find sickness. We want strength and we find weakness. We want beauty and we find horror.

But we neither can nor will settle for this state of affairs. We are driven by who knows what—maybe it's the Holy Ghost—to complain about this discrepancy, to oppose it, and to transcend it. We write about our experience, and we sing about it, and we reenact it because we think that somehow if we can stand off from it and get a look at it, we can get ahold of it once more. We signal our awareness of perfection by making something approximating perfection out of our experience—something true, beautiful, good, and incorruptible. Myth is one version of this effort.

Distance and Identity in Myth

I do not think the words *art* and *myth* are synonymous, but perhaps myth stands at the pinnacle of the narrative art. In it you will find more or less perfectly manifested what is implicit in all art: distance from the immediate but identity of substance. Myth stands off from our experience, but it is *about* our experience.

Perhaps a distinction needs to be made here. We should speak of *high myth* when we are talking about those great tales that come out of the Mediterranean and the North, since the loose term *myth* can refer also to the controlling atmosphere or set of ideas or pool of presuppositions that govern an era. The twentieth century, for example, operates within a secularist myth. The Middle Ages operated inside a Christian one. And so forth.

You get in high myth a fairly pure example of what art is about: distance and identity. Perhaps this is why you used to have frames around paintings. Such and such a scene or person or event was "in there," and you, the viewer, had leisure to regard it and contemplate it. You were free from any entanglement. By the same token, when you read one of the older novels you can look *at* the experience being described precisely because you aren't called upon to sort it out. Of course, part of the genius of the whole thing is that you *do* get involved. But it is an involvement that is not cluttered by having to attend to a thousand trifling details. You are free to get a grip on things exactly because you are at a remove from them.

By the same token, if we move the world of myth away from the immediate, out of the twentieth century or the nineteenth or the eighteenth or the tenth, out of our calendar completely, we disengage it from the fuss of our world, and by thus setting it free from our time, we set ourselves free with respect to it. For time may be *the* tragic dimension of human experience. It is the agent and vehicle of change and decay and death. If we can get free from time, we can approach bliss. This is why poetry and the promise of paradise are so attractive to us. They all offer an escape from time. And the escape seems to be an escape *from* the unreal, from the transitory and evanescent, *to* the solid and immutable, that is, the real.

So we need distance, probably both chronological and geo-graphical. We like the formula, "Once upon a time in a far off land." That's the best opening for a story—there's no question about it. For at that point we can settle in. There's no danger of any clutter and intrusion from the immediate world. If we sat down to read a story that began "At eleven o'clock on the morning of Friday, October 16, 1970, in the living room at 210 East Seminary in Wheaton, Illinois, an old crone began to stir her brew," we'd say, "Wait! Stop! It won't work. It's no good." The trouble is that we know that room. It's too defenseless against the postman and plumber and electrician, and we don't want *them* in our midst.

The Fate of Myth in the Modern World

Of course, it will be observed here that most of the writing that engages our attention now *is* realistic in this way. Isn't *this* art and therefore a form of myth? What about Updike and Saul Bellow and all the fiction that gets published now, to say noth-ing of cinema and theater? The whole avalanche of contem-porary imagery tumbles out of our living rooms and kitchens, and bathrooms and bedrooms. What about all this? Can't things be local and contemporary?

It may be here that we come upon the trouble that the mythmakers and storytellers have nowadays, and indeed the trouble with the whole era. For they have to make their images out of what their world is made of. There has to be some identity of substance between what they make and what we know, so that we can recognize it. And it turns out that the stuff our world is made of won't shape up into high myth. Oh, you can make something out of it—cigarette ashes and tiny situations—but you can't get anything huge and wonderful and breathtaking and beautiful.

Why not? Because the world that gave birth to the high myths—to those huge worlds of story that are remote from us but terrifyingly close—that world has disappeared. It has disappeared under our interdict. For we have decided (sometime in the Renaissance it was and we finished the job in the eighteenth century) to recreate the world. It's a very small one now, limited as it is by microscopes and telescopes and computers, and asphalt parking lots at MacDonald's hamburger stands. And it's a horror. It is, above all, boring, for mystery has fled from it. We have announced to anyone who cares to listen— and somehow one imagines that the angels and elves aren't all that enthralled by the information—that we can explain everything. We know what our forefathers never guessed: that if you take things apart you can explain them and thus master them. And we're dead right. You certainly can master them. The only difficulty is that the thing you've got the mastery of is a pile of pieces all taken apart. We haven't found the spells (since we don't believe in spells) to put them back together again. We're in the position of all the king's men in "Humpty Dumpty."

By the eighteenth century the myth became sovereign that the analytic and rational capacity is absolutely adequate for unscrambling the mystery of the universe. Somewhere in the process the gods fled. The irony is that in the very effort of modern art to disentangle human experience from the transcendent, human experience turned to ashes. In painting and sculpture the focus is on less and less, until indeed there is less there than meets the eye. We are told that we must no longer ask what a work of art *means*, since all that matters is that it *is*.

The problem of the modern writer is obvious. He can't make bricks without straw. He can't make a rope out of sand. He can't create heroes and evoke courage and nobility and courtesy out of the materials that his world furnishes him. He may feel that what we have now is the truth of the matter.

On the other hand, the modern writer may be unhappy with the way things are. He may, like François Mauriac or Flannery O'Connor or Tolkien, think that the time is out of joint, that what we have is most emphatically *not* the way things are, in which case he can try various things. He can try to find tiny pieces in the pile that is left of the world in the twentieth century—pieces which, if put together in a certain way or held up to a certain light, may bring back an old memory that once upon a time it wasn't broken like that. Or, like Flannery O'Connor, the storyteller can hail us, shout at us with frightening images to try to remind us that what we've made is not, in fact, very satisfactory. Or, like Tolkien, the mythmaker can step away from things and hold up for us some unabashedly ancient shapes, since he can find nothing at hand that will suit his purpose. When we have entered Tolkien's remote world we find that it is a true one, and therefore true of ours.

But apart from a few plucky spirits like this, what are the mythmakers giving us? You wonder whether the poets and artists are really fulfilling their ancient office, which is to see further than the rest of us, to see the mysteries and bear witness somehow to what they see in an imagery drawn from our world.

The Necessity of Myth

If we believe that the pile of broken pieces is a late and false creation, and that the world the old bards knew was, in fact, the world where our real life lies, then it must be confessed that, reactionary as it sounds, a return is indicated. At least some sort of return. Remember that not all returns are bad. A return to health after sickness, a return to shore after a voyage, a return to home after estrangement, to liberty after prison—these are salutary returns. Let's have no cant about reactionism.

The chances of a writer finding inside the modern world an imagery that will suggest the big, real, whole world are slim. The writer will have eventually to lift his sights away from the shards and catch once more the vision that was born in olden days when an imagery of heroes and elves and gods was alive. He'll have to search for it with all his heart, and he will, if he looks hard enough, find at least something. He'll find that, despite the cold and lethal myth that holds the whole world in a frosty sovereignty, there are pockets of warmth and life. The old vision, the vision that was affirmed in the high myths, is kept alive and nourished in the households of good and humble people everywhere. And (we wish it were true) in the church. At least it is still celebrated in the church, for we still sing *Kyrie* and *Gloria* and *Sanctus*, and break bread and pour wine, and call them the body and blood of God.

The human spirit at its best is impatient with the small and local and fragmented. It demands images of greatness and wholeness. The world of the imagination that I have called myth is a repository of such images—images of courage and glory and mystery and romance and deity and heroism. Excursions into that world are never a flight away from reality; they are, rather, a flight to reality.

A Christian View of Tragedy

E. Beatrice Batson

Of all literary forms, tragedy has through the centuries elicited the most discussion. It has, moreover, generally been regarded as the most pro-found of all literary forms, and it has proved particularly effective in moral and intellectual stimulation.

At a purely descriptive level, there has been overall agreement about the basic ingredients of tragedy: an exalted hero who faces a dilemma, human choice and error, suffering and catastrophe, and moral or in-tellectual perception. There has even been a consensus in interpreting some of the deeper meanings of tragedy: it portrays caused suffering (the hero makes a wrong choice), it simultaneously asserts human great-ness and human limitation, it affirms human choice, and (though here the consensus begins to break down) it implies cosmic justice.

Along with these agreements, however, tragedy has been a subject for scholarly controversy. Most controversial of all is the question of whether there can be Christian tragedy. The following essay surveys the issues in the debate and explores the conditions under which we can call tragedy "Christian."

The Debate about Christian Tragedy

When critics as dissimilar in stance as I. A. Richards and A. C. Bradley have argued that Christianity and tragedy are

211

incompatible, it may be ill-advised to challenge so authoritative a claim. Yet, the question of what Herbert Coursen calls that debatable *genre* known perhaps oxymoronically as "Christian tragedy" is still very much alive.

Eliseo Vivas emphatically declares that he has become more and more opposed to the efforts of distinguished critics to cut down to the comfortable size of a "myopic theodicy" some of the "boldest, most unfettered, most courageous, profoundest, yet darkest products of the human imagination." Equally strong is E. I. Watkins's view that tragedy involves the tragic conflict, and the tragic conflict in turn involves presuppositions of a non-religious interpretation of life.

Contrastingly, G. Wilson Knight looks at the structure of tragedy as displaying the entire Christian story, including the final victory; thus the tragic hero is seen as a "miniature Christ" undergoing a calvary and a resurrection. In sympathy with the possibility of *Christian* tragedy, Roy Battenhouse, a prominent theological critic of Shakespearean tragedy, theorizes that there are many Biblical analogues in Shakespeare's dramas but holds that these are frequently unwitting parodies of aspects of the Christian story.

Recurrent discussions by those who seem to stand simultaneously on both sides of the question also abound. In his work, *The Vision of Tragedy*, Richard Sewall urges early in the book that instead of negating tragedy, or taking man in a leap of faith "beyond tragedy," Christianity in actual practice, historically, has provided a matrix out of which has come, since the beginnings of the Renaissance, a prodigious amount of tragic expression. Approximately one hundred pages later in the same book, he states that "the incompatibility of tragedy and Christianity is inescapable." He further says that he uses the term "Christian tragedy" as a useful way of referring to tragedy "written in the Christian era which bears the mark of Christian thought and feeling, however short it falls (and to be tragedy, it always does) of the doctrines of the Church."

Each of the aforementioned critics, and numerous others who present variants on their positions, consider the possibility of Christian tragedy to be an issue worthy of serious discussion. Ronald Crane, however, calls the matter "a pseudo-issue," one which is made to look like an issue of fact but which has no identifiable reference "outside the game of dialectical counters in which it has arisen." Those who believe the question to be genuine and in need of clarification are unwilling to dismiss it as dialectical acrobatics or semantic quibbling. Crane is, however, of greater assistance than his apparent dismissal of the question might suggest. Later, I shall return to the heart of his argument as a means of getting major aspects of the issue in focus.

Toward a Definition of Tragedy

Before thinking further on the possibility of Christian tragedy, we must first come to an understanding of tragedy. In its popular and everyday use, "tragedy" is a synonym for disaster or calamity, but my concern is not with that imprecise usage. Like other literature, tragedy is structured and interpreted human experience, and it discloses by indirection. So whatever may be the understanding of a wider reality, it should come by way of the tragedy's own reality. Yet, tragedy, with its own reality, is a distinctive kind of experience that needs to be distinguished from other human experiences.

In attempting to define tragedy we face the risk of thinking of it in such a generous manner that we include all serious and profound art, or in such a restricted way that we thrust away works which have no right to be called anything other than a tragedy. If one of our primary concerns is to discover the distinctive kind of experience shaped into a form, we then have a place to start. Tragedy begins with a certain kind of person in a particular kind of situation. This person is capable of making choices, which he does because of the kind of person he is. The consequences of his choices lead to suffering and usually to perception and death. Not always does the pattern develop as consistently as the definition suggests, but in both pre-modern and modern tragedy, it is remarkable how frequently the shaped experiences unfold in this manner.

In tragedy the "certain kind of person" *may* have high social position, but he *must* have greatness of spirit. He undertakes an action of such magnitude and seriousness that it has life-and-death consequences; by that action, subject to his "particular kind of world," he becomes both agent and victim and inevitably comes to grave suffering. His suffering is not a weary submission nor is it a joyful acceptance; it usually springs from a desire to know the full meaning of his ultimate commitment or of the action which he undertakes. When perception occurs, the tragic protagonist knows where he is and how he got there. If death occurs, as it usually does in tragedy, it is no cause for despair, for as Northrop Frye states in *Fools of Time*, "In the tragic vision death is, not an incident in life, not even the inevitable end of life, but the essential event that gives shape and form to life." When tragedy does show reconciliation and triumph, and I believe it frequently does, I disagree with Oscar Mandel that reconciliation, submission, attainment of peace or the "redemption of the protagonist" and the like are "post-tragic episodes." What he suggests is that tragedy is not necessarily coterminous with the work of art as a whole. I prefer not to fragment, but rather to see the dramatic action in its entirety: an individual makes a choice which unfolds in staggering consequences; there is always great loss, but all is not lost, and the dramatic action may reflect this.

To summarize, tragedy is a narrative form of literature in which a tragic protagonist who possesses greatness of spirit commits himself to an undertaking of great magnitude within a given situation and as a result comes to spiritual suffering usually followed by perception and death, and possibly by "redemption."

If there is a possibility of Christian tragedy, it must first be tragedy; if it is also true, as various critics believe, that tragedy adapts itself to the thought and ethos of every age, including the Greek pantheon, Christianity, feudalism, skepticism, and existentialism, there is a strong possibility that the term "Christian tragedy" is not so strange. Let us return, as I earlier promised, to Ronald Crane's argument and try to determine whether he might be of greater assistance than his apparent dismissal of the validity of tragedy as Christian suggests.

The Need to Let the Text Speak for Itself

Crane distinguishes two essential modes of critical procedure; consequently, he provides a means of getting the issue in focus. The "Abstract" mode begins with an hypothesis about nature, the supernatural, man, literature, and other important topics, only to discuss specific literary works in terms of this theory or hypothesis. In contrast, the "Matter-of-Fact" procedure begins with "the Fact" of some actual literary form and, on the basis of what happens in the specific work, determines the necessary causes of the events or facts. In brief, the primary emphasis is on the created work rather than upon some theory or hypothesis about literature or other interesting subjects.

Attempts to clarify the possibility of Christian tragedy have usually proceeded by way of the "Abstract," and Crane is partially right in suggesting that, so conceived, the issue only admits of a solution not entirely pertinent to the work.

What Crane calls "Abstract" is similar to what Oscar Mandel calls "derivative." Mandel suggests that a derivative view of tragedy postulates an *a priori* order, usually ontological, of which tragedy is an expression. It is not an ontological order that troubles Mandel; he readily admits, in what he calls a "substantive" definition of tragedy, that if a "substantive critic," who begins with the work of art itself, discovers an ontological order, the order is precisely *in* the work. Emphases may vary, and the "substantive critic" may look at literary works from opposite poles and from different approaches, but he begins with the *art work* and focuses on its constitutive elements.

What both Crane and Mandel see is significant: an insistence on certain prescribed, *a priori* categories for viewing and interpreting all tragedies—or all literary works—may possibly be substituted for a careful study of component features inherent in the work. To fit a giant to the bed of Procrustes is no problem if we cut off his legs; to superimpose preconceived notions on great writings is a simple matter if we find selections which echo our stance.

What Makes Tragedy Christian?

Can some tragedies be called Christian without neglect of component parts of their substance and without leading to the false assumption that form and content can be separated? If Christian tragedies already exist, this question has to be answered affirmatively. If they do, why are some good thinkers understandably uncomfortable with such a term?

In an age when designations like "Christian" writer, "Christian" magazine, "Christian" novel, "Christian" bookstore, "Christian" radio and television, "Christian" school, "Christian" hospital, and a host of other "Christian" creations are thoughtlessly tossed about, it is no wonder that many are wary of even raising the question of the possibility of Christian tragedy. That there is carelessness in using the word "Christian" as an adjective I readily admit; that there is abuse in proceeding from the "Abstract" and the "derivative" is equally true. But neither carelessness nor abuse obviates the legitimacy of calling a tragedy Christian if the features inherent in the work so warrant. Caution is imperative, however, as we stress "constituent elements" or "component features" of a given work. Whatever we may think of Leslie Fiedler's literary criticism, it is essential to hear his argument that the "pure" literary critic, who pretends to stay inside a work all of whose metaphors and meanings are pressing outward, is only "half-aware." In his judgment, "half-aware" critics deceive in that they cannot help bringing moral and metaphysical judgments into their "close analysis." I suggest that we discover as accurately as possible what is involved in the "pressing outward" by way of the work itself or that we discover, as I earlier suggested, a wider reality through the work's own reality. To carry on the hard work of studying the subtleties of plot, characterization, and development; the intricacies of images, rhythm, and syntax; and the complexities of the paradoxes, tensions, and nuances inherent in the interpreted experience is our first responsibility. When we engage in this pursuit, we are better able to show that the work might possibly be called a Christian tragedy. It is obvious that some good thinkers prefer to take another route which, in my judgment, helps to induce the criticism that Christian tragedy or any Christian literature exists only through the heavy-handed efforts of those who squeeze the work into their Christian patterns and systems.

Strong scholars have been known to offer theories which insist on certain Christian doctrines as scalpels for paring away at literary works. Randall Stewart, for whom I have unstinting admiration as my former teacher, sets up five basic doctrines of Christianity, with special focus on original sin, and examines writings from this perspective. With these dogmas in hand, he says in *American Literature and Christian Doctrine* that Faulkner should be regarded as one of the most profoundly Christian writers in our time. To argue with his conclusion is not my desire. But when he says that everywhere in Faulkner's writings there is "the basic premise of Original Sin; everywhere the conflict between the flesh and the spirit" and then adds that one finds the "trial by fire in the furnace of affliction, of sacrifice and the sacrificed, of redemption through sacrifice" and concludes that "man in Faulkner is a heroic, tragic figure," I submit that *how* Stewart arrives at his conclusion is dubious. If after careful scrutiny of the actual intricacies and inner movement of the work, he discovers that it brings into being particular insights on Christian dogma, his conclusion would be more convincing, but his statements fail to reveal a special thrust in that direction.

On the other hand, some would have us believe that we have Christian tragedy if the work depicts characters with a Christian mentality or Christian attitude. If this be true, then to accumulate statements made by numerous characters in Shakespeare's *Hamlet* (and I will return to this drama for support of my own position) would quickly settle the question. In the opening scene, Marcellus remarks that no spirit dare stir in "that season . . . / Wherein our Saviour's birth is celebrated" (I, 1, 159). Concerned over Hamlet's safety, Horatio says, "Heaven secure him" (I, v, 114). During Ophelia's madness, she says, "And of all Christian souls, I pray God. God buy you" (IV, v, 193). The Queen begs Laertes concerning Hamlet, "For love of God forbear him" (V, 1, 296). Hamlet asks Ophelia to pray for him, "Nymph, in thy orisons / Be all my sins remembered" (III, 1, 89). When Hamlet sees the gravediggers toss up the skulls, he remarks, "This might be the pate of a politician . . . one that would circumvent God" (V, 1, 86). How these various statements are handled is the huge task facing any student-scholar. Can we call a drama Christian simply because there are attitudes in the play which are frequently displayed by Christians?

Or, is the question clarified when we show analogues between a given work and the Bible? If we show that Lear's "opening ritual is a parody of God's giving the earth to unfallen man," or that Cordelia in the first scene of *King Lear* "represents that part of the outer mystery which expresses truth but which, like Christ, must . . . resonate against the inner mystery of man," or that Cordelia's muteness before Lear parallels Christ's silence before Pilate, or the kneeling of Lear to his "child, Cordelia" is a parallel to the kneeling of the Magi before the Christ-Child, may we call this tragedy Christian? Or, in *Othello*, is it sufficient to observe that the meek Desdemona parallels the meek who would inherit the earth of whom Christ speaks, or that the temptation of Othello by Iago reflects the struggle between Satan and the two great victims of temptation, Adam and Judas? These analogues, and scores of others that critics have found, are interesting to ponder and may be profitable to discuss, but I have doubts, not only of some of the analogues, but also of their being a valid basis for calling tragedy Christian.

Equally confusing is the view that extrapolates "spiritual values" from literary works and points to these as indications of the redemptive or Christian essence of the work. George Morrison says of *King Lear* that nothing is more beautiful in Shakespeare than the purification of the soul of Lear under "the slings and arrows of outrageous fortune." Of the same play, Ernest Howse says, "to turn from Lear in the first act is like turning from a Saul of Tarsus to a Paul the Apostle." Howse's musings on Lear close with the statement that in so much of Shakespeare "we can always see above the darkness to the sheen of everlasting light." These private responses may bring satisfaction to the individual reader, but they fail to show the relation between the *how* and the *that*.

With the many penetrating insights that have come from the Religion and Art Movements, there is among some of the leaders more of a theologian's concern with culture than a critic's analysis of a literary work. Nathan Scott, for example, views contemporary literature primarily as a vehicle of the "ultimate concerns" which define "the spiritual situation of our age." He sees despair, alienation, and estrangement in almost all of the works he discusses. In Sallie TeSelle's words, he becomes "what might loosely be called a theologian of culture." To castigate Scott for doing what he set out to do is by no means my desire. His preoccupation with both religion and literature could, however, greatly assist in the clarification of the relationship between them had he spent more time on the painstaking explication of the text.

At polar opposites to Scott are those who insist that no literature, and certainly no tragedy, can be Christian unless it contains specifically Christian language or names Christian doctrines. If we take this view, we will have to exclude the Book of Esther, many of the parables, and numerous works of literature, including Gerard Manley Hopkins's magnificent poem, "The Windhover." In the subtitle of the poem, there is only the slightest hint that the poem is a metaphor of the crucifixion, but even that slight hint is unnecessary. The poem shows the majestic flight of a powerful bird who dies in flight but whose death is more powerful and more brilliant than his life in flight. How does Hopkins show this? He conjoins a complex and intricate net of images and lets the poem "tell" without external impositions. What is most essential, in my judgment, is that "The Windhover," as Sally McFague says, is so magnificently made that the pattern of the majestic flight and the violent death can be sensed simply from the rhythm of the words apart from any meaning we may wrench from them. Hopkins does what many writers do: he chooses the familiar and the natural to get to the transcendent, and he does it artistically. But another angle to remember, in addition to the beauty one sees in Hopkins's poem, is that the incarnational view of reality means that life, with its varied experiences and in all its problematic, historical, and messy reality, can also be the focus of the most profoundly serious and utterly sublime literature. To celebrate finite reality in its multi-faceted features is in the final analysis the business of all art.

To summarize, I have said that art shapes and interprets human experience. I have also contended that literature is not to be called Christian through impositions from without even though I have stressed that the reality of a given work may press outward to a wider reality. It is not necessarily Christian terminology, extrapolated Christian values, or theological interpretations of a culture found in the work that clarify the question. Equally significant is that the incarnational view of reality opens all human experience to the writer. If this is true, it must also be true that tragedy may be essentially Christian. The stronger claim is that only the Christian vision can truly sustain tragedy's paradoxes.

There is paradox in tragedy, and one of the greatest is that the form is constant and ever-changing. This paradox is only proof of the power and scope of tragedy. Choral odes give way to dialogue and free verse, furies become ghosts, and the sporting Greek gods give way to Jehovah, but changes in format fail to conceal the tragic concept. The presence of paradox of whatever kind is no rebuttal to the claim that tragedy may be Christian. So, I submit that Christian tragedies exist. By Christian tragedy I mean the celebration of finite reality in its metaphorical relation to Infinite reality or Christian reality.

Some Examples of Christian Tragedy

The Bible contains some of our greatest examples. The story of Jonah, for instance, shows great devastation of spirit, but the dramatic story of Saul embodies the essence of tragedy. The tragic concept is there. A certain kind of man is Saul, one of exalted status who was "anointed by Samuel," after which he was "turned into another man," and one "upon whom the spirit of God came mightily." But there is another angle. It is a "condition of being," to borrow Northrop Frye's phrase, which will be a prelude to his major choice in his situation. In Gilgal he waited for Samuel to come to offer burnt offerings, but as he waited his troops were scattering from him. Rather than continue waiting, Saul offered the burnt offering himself, only to be told by Samuel, when he arrived, that he had not kept the commandment of God and that his kingdom would not endure. But Saul had thought that the urgency of the moment demanded that he take matters in his own hands.

The prelude gives way to the tragic choice in which Saul disobeys God's command to destroy everything belonging to the Amalekites. He destroys what was worthless and spares what was good, and tells Samuel, "I have performed the commandment of the Lord." The tragic choice leads to consequences; the most enormous consequence is in these words: "the spirit of the Lord departed from Saul, and an evil spirit from the Lord tormented him." Even as the ugliness of his character becomes more manifest, Saul continues to fight. Yet there is a time in his encounter with David when he catches a peep of what he is. When David refuses to kill him, Saul weeps when he recognizes David's voice and says to him, "You are more righteous than I, for you have dealt well with me, while I have dealt wickedly with you." The tragic action of the story of Saul ends with his death by suicide.

The data which the story of Saul so unmistakably provides ought to help settle the question of the possibility of Christian tragedy. For further support, I should like to study briefly at least one of the tragedies in the New Testament—and there are many, especially in the parables. I should like also to choose a parable that some would say does not end on a tragic note. As I have stated earlier, however, I do not believe that a triumph should be called a "post-tragic" episode. To the frequent charge that if a work ends triumphantly it is comedy, I can only say here that comedy focuses on a community and on a new beginning. What happens in tragedy is a climactic shock, primarily in one life, but also as that life touches society. There may be, and I believe that there sometimes is, a triumph and a re-ordering. There is no such thing as going back, but there is the possibility of going forward; loss is never gain, but loss does not prohibit the possibility of gain. Martin Jarett-Kerr undoubtedly saw the possibility of triumph when he says, "Only in a world where real tragedy is possible is redemption also possible." He also says that perhaps the reverse is also true: "Only in a world where redemption—and therefore damnation too—is possible is tragedy also possible." Christ must have thought of this before Martin Jarett-Kerr, for not only did he tell the parable of the wedding feast and the five foolish virgins, but also the parable of the prodigal son.

What we see in the parable of the prodigal son is the familiar in a new context. A young man, undoubtedly discontent with his father's home, chooses to take "all he had" and go into a "far country." His choice leads to consequences: he spends all that he has in riotous living, a famine arises, no one gives him a thing, he takes a job feeding swine, and he would gladly have eaten their food. But the consequences did not stop here, for he came to himself. He responds to "being in time," and shows even here a victory over the B. F. Skinner boxes. He realizes how he got where he was, he is sorry for what he has done, and he decides to return to his father's home, where he not only receives extraordinary love from his father but a succession of unmerited gifts. He does not die; he is alive, and this "tragic parable" ends in triumph.

I am not suggesting that Christ calls those days in the "far country" anything less than loss; but the parable ends, after the loss, in great rejoicing. This parable too is a tragedy and provides further evidence for the possibility of Christian tragedy.

I wish now to turn to two tragedies outside of the literature of the Bible. Tolstoy's *Anna Karenina*, Dostoevski's *The Brothers Karamazov*, Eliot's *The Cocktail Party* and hosts of others should be considered, but I select for brief study *Murder in the Cathedral*.

From Thomas à Becket's first message of "peace," it seems that he perceives his choice and his suffering in the seven years of exile previous to the play: "They know and do not know, what it is to act or suffer. / They know and do not know, that action is suffering / And suffering action. / Neither does the agent suffer nor the patient act. But both are fixed / in an eternal action. . . ."

Thomas is awake to the deed to be committed; there is no temptation in his first three tempters. He knows he is not in England to forget his position, to compromise, or to intrigue. But he was not quite prepared to be so blatantly met by himself or so openly confronted by a cancerous grain of his own thought. This twin-tempter, the fourth tempter, is unexpected because he steps from Becket's soul. The temptation causes bitter suffering and a struggle. For the next twenty-three days Thomas will remember in silence the meaning of their interviews: "the right deed for the wrong reason." In this play, Eliot wants us to see the perception, not the perplexity and not the murder. Temptation is no more; he orders his church doors opened, though he knows it will invite beasts. The beastly disorder of the chorus becomes a triumph chant:

> It is not of time that my decision is taken
> If you call that decision
> To which my whole being gives entire consent.
> I give my life
> To the Law of God above the Law of Man.
> Unbar the door! unbar the door!
> Now is the triumph of the Cross!

Death awaits, of course, but the play ends with a choir singing a *Te Deum* while the chorus utters the last lines.

The story of Saul and the parable of the prodigal son show that there are tragedies in the Bible; indeed, the tragic concept is an actual part of Christianity. Choice leading to consequences is certainly at the center of the dramatic action of tragedy; it is equally at the heart of the Christian life.

Murder in the Cathedral dramatically depicts the bitter struggle and costly price of one who in Thomas's words "loses his will in the will of God." With the serious and complete action ordered toward Christian ideals and teaching, there is little difficulty in calling the play a Christian tragedy. But there are numerous works that may not depict as clearly a Christian orientation as T. S. Eliot's play, but do show at various levels a "wider reality," or preferably a Christian reality.

Shakespeare's *Hamlet* affords fertile ground for studying these various levels, and an observation of these levels will show that lines may be drawn too rigidly between "Christian" and "non-Christian" works. The painstaking study of the dilemma, choice, dramatic action, images, and significant themes of *Hamlet* will, I believe, lead one to think of it as a Christian tragedy. To explicate the tragedy fully is beyond the scope of this study, but these few brief statements are essential.

A supernatural agent enjoins a young man, who is both active and contemplative, to get revenge on a murderer. He must act responsibly in a world diseased by sin and filled with wrong; he must punish regicide and cleanse Denmark. To kill a murderer is simple; to root out evil is complex, and he must not act in a spirit of revenge. The initial movement of the play comprises Hamlet's attempt to discover why *he* should rectify the wrongs and whether the prescribed remedy came from the right authority. When, after the Mousetrap play, Hamlet finds Claudius at his prayers, he fails to kill him—for the wrong reason. He will wait until he is sure of sending Claudius' soul straight to hell. But if he does kill Claudius with such intention, he will almost certainly damn himself. In killing Polonius a bit later, Hamlet becomes both "minister and scourge." As a result of this murder, the king has him shipped to England.

The tone of the play now moves toward a deepening Christian thrust. With increasing clarity, Hamlet perceives that the way to his goal lies, not in self-centered action, but in putting himself in God's providence. He learns of the "divinity that shapes our ends," that "there is a special providence in the fall of a sparrow," and that "readiness is all." Possessed of such a vision, Hamlet carries out his commission. All that Shakespeare packed into that final act, I think we can never quite exhaust, but manifold images throughout the play as well as the dramatic action, including the large themes of good and evil, the mystery of death, and the problem of guilt, all point toward Christian reality.

Christian tragedy, then, as I have tried to show, is concerned first with its own reality, with the plots, images, characters, and meanings that constitute it. Its own reality presses upward to Christian reality, and it is the task of the careful reader to discover how and to what extent finite reality metaphorically refers to Infinite reality. To what extent Infinite reality will be manifest will depend upon the given work of art. The presence and power of a personal God are obvious in *Murder in the Cathedral* as well as the dedication and love of man for God. Shakespeare's *Hamlet* depicts transcendence, but the personal nature of this transcendence is not as clear-cut as in Eliot's drama; Christian reality, however, still engages our attention. I see no reason for leaving *Hamlet* among the Revenge tragedies; it has a Christian vision and Christian substance.

I have also suggested that the Bible affirms the seriousness of the tragedian's preoccupation with the experiences of the individual who makes a choice which always has consequences. The Bible too contains tragedies. It sanctions the probing and interpretation of human experience.

To discover the vision or outlook of the particular tragedy is the work of any critic, and he will honor his profession by suggesting what a work says through the way it says it. He will equally honor his profession by calling a tragedy Christian when it declares itself to be so.

Can Satire Be Religious?

Harry Boonstra

The most general way to organize the content of literature is to say that it deals with two topics: anxiety about the world's woes, and longing for a better world. Viewed from the perspective of Christian theology, we can discern two doctrines underlying literature as a whole: the fact of the Fall, and the hope of redemption.

Satire is the vision of a fallen world. It is the exposure of human vice or folly through ridicule or rebuke. In order to analyze a work of satire, one examines four elements: first, the object(s) of attack; second, the satiric vehicle in which the attack is embodied (e.g., story or character); third, the tone (e.g., biting or light and humorous); and fourth, the satiric norm, or standard of truth or goodness by which the object of attack is criticized. The following essay, while dealing specifically with religious satire, can be applied to satire in general.

What Is Satire?

The old cracker prayed on, "Lord, Lord, dear Lord, since I did not have a nice old colored mammy in my childhood, give me one in heaven, Lord. My family were too poor to afford a black mammy for any of my father's eight children. I were mammyless as a child. Give me a mammy in heaven, Lord. Also a nice old Nigress to polish my golden slippers and keep the dust

227

off my wings. But, Lord, if there be educated Nigras in heaven, keep them out of my sight. The only thing I hate worse than an educated Nigra is an integrated one.
—From *"Cracker Prayer" by Langston Hughes*

The brief excerpt above is part of a marvelous spoof on racial religiosity. It immediately raises questions one tends to ask of other religious satire. May one ridicule sacred subjects? To what end? Are there taboo subjects? What tone does one adopt?

Before scrutinizing these and other questions, let me supply a brief working definition of satire. Satire exposes and points out human foibles, errors, and incongruities; it does so in a playful, humorous manner; it often involves ridicule of its subject; it makes use of a number of techniques, of which irony and exaggeration are the most common; it aims at the correction of mankind. Religious satire deals with religious, theological, biblical, and churchy topics.

Religious Satire as a Form of Polemical Writing

Many Christians feel uneasy about the reading and writing of satire, especially religious satire, because it does not seem a serious enough vehicle for religious topics. The whimsy of satire seems inappropriate to the sacredness of the faith. These Christians are often not against controversial writing per se. For example, if I should write a treatise against dispensationalism, or against fraudulent religious advertising, or against shoddy country music, they would not consider such writing inappropriate. Of course, they might disagree with me and defend their silent, trumpetless raptures or their walk-where-Jesus-walked-stay-at-the-Capernaum-Hilton commercialism, or their "Jesus, Drop-Kick Me Over the Goal Post of Life" song, but they would not think it inappropriate for me to defend my point of view and write my argumentative essay. But to many people the treatment of dispensationalism or Calvinism or prayer or any other religious topic in a satiric vein seems to violate religious propriety.

I defend satire. I defend it because satire attempts to expose that which is false and, at least implicitly, to set forth an alternative. Religious satire points out what is amiss in Christian walk or belief, and it may suggest a more biblical view. Religious satire is thus in the company of argumentative, polemical literature. And, certainly, polemical Christian writing has a long (if not always venerable) tradition. Through the centuries Christians have disagreed with each other, and have said so—sometimes with Arnoldian sweetness and light, sometimes with more than a touch of vinegar.

The pigeonholing of satire as controversial literature can perhaps be illustrated best with a few examples. "Holy Willie's Prayer" by Robert Burns and "Cracker Prayer" by Langston Hughes castigate those Christians who plead special rights with the Lord and use their prayers to settle scores with their enemies. If there are such Christians and such prayers, then they ought to be exposed—and this can be done by a sermon, by a *Moody Monthly* article, or by satire. Or take Dutch immigrant Calvinists. They were often extremely narrow and intolerant in their views of other Christians. Such an attitude often betrayed an unbiblical exclusivism which could be exposed either by an Arminian apologetics or by a satiric piece as found in Peter De Vries's *Blood of the Lamb*.

I could easily continue with other examples where an error could be exposed either straightforwardly or satirically. Since the intent is similar, at one level at least, satire can be seen as a species of polemical writing.

One similarity between satire and general polemical writing is worth pointing out. The charge is often made, and rightly so, that satire exaggerates, presents only one point of view, does not give a fair hearing to the opponent, and intimates the superiority of the author. But here again, I suggest that satire may have such traits in common with other controversial writing. Calvin, Luther, More, Eck (just to limit the examples to the sixteenth century) used hyperbole and exaggeration, did not allow other alternatives, and were convinced of their theological superiority. I am not necessarily arguing here for the propriety of such strong polemic, but I do want to stress that satire shares certain characteristics with other argumentative modes. And, incidentally, I often prefer the sharpness of satire to that of the "straight" polemicist, because the former at least has the grace of wit. Also, the satirist may ultimately be more aware of his exaggeration and superiority—it is part of his technique, a pose he may not take too seriously, whereas the polemicist's dead earnestness does not allow for such a distance.

Satire in the Bible

A book that warns us not to sit in the seat of the scornful and scoffers would not seem to be the most promising source for satire, or a guide for satiric writing. Remembering what happened to Goliath and Rabshakeh, one ought to be careful to emulate some of the satirists of Scripture. But there are other examples that can perhaps be instructive.

Probably the best known example is Elijah's sarcastic encouragement of the Baal prophets: "Yes, you have a god, but he's probably taking a snooze." The spirit of these remarks is reminiscent of our Lord's laughing at those who exalt themselves against his rule (Ps. 2). Such laughter awaits those who are foolish enough to play around with holiness.

But often the barbs are aimed at God's own people. In Jeremiah 8:7 God ridicules his people by contrasting their knowledge with that of the stork, turtle, and swallow who can discern their appointed time, which the people cannot. Isaiah similarly mocks the people who try to divine the truth from the wizards who can only produce a silly peeping and muttering (8:19). Earlier (3:16-26) he has a scathing portrayal of the women of Jerusalem. Although there's very little wit here, the balance of ornamental spices, belts, and coiffure with stink, rope, and baldness does have sardonic intent.

Elsewhere God turns his sarcasm on erring servants. Jonah's pique, first at seeing his enemies spared and then at seeing his parasol destroyed, is greeted with the Lord's incredulous, "Do you well to be angry?" (4:4, 9). And Job's challenging "Let the Almighty answer me" (31:35) is greeted by the Almighty's "Where were you when I put my tape measure around the universe?" followed by the refrains of "Can you . . ." and "Have you been there?" and "Deck yourself with majesty" (chapters 38–41). Of course, Job had previously withered his comfortless friends with "No doubt, you are the people, and wisdom will die with you" (12:2), and he later called them, in effect, "windbags" (16:3).

Of a somewhat different nature are some of the Proverbs. One thus nicely characterizes our taste for juicy gossip: "Gossip is so tasty! How we love to swallow it" (26:22, Good News Bible). Or the delightful satire of the lazy man who shuts off the alarm clock and says, "I better not go to work today; there may be a hungry lion out on the street!" (26:13). And, although much of the advice and reprimand of Proverbs seems to be addressed to males, women are not totally neglected, as in the unflattering comparison of a nagging woman to a leaky roof (27:15).

Christ's lampooning of the Pharisees is, of course, well known, but familiarity may have dulled us to the vignette of a church elder depositing his twenty-dollar bill into the collection plate to the accompaniment of a trumpet fanfare, or of another with a camel traveling down his esophagus while he's busy straining a fly out of his drink.

At other times the satire consists more of situational irony. Job's friends, for example, are portrayed in such a way that much of their characterization seems satiric. Since their argumentation is largely undercut at the end, the presentation of their sober, serious, long-winded rhetoric appears ironic, at least in retrospect. So with Jonah. Here we have a reluctant preacher who is shamed into prayer by pagan sailors, who pleads the mercy of God in an abdominal prayer, but then he sulks when that same mercy is extended to others. Jonah certainly must be counted as one of the most effective revival preachers in history, but also the most unhappy with the decisions he elicits. And I can't help but think that both the human author and the Divine Inspirer must have been aware of the ironies of our reluctant and pouting itinerant preacher.

But enough of examples. Is there any pattern here? Any similarities? Yes. The examples all conform to part of my definition of satire: an attempt at reproof and correction through humor or ridicule. Certainly Elijah wants to expose the Baal prophets, and the Lord reproves his stubborn people and his balking prophet. So the proverb preacher inveighs against nagging and laziness, and Christ against nit-and-fly-picking hypocrisy. And the ridicule runs the gamut from the Lord's gentle mocking of Jonah: "Do you well?", through Job's sarcasm against his friends, to Elijah's taunting of the Baalites. In all of these examples the ridicule is carried by different kinds of humor or wit—sometimes through exaggeration, or a far-fetched comparison, or simply by demonstrating an incongruity, such as Jonah's being more concerned about his sunburn than with God's fire raining down upon the children and animals of Nineveh.

Do the Scriptural examples also provide us with guidelines for critiquing or writing satire? The Bible is obviously not a handbook on religious satire, but the examples do provide some general guidelines. One guideline is a warning: satire, as in the case of Rabshakeh, can be used as scoffing against God, and is abhorrent to the Lord. But satire is also used as a means of reproof of God's people, pointing out inconsistencies between word and walk, calling the people back from error, exposing the folly of their conduct—often by shocking or surprising them into a recognition of their faults through ridicule or through an unexpected twist of words. Since people today continue to be foolish, hypocritical, selfish, silly, pompous, also in their religious lives, there continues to be a role for the satirist to expose such foibles.

The Limits of Religious Satire

Thus the biblical record suggests that satire can be appropriate. There are, however, some constraints on the Christian satirist who also wants to observe the mandate to speak the truth in love. Even though I do not wish to propose formulas or prescriptions for religious satire, let me suggest some limits which ought to be observed.

Satire is directed at a target. The target may be, for example, a belief, institution, action, product, or person. What are the constraints for the Christian satirist when considering these targets?

First, a consideration of the "person target." "Holy Willie's Prayer" was, presumably, an attack on a strict Scottish elder, William Fisher. Byron's "The Vision of Judgment," which is partly religious satire, skewered King George III and Robert Southey. Less specific are the personal targets in *Elmer Gantry* and "Cracker Prayer," although both Lewis and Hughes had real-life models in mind.

Are such attacks on specific people appropriate for a satirist who also wants to observe charity? I suggest that, as a general rule, the lampooning and maligning of a person's character, motives, or spirituality is outside the pale of Christian charity. Instead, the Christian satirist ought to focus on beliefs, views, writings, and practices. Perhaps the old distinction between the sin and the sinner is applicable here. Interestingly, Elton Trueblood, in *The Humor of Christ*, suggests that Christ's satiric attacks on the Pharisees were against the Pharisaic spirit, rather than against individual Pharisees.[1]

Of course, one cannot fully separate a person from his or her opinions and writings and actions. Most people will identify themselves with their expressions, and thus will feel personally attacked when their writings or lifestyle or opinions are assailed. (An instructive exercise would be a reading of the letters

---

1. Elton Trueblood, *The Humor of Christ* (New York, Harper & Row, 1975), p. 51.

of response in the *Wittenburg Door*, a magazine which specializes in religious satire. Obviously, even though the satirist may not have intended to malign a person, the responses indicate that the criticism was indeed taken personally.) Nevertheless, it remains true that satire, as other polemical writing, ought to be very careful in its aim, and not attempt to assassinate character.

If personal attacks are not appropriate for the satirist, what about other religious subjects? Again, there are limits, but also ample scope for the satirist. Certainly, we should have proper respect for the Lord's ordained vessels, but don't the shenanigans of some ministers invite healthy laughter? Our faith is sacred, but the expression of that faith can get very ludicrous. Prayer is our avenue to the Lord, but those who pray can often distort God's truth. Sex is a gift from the Lord, but some people are so nervous about it that they have to interpret the Shulamite's breasts in the Song of Solomon as symbols of the Old and New Testament. Death is too serious a subject to joke about, but American's expensive funeral cosmetology may be a moral stench.

You see my point. In some way all religious subjects are sacred and demand reverence. But once these subjects have been appropriated by us, they have a way of going awry, and then the satirist's job is to show the incongruities of our ways. Perhaps biblical subjects and incidents should not be satirized (certainly not the way Mark Twain does in his *Letters from the Earth*), but even here there are incidents which can be highlighted with a humorous twist. Thus, although reverence would forbid us to satirize the Lord and his name, no other facets of our religious and moral life can be considered taboo in themselves.

Instead of imposing a taboo on subject matter, it is more instructive to consider the *tone* of religious satire. Some definitions of satire are framed in such a way that no Christian could ever commit writing it. Such definitions focus nearly exclusively on the destructive, vicious potential of satire, in which the writer vents his spleen, is motivated by personal spite, and mercilessly goads his victims. But the satiric spectrum is much wider, and the definition just mentioned presents only one end of the spectrum. Satire can be jovial as well as vicious, mild as well as bitter, zany as well as malicious, and provoke a chuckle rather than a sneer.

Thus tone and spirit and intent become crucial features of religious satire, and the Christian satirist is to steer away from the end of the spectrum which is characterized by derision, contempt, malice, vindictiveness. Of course, the true testing comes not in prescription and formula, but in the evaluation of the actual piece.

Perhaps some readers feel that by now I have allowed Christian satire such a narrow scope that I have blunted its barb and am left with only a genial kidding, an amused, harmless chuckle which doesn't disturb anyone. Such is certainly not my intent. Satire has to maintain its bite, and the proverbial "soft answer that turns away wrath" (Prov. 15:1) and "sweetness of lips" (16:21) are not the only way to expose error in the church. Just let me remind you again of Isaiah, Jesus, Paul and the Proverb writer himself, who often spoke with a good dose of stringency and tartness.

Laughing for God's Sake

Finally, it is helpful to view satire in a wider context of laughter. Theories of laughter and of the comic have been seriously discussed by many scholars, of whom Bergson and Freud are perhaps the most famous. Laughter in the Christian life has also been explored in some detail. A delightful exposition is Nelvin Vos's book, *For God's Sake Laugh*[2]; the collection of essays titled *Holy Laughter*[3] is also helpful. Those who want

2. (Richmond, Va.: John Knox, 1966).
3. M. Conrad Hyers, ed. *Holy Laughter: Essays on Religion in the Comic Perspective* (New York: Seabury, 1969).

an epistemological, philosophical, theological systematics of humor can consult some of those works. I merely want to give a few pointers.

Since satire tends to look at the absurdities of life, satire can be readily employed by those who consider life to be absurd. Much of the theatre of the absurd and contemporary black humor, for example, can be read as a satire on life. Life is stupid and meaningless, and a sardonic grin is the best face one can put on it all. Without belaboring the point, let me just state that this kind of satire, which considers life to be basically a bad joke, cannot originate from a Christian who takes creation and redemption seriously.

Those Christians who hold that humor and laughter ought to occupy, at most, a very small corner in the Christian life, are off the mark. Laughter, a sense of humor, are fitting parts of the Christian armor, even though St. Paul did not specifically prescribe it for the Ephesians.

Laughter is liberating. It frees us from the snares of smugness and rigidity and from being imprisoned in our own little worlds. Laughter keeps us from taking ourselves too seriously. Certainly we need earnestness and idealism, but a context of humor can make us wear our earnestness a bit more graciously, because it makes it easier for us to admit error, to face shortcomings. The gift to be able to laugh at self shows awareness of limitations, both personal and intellectual. One wonders if a good sense of humor might not have prevented about half of the church's schisms and secessions.

Laughter is not at odds with contrition and forgiveness. Certainly, contrition is often accompanied by tears, but at other times a hearty laugh may be as appropriate. A husband and wife exchanging poisonous remarks because they began to quarrel whether a toothpaste tube ought to be squeezed or rolled may well begin their mutual confession by laughing at their silliness, which can change into the laughter of acceptance and forgiveness.

Laughter is closely tied to the notion of playfulness. Both laughter and playfulness are childlike. And in turn laughter, playfulness and childlikeness are related to creativity. In this connection let me allude to two Scripture passages: the one about Christ urging us to become like children, and Proverbs 8, where Lady Wisdom, as a newly created child, is delighting with the Creator in the imaginative shaping of the universe.

There is a theology of laughter:

> . . . God did and does have the last laugh. Once in Eden and later on Golgotha, the demons thought they had made the whole plight of man one of never-ending seriousness. The monster death was allowed to close its jaws, and then, suddenly, it burst asunder, teeth, jaws, and all, with a party-balloon bang.
>
> To witness that man can be free from sin, the devil, and the world, what could be more appropriate than to laugh—to laugh, for God's sake?[4]

And to complete the divine comedy we also need the vision of the New Jerusalem—without tears, but with singing, harps and guitars, eating and drinking at the banquet of the Lamb, with full-throated laughter.

The Christian life often demands tears and sobriety, but these are not the ultimates. Joy, laughter, playfulness—these are not optional elements, but fundamental aspects of the redeemed life. And such a life provides a context for the right kind of laughing at ourselves, such as satire can help us do.

The Uses of Satire

Satire is not essential—but it can be useful and can promote health in the body ecclesiastic. I have already illustrated various uses of religious satire, but there are many others. Just think of some rather typical situations. The traditional role of the

4. Vos, *For God's Sake Laugh*, p. 70.

pastor who is revered and hallowed and sometimes feared, has built-in potential for pomposity and pretensions. A preacher writes seriously that the mark of a good Christian family is the wearing of bibs by children that say "I love my preacher." Another minister seems so devoid of mortal blood that even his wife calls him "the reverend." The satirist can perform a useful function in exposing the earthenness of such vessels.

Again, we are a people who take our faith and our Bible seriously. We should. But then we begin to take our particular interpretation of it equally seriously. We get theologians who speculate how many angels can waltz on the point of a needle or modern-day biblical mathematicians who can manipulate Kissinger's name to make it read 666. There once were Dutch Reformed folk who became concerned when their new minister smoked neither pipe nor cigar, since that made him suspiciously similar to the Baptist minister who was not only an Arminian, but infralapsarian. And one cannot help but think of a Bible Belt morality which preached against pipe smoking, while it lynched and castrated people whose mortal sin it was to be born black.

Then there are the profiteers who find that the gospel of self-denial is a rich source of treasures that are susceptible to moth and rust. Here too we have an ignominious tradition of selling indulgences and plastic dashboard saints, of promoting Christian charm for the right price, and sponsoring Holy Land tours that partake more of Mammon than Yahweh.

Foibles, silliness, blind spots, incongruities. And what does satire do? It exposes fraud, deflates sanctified pomposity, slays holy cows, pricks inflated pious balloons, puts a banana peel in front of the unctuous posture.

Thus the kind of satire I have been describing does not mock the serious things of life, but rather people who take themselves too seriously—not God, but man's ecclesiastical idols; not God's Word, but man's interpretations of that Word; not the faith once delivered to the saints, but the sometimes silly caperings of those saints.

And we will not bestow on our satirists honorary doctor of divinity degrees, nor name our libraries after them, or even give them imitation-leather-gold-trimmed King James Bibles. But they do deserve our applause when they expose what we think to be the moral blemishes of the church and our uneasy smile when they hit targets dear to us.

The Religious Meaning of Comedy

Nelvin Vos

Although tragedy has held the most fascination for literary theorists, there is general agreement that comedy most accurately embodies the Christian message. In the following essay, a Christian authority on literary comedy explores how this is true.

Comedy means two things in literature. It refers, first, to a type of story or plot. A comic plot is U-shaped, beginning in prosperity, descending into tragedy, and rising again to end happily. The first phase of this pattern might be omitted in a given story, but the upward movement from misery to happiness is essential. The comic plot consists of a series of obstacles that must be overcome before the happy ending can occur. Often these obstacles are blocking characters who prevent social progress or happiness. In comedy the hero is gradually assimilated into his society, while in tragedy he is gradually isolated. The typical ending for a comedy is a marriage, feast, or reconciliation. The following selection illustrates how this comic pattern exists in Dante's Divine Comedy *and in the Bible, especially the gospel.*

This selection is taken from Nelvin Vos, The Drama of Comedy: Victim and Victor *(Richmond, Va.: John Knox, 1966). In addition, Professor Vos has explored all sides of comedy in a book whose title is worth a dozen essays on the topic:* For God's Sake Laugh *(Richmond, Va.: John Knox, 1967).*

Comedy also means the humorous, and here, too, there are con-
nections between comedy and the Christian faith. In the words of Flan-
nery O'Connor, "Only if we are secure in our beliefs can we see the
comical side of the universe." The laughter of a writer such as Chaucer
springs from faith in the ultimate order of a world that is not, after all,
the final reality, Or as C. S. Lewis says of Edmund Spenser, "He was
often sad: but not, at bottom, worried"; he was under no illusions about
what is wrong in the world, but he did not regard history as the whole
story.

The Religious Significance of Comedy

To assert that the investigation of dramatic comedy is of
literary importance is to go counter to much of the tradition
of criticism. Aristotle's admission that comedy was not at first
treated seriously[1] foreshadows a persistent critical attitude
toward comedy, for almost all histories and studies of drama
operate on the supposition that the only important form of
drama is tragedy. The study of tragedy has had a long and
distinguished history, but the assumption has frequently been
that comedy is best approached, if at all, by not treating it
seriously.

To assert further that the investigation of dramatic comedy
is of religious importance is to challenge much of the Christian
tradition. The early church fathers, as well as many of their
later counterparts in Europe and the United States, vociferously
opposed the comic representation of men and events. In the
last decade, considerable interest has been shown in the relationship of Christianity and tragedy; but with notable exceptions, the affinities between comedy and religious perspectives
have not been explored. Here the assumption has been that the
often frivolous and immoral world of comedy is best ignored.
Thus both the literary importance and the religious significance
of comedy have been neglected.

---

1. Aristotle. *Poetics*, 1449b.

One of the ways out of this impasse is to propose that what is both necessary and desirable is a new dialogue between comedy and the Christian faith. My argument therefore is that the structure of dramatic comedy and the structure of Christ's passionate action bear an analogical relation to each other and that a study of these two orderings of experience may deepen our perception at once of the essential meaning of comedy and of the Christian account of human existence.

No greater problem faces the student of comedy than the obvious question of what it is. Both the history of literary theory and the nature of comedy itself, however, discourage formal definition. The loss of Aristotle's treatise on comedy at the very beginning of Western literary history symbolizes the extreme paucity of guidance which the tradition represents in the field of comic theory. The diverse works of comedy ranging from Aristophanes through Dante and Shakespeare to Shaw and Beckett have also served to remind us, as Dr. Johnson did, that "comedy has been particularly unpropitious to definers." It is too simple to refer to Horace Walpole's epigrammatic formulation: "This world is a comedy to those who think, a tragedy to those who feel." We are not very deeply impressed by Plato's suggestion that tragedy and comedy are identical[2] or by Aristotle's notion that they are opposites.[3] Nor does the proposal that one form moves us to tears and the other stirs us to laughter seem to take us to the heart of the matter.

My presupposition is that the essence of dramatic comedy is, first of all, neither social nor philosophical, nor even narrowly literary, but rather religious. Both tragedy and comedy seek to delineate a broad and inclusive meaning in human experience, to open up panoramic perspectives by which to discriminate and understand it.

The most abstract generalization one can make about the structures of tragedy and comedy is that both focus on the

---

2. Plato. *Symposium*, 223.
3. Aristotle. *Poetics*, 1449a.

relation of the finite to the infinite, on what man conceives to be the ideal of existence. Tragedy and comedy begin with the same framework: a protagonist with finite limitations and infinite possibilities who is moved by a multiplicity of forces working within and around him. Man knows he is bound to the finite, yet he aspires toward and pretends to achieve the boundless and perfect. He strains under the incessant twin temptations, either of imagining himself a god or of resigning himself to the status of a beast. Man is both a part of the universe, and apart from the universe. Ethically and aesthetically, he lives constantly in the presence of two worlds which are nevertheless one: the world as it is and the world as it ought to be. Man is entangled in the confines of the here and now, and yet he is also a creature who possesses an ultimate concern. This ultimate concern, this conception of what is infinite, is the common element within tragedy and comedy, for the structures of tragedy and comedy are rooted in man's attempt to understand his nature and his destiny.

The structure of tragedy arises out of some great effort to close the gap between the finite and the infinite, and the tragedy lies in the protagonist's final realization of the incommensurability between the two. He strives against every condition of his finitude. What is represented in tragedy, as Richard Sewall has said, is "man at the limits of his sovereignty—Job on the ash-heap, Prometheus on the crag, Oedipus in his moment of self-discovery, Lear on the heath, Ahab on his lonely quarter-deck."[4] The tragic hero's intensely painful suffering is brought about by extreme impatience with the fundamental limitations of his creaturehood. The tragic protagonist is constantly warned to observe the restraining boundaries, but his passion is not easily tempered by the counsels of prudence. And, through tragic foreshadowings and ironies, the spectator is gradually made aware of how hopelessly remote his goal is. It is tragic

---

4. Richard B. Sewall, *The Vision of Tragedy* (New Haven: Yale University Press, 1959), p. 5.

that a hero could have avoided catastrophe, and did not. What moves the tragic protagonist is his will for self-consummation, and the inevitably tragic result is self-destruction.

The structure of comedy also arises out of an effort to close the gap between the finite and the infinite and, here, the comedy lies in the protagonist's final realization of the disappearance of the chasm between the two. He accepts every condition of his finitude. For comedy stands, as Father William Lynch says, "with full, cognitive confrontation, and remembrance, in the presence of man, down to the last inch of the little beastie."[5] Though the comic man may suffer, he is patient with the fundamental limitations of his creaturehood. He constantly keeps himself within the restraining boundaries, and, however difficult his situation may in a given moment become, the spectator is made aware through "comic assurances" that the entire action will not end in the worst possible manner. It is comic that a fool cannot help being a fool, but, fool though he be in accepting his creatureliness, he does at least manage to last; as one critic has remarked, "You cannot kill a comic hero."[6] What moves the comic protagonist is his acceptance of self-renunciation, and the inevitably comic result is self-preservation.[7]

Tragedy and comedy, then, make a kind of contrapuntal music in man's whole effort to understand the basic dilemma of his existence, the incommensurability between the finite and the infinite. Both are dramatic orderings of human experience, comprehensive views of man and his world; and each presents a radically different response to man's nature and destiny.

5. William Lynch, *Christ and Apollo* (New York: Sheed and Ward, 1960), pp. 91-112.

6. Albert Cook, *The Dark Voyage and the Golden Mean* (Boston: Harvard University Press, 1949), p. 42.

7. I am indebted to Susanne Langer, *Feeling and Form* (London: Routledge and Kegan Paul, 1953), for the terms to describe tragedy and comedy: self-consummation and self-preservation, p. 351.

The Structure of Comedy in Dante's Divine Comedy

A. C. Bradley has observed that tragedy is "pre-eminently the story of one person, the 'hero,' "[8] and thus the tragic redemption occurs in Oedipus, in Hamlet, in Willy Loman. But in comedy the protagonist is subordinate to the social ethos, the society is redeemed in the man, and the society is to be "the redeemed form of man" (to borrow a phrase from the elder Henry James). Comedy assumes that society must be made to work, that men must somehow learn to live together. The tendency of comedy is to include as many people as possible in its final society. The extreme individuals expel themselves from the new society: Alceste and Shylock leave the stage, muttering about harsh injustice. But most men are pardoned at the end of comedy. Men are reunited who were long separated not only in geographical distance, but also in social and moral distance. And the new society often celebrates with revels: nuptials, banquets, and dances.

The common element in all these social actions is love: love of fellowmen, family love, and most of all, the love between a man and a woman. For the most specific manifestation of the social dimension in comedy is love in all its forms, from the highly intellectualized to the blatantly sexual. Reconciliation, especially in the form of love, is the presiding genius of comedy, just as alienation, especially in the form of death, is the reigning presence in tragedy.

The definition of the relation between comedy and the Christian faith therefore can best be furthered by using as guidelines two texts in which the motifs of reconciliation and love are central: Dante's *Divine Comedy*, and the biblical narrative.

Dante's work, as Jefferson Fletcher points out, is "the most perfect of all comedies in that its curve of amelioration rises from the absolute zero of damnation apparently assured to the

---

8. A. C. Bradley, *Shakespearean Tragedy* (London: Macmillan and Co., 1961), p. 2.

maximum of blessedness."[9] Dante's own description of *The Divine Comedy* is still more vivid: "Hence it appears that the present work is called a comedy. For if we look at the matter, it stinks and is terrifying to begin with, being *infernus*; in the end it is happy, pleasing and to be desired, being *Paradisus*."[10]

Dante's journey thus is similar to the order of salvation, for the religious and literary movement of the comedy parallels the chronology of the Christian life as described in such documents as the Heidelberg Catechism and the Westminster Confession: from Sin and Misery through Salvation to Gratitude. On the literal level of the drama, the quest of the seeker on the way of purgation begins with the impotence of the will and ends in perfected nature. On the allegorical level, the quest on the way of illumination begins in ignorance and ends in perfect vision. Finally, the journey on the way of union begins in absolute separation from the object of desire and concludes in complete union.

The *Inferno* accurately reflects the story of the comic victim. A kaleidoscopic view of the soulscape of the *Inferno*, and thus of the mythos of the comic victim, would include the elements of horror, strife, contention, isolation, detachment, hopelessness, dehumanization, bestiality, sin, estrangement, incongruity, nightmare, the Fall, weeping, and despair. The atmosphere of hell is pervaded by a sense of correspondence between the punishment and the sin. Dante, in a satirically comic way, has placed the victims in a world which is a grotesque exaggeration of their desires. The greatest desire of those in the *Inferno* is freedom, but instead they are in complete bondage. They are victims, comic victims.

Dante's intention and effect are thus amazingly similar to the comedian of the Victim: both render dramatically the state of man in the absence of the infinite. The shock of parody and

9. Jefferson B. Fletcher, *Symbolism of the Divine Comedy* (New York: Columbia University Press, 1921), p. 228.

10. Dante, *Eleven Letters*, trans. C. S. Latham (Boston: Houghton, Mifflin, 1891), paragraph 10.

the grotesque exposes the comic flaw of finitude, of man's placing all his faith in himself. The vision of hell therefore is preliminary to the other visions, for infernal death must precede rebirth and reconciliation.

If the *Inferno* is Sin and Man and Misery, and the *Paradiso* is Glory and God and Happiness, then the *Purgatorio* is in many respects the center of the *Comedy*, for in this canticle the change from absolute damnation to absolute bliss takes place. The unique contribution of Dante at this point in his understanding of grace, of how the finite from the *Inferno* reaches the infinite in the *Paradiso*. The process is purgation leading to reconciliation, with grace as the power and Beatrice as the agent. The grace the souls receive is the ability to accept the punishment (confession), to accept forgiveness (contrition), and to accept the transformation (satisfaction). And Beatrice is the vehicle by whom grace and reconciliation are given to Dante. She does not save him, but it is only through her that he is saved.

The underlying reason for the misery of Inferno was the pervasiveness of sin. The underlying reason for the happiness of Paradise is the presence of God. Here the union of the finite and infinite is complete. Here the central word is neither freedom as in the *Inferno*, nor salvation as in the *Purgatorio*, but knowledge. The result of Dante's beatific experience of beholding the heavens and their King is illumination. He is united to the Source of all truth, to the Eternal Light. Dante realized, in other words, that the *eschaton* of Christianity and comedy is identical: the arrival at total knowledge, full forgiveness, complete joy, and perfect love.

In the movement of his work Dante not only employs the journey as a pattern of the Christian life, but he also clearly indicates that the movement in *The Divine Comedy* is an analogue of the divine action of Jesus Christ: the movement from misery to happiness. For the structure of the *Comedy* indicates that Dante is in some sense retelling the story of the Christ, and, in so doing, is viewing it as a comedy.

The first clue is the time sequence used in the *Comedy*. Dante is very insistent that the reader understand the action begins on Maundy Thursday. The darkest three hours in history, the hours of the Crucifixion of Good Friday, occur while Dante is wandering in the dark wood with the three beasts. The time Dante spends in the *Inferno* until he sees Satan is identical with the time Christ spent in the tomb. The end of Canto XXXIV of the *Inferno* marks the dawning of Easter Sunday. Purgatory continues until Wednesday noon. And the *Paradiso* ends on Thursday, not only a full week later, but also the day of Ascension.

It is clear, therefore, that, on all three levels of the drama, the work of Christ is understood as a comedy: literally, in his earthly body a comedy begins in a manger and ends in the triumph of the Ascension; allegorically, in his mystical body a comedy begins outside Eden and concludes in Paradise regained; and, analogically, in his sacramental body a comedy begins in the breaking of bread and ends in the festive union with the redeemed. Thus there is an inherent relation between the Christian and the comic dimensions in *The Divine Comedy*, for literature's richest comic structure employs a christological pattern of events.

The Comic Pattern of the Christian Faith

The English theologican Hugh Bishop remarks that "the story of the human race is a love story: the story of how man was made for God, and then proved to be unfaithful and deserted him; until at last, after an almost incredible series of heroic adventures, our divine Lover succeeded in rescuing us."[11] The Christian understanding of existence, particularly as it is expressed in the biblical narrative, presents the most outstanding example of the comic mythos.

11. Hugh Bishop, *The Passion Drama* (London: Hodder and Stoughton, 1961), p. 11.

Indeed, the entire biblical narrative revolves about the themes of love and reconciliation, for the gospel of reconciliation and the celebration of love are at the heart of the Christian faith. The extreme individuals—such as Judas and the unrepentant thief on the cross—expel themselves from the new society. But both the repentant thief and the prodigal son reenact the comic ritual of pardon and forgiveness. Men are reunited who were long separated, and, in celebration, the participants feast on the fatted calf or convene in Paradise: "Today you will be with me in Paradise" (Luke 23:42). The action of the biblical drama ends in marriage, in "the marriage of the Lamb" (Rev. 19:7, 9). For the love affair between Christ and his Church is the primary strand in the Christian understanding of history.

And this fellowship of love, the Church, was established only after the atoning actions of the sacrifical love of the Cross and the triumphant victory of the Resurrection. For the biblical drama begins, as do many comic actions (think of the law of killing Syracusans in *Comedy of Errors*, the law of compulsory marriage in *Midsummer Night's Dream*, the law that confirms Shylock's bonds, and the attempts of Angelo in *Measure for Measure* to legislate people into righteousness), with the presence of a harsh law, the Old Testament law of bloody sacrifice. But, as in all comedy, law and justice and death finally give way before love and merry life. The goal of the universe, according to the Christian perspective, is the end of all estrangement, the fullness of reconciliation in Christ.

Thus the whole drama of salvation history, from Abraham to our own day, could well be understood as God's effort to reconcile man to his neighbor, and to his own desperate self. To this end were the Exodus and the Covenant, the Law and the Prophets, and the whole controversy of God with his people, culminating in him who lived and died and again lives in freedom from man's universal subjection to the power of death, sin, the devil, and the world.

And once more we are led inevitably to the central role of

Jesus Christ who did not only preach a gospel of reconciliation and love, but, more importantly, lived and died and lives again in a ministry of reconciliation. In him there is no quarrel with the conditions of existence. There is no discontent, or querulousness, or rebellion. There is no radical inconsistency, no humbling division of the soul against itself. There is no attempt either to transcend the human or to escape it. Rather, there is a glorying in the finite, an example of reconciliation in living and in dying, in festive celebration and in loving sacrifice.

A comic character sits; the tragic hero strides nobly over the stage. The man of comedy eats; such a matter is too mundane for the tragic hero to do in public on stage. Can one imagine Hamlet or Macbeth sitting as they deliver their soliloquies? Can one imagine Oedipus eating on stage or Falstaff not eating? And now, in a comic translation, reflect on these statements: "Seeing the crowds, he went up on the mountain, and when he sat down his disciples came to him" (Matt. 5:1); "This man receives sinners and eats with them" (Luke 15:2). He said, "The Son of man has come eating and drinking" (Luke 7:34), and he sat and ate with Zaccheus, with Mary and Martha, and with the thousands. Both before and after his resurrection, Christ sat, and he ate with his disciples many times, including the great final occasion of the Last Supper which was both a Sacrifice and a Feast. And immediately after the Supper, he promised that he would appoint a kingdom for his followers "that you may eat and drink at my table in my kingdom, and sit on thrones judging the twelve tribes of Israel" (Luke 22:30).

But it is in the Christ's death and resurrection that we most clearly see the work of reconciliation and love. The Cross, therefore, fulfills similar demands, and effects similar results as the act of reconciliation in comedy. What F. W. Dillistone indicates about the Cross has an analogical relation to the triumph, the acceptance, and the persevering quality of the protagonist of comedy. The Cross, writes Dillistone, is "the place of the supreme and decisive triumph over all the forces of evil . . . , the place of the full and complete forgiveness of sins . . . , and the place of constant renewal."[12]

Reconciliation, then, comes only through self-sacrificing love, through complete identity with the other, even unto death, symbolic or actual. In tragedy, the heroes live and die only for themselves; in comedy, Shakespeare's fools and clowns, Chekhov's buffoons, and Beckett's tramps live for one another, and, if they die, it is in sacrifical love for another.

The comic perspective perceives that the structure of life is a tension of sacrifice and festivity. In such a structure of antimonies the man of faith has always moved. To him nothing finite is infinite, nothing limited is ideal, nothing actual is wholly logical. He accepts all this because he cannot change it and would not wish to. He accepts the irreconcilables of the real and the ideal, the finite and the infinite, which indicates that his stance is one of faith. His world is not the world of sentimentality in which all opposites are absolutely irreconcilable, but primarily the world of the man of faith is one in which the coexistence of opposites in all their complexities is accepted. He knows that man cannot stand too much order, for rigidity and pattern lead only to tragedy when facts burst out of systems, and categories begin to break down. But he knows also that man cannot stand too much disorder, for chaos and chance lead only to tragedy when meanings cluster in a unity, and concepts focus into connecting relationships. And thus the man of faith has a profoundly comic consciousness of things, for he is cognizant of the meaning of the human, of what it means to be reconciled to the finite.

For man's attitude toward his own finitude provides still another way of distinguishing the various structures of comedy. What David Grossvogel cites the historian Lanson as having said of medieval man is perhaps helpful in illuminating the relation of the religious and the comic for all of Western man:

---

12. F. W. Dillistone, *Jesus Christ and His Cross* (Philadelphia: Westminster Press, 1953), pp. 125, 128, 154.

He has three sensitive parts: his skin, his purse, his woman; to be beaten, robbed, deceived, are the three misadventures that make him laugh when they happen to others. . . . And these three sensitive parts are the realistic surfaces that prefigure the primal fears of man: anxiety before Death, before Man, before the Flesh.[13]

Each of these fears is rooted in deep religious feelings. And what dramatic comedy does is to represent first the loss of these fundamental human possessions and then their subsequent recovery. What uniquely marks both the religious and the comic worlds is the experience of reconciliation, the movement from loss and alienation to the arrival of "at-one-ment" with self, society, nature, and the infinite.

Because the man of comedy is essentially human, he is aware that only the serious man can really laugh; the rest only mock or giggle. He is not afraid to laugh because he realizes that the grossly human and the grandly sublime within himself are wonderfully and repugnantly mixed. His awareness includes a deep sense of sin and unworthiness, as well as a profound sense of joy and blessedness. He celebrates because he has been reconciled with the Father.

For the comic perspective and the Christian faith are strangely and wonderfully mixed when we accept Saint Augustine's assertion that "He was for us both a Victor and a Victim—a Victor because a Victim."

13. David Grossvogel, "The Depths of Laughter: The Subsoil of a Culture," *Yale French Studies*, vol. 23 (Summer 1959), p. 66.

A Biblical View of the Novel

Rolland N. Hein

One of the most universal human impulses can be summed up in four words: "Tell me a story." Stories are one of the chief means by which people have wrestled with and made sense of their experiences in the world. The stories that people tell and listen to, in fact, are one of the clearest expressions of how they perceive the world, and of what they fear and long for.

The oldest stories were myths —stories about the gods. As Western literature developed, myth gradually gave way to romance, which has been replaced by the novel. While the following essay focuses specifically on the novel, it makes wide-ranging comments on all forms of imaginative literature.

The essay illustrates some essential features of Christian literary criticism. These include (1) a reliance on both biblical doctrine and biblical example in answering questions of literary theory; (2) the assimilation of extrabiblical texts (such as Aristotle's Poetics) into a Christian frame of reference; (3) a recognition of the ability of the imagination to reveal and receive truth; and (4) the ability to interpret literary texts in the light of a Christian view of reality.

The Novel: A Vision of Human Experience

What has the Bible to say to me as a reader of novels? Does it condemn me, as some of the Puritans thought, because I take seriously what in their view is essentially lies? Or does it have nothing to say to the point, so long as I keep my moral convictions in tune with its precepts? Perhaps there is something to be said for the secular-sacred dichotomy after all. But suppose I am committed to the integrative approach to life, convinced that everything I do is at least in some sense sacred? If the Scriptures do indeed govern all of life, they must give me some basis for criticism of the serious novel, making my perspective distinctively Christian. The critic who is determined to work in full harmony with the biblical revelation will find, it seems to me, at least five working principles.

The first principle should dismiss any uneasiness he may feel in working with the novel genre at all. It is that God himself places an astounding value on human experience. And the real qualities of human experience are the serious novelist's prime concern.

How many students of Scripture have been adequately impressed with the attention the Bible gives to man's experiences, both in poetic analyses (e.g., the Psalms) and in historical narratives? The Spirit chose to *show* us as a prime means of teaching us. He filled his revelation with narrative after narrative: Adam, Noah, Abraham, Isaac, Jacob, Joseph, and on and on to John and his great visions on Patmos. Christ's favorite tool for teaching was the parable. The Scriptures are together one great historical plot, with God the protagonist and the biblical personalities his foils. In the beginning he is presented creating all things, and in the end renovating and recreating all things, and all between he is shown momentously intervening in human history, moving it to its certain denouement. The manner of these interventions should strike all Christians with great force. The Bible is centrally concerned with presenting the raw material of human experience. Underlying its entire form is the quiet, persistent assertion that concrete human experience—its particular events—is of profound importance.

To study these incidents carefully and work toward theological generalizations is necessary. But the Spirit does not intend this to be man's whole response to his revelation, nor indeed the primary one. The Spirit uses various aspects of Scripture to bring man to truth. The Bible is able to grip the heart through the imagination, and through his imagination man can very directly approach truth. If the mind of man is to grasp the full truth of Scripture, it must not stifle the imagination's power to recreate the experiences of particular men. Since God is a God of movement in the concrete world, kinetic rather than static, revealing himself more in the affairs of men than in their abstractions, the story form is an essential vehicle for communicating the truths of life.

To approach truth through the imaginative re-creation of human experience is the object of the serious novelist. I can hear someone objecting: "Your comparisons between novels and the Bible are hopelessly invalid because the Bible is history, whereas fiction is merely the product of imaginative fancy. No practical Christian should take fiction seriously, no matter how beautiful it is as literature. Good novels may entertain harmlessly, perhaps, but that is all they are good for." So we are getting back to the objection of certain Puritans: the novel is lies.

My objector really owes it to himself to read some of the classic discussions of the relation between truth and works of the imagination, such as Aristotle's *Poetics*, Shelley's *Defense of Poetry*, and Joseph Conrad's Preface to *The Nigger of the Narcissus*. To summarize: the novel presents an imaginative vision of life in order to tell higher truth. This is the compelling quality of the serious novelist's vision: he has something true to say about life, but he can say it only by embodying it in an imaginative projection of life in an imagined real world. What a novelist says instructs, and that profoundly. It is a gross mistake to view the novel only as entertainment, or indeed to erect an apologetic for any literary genre on its aesthetic qualities alone, as if it could be divorced from practical life.

Granted, not all novels teach truth, and not all novelists are even interested in pursuing truth. Poor novels have a large capacity to impress the imagination with untruth and evil. But the existence of many cheap, escapist, and depraved works must not persuade the Christian to reject the entire genre. Part of his responsibility to his world is to bring to bear upon the novelist's visions his deep conviction that all of human experience can be redeemed.

The Novel and the Quest for Understanding

The Bible not only esteems human experience highly; it also sanctions full and uninhibited probing of the meaning of that experience. The second principle the Bible conveys to the literary critic is that man, an inveterate questioner, has full right to pose and boldly ponder all his hard questions about the whys of experience. Consider the Book of Job. Job is the completely honest questioner. He faces his experience inductively and fearlessly demands answers. And God in the end commends Job, nowhere condemning his inquiring spirit. Serious novelists such as Melville and Dostoevsky show a similar spirit. They are in a sense modern Jobs, imaginatively posing the hard questions of the meaning and nature of life in deep agony of mind.

In his attitudes and pronouncements as well as in his open questions Job anticipates the types of deep concerns man has in our own time. When he laments, "the arrows of the Almighty are within me, . . . the terrors of God do set themselves in array against me" (6:4, ASV), one thinks of novels of Thomas Hardy that make a similar remonstrance, such as *Tess of the d'Urbervilles*. Job expresses with poetic force the theme of alienation, so poignantly portrayed in many modern novels of existentialist cast: "He hath put my brethren for an alien in their sight" (19:13-15, ASV). And Job anticipates the concern of modern writers such as Nelson Algren who have delineated the plight of the ghetto: "From out of the populous city men groan, and the soul of the wounded crieth out: yet God regardeth not the folly" (24:12, ASV). This listing could go on at length.

Job is not only a book of laments, however. It also moves toward a conclusion that is far reaching and complete. Both the movement and the conclusion should be of interest to the student of the novel. They yield him a third biblical principle: the Bible presents us with a model of movement that is in a sense archetypal and that is all but inevitable in any narrative of serious purpose. The pattern is that of spiritual quest that leads to illumination, of moving from problem to solution or meaning within an imagined real world. There is hardly a serious novel that does not at least suggest this pattern. And even the most vulgar fiction sees man in quest, though he be depicted as an animal seeking bestial satisfaction through violence and sex.

The end of Job's quest is fulfillment on the highest possible plane. He reaches the ultimate illumination: confrontation with God. The result is that Job is fully satisfied, but not with rational answers. Instead, God meets him with more questions, for God is subject, not object. Job's satisfaction derives from an experience with the One who is the true God, an experience that encompasses his whole person. His mind is not allowed to analyze God as it would some objective phenomenon. What Job learns is that he is a being with distinct limitations, that all of reality—not just evil and suffering—is veiled in mystery for man. In thus depicting man as a restless, questioning being who can find satisfaction only in God, the Book of Job offers the Christian critic of the novel an invaluable biblical base from which to operate.

Job experienced an illumination of high degree, from the Voice of Ultimate Truth. Novels, by contrast, present human insights into human situations. They concentrate upon particular problems of human experience and move toward insights that, from the Christian perspective, may be partial.

The novel, however, does not work with the enigmas of experience as a detective story would, moving mechanically
toward neat solutions. Rather, the novel allows experience to
retain its open-endedness while offering insights into how one
may order his life more satisfyingly. Novels that succeed in
illuminating large numbers of readers will endure, outlasting
their generation and their literary period to join that body of
literature which seems to transcend time. This body endures
precisely because generations of readers agree that these works
give them certain insights into the human situation.

The Christian Critique of Novels

The fourth principle the Bible offers the critic gives him an
important approach to the actual task of evaluating the literary
worth of a given novel. It is that true meaning resides in form,
and that any statement about the theme of the narrative must
be supported by the form. This support must be convincing
and aesthetically satisfying. Take, for instance, the Joseph story.
It is history, but the principle it illustrates applies with equal
force to serious fiction. Joseph himself announces one strong
theme of the narrative in Genesis 50:20. Speaking to his brothers, he asserts: "And as for you, ye meant evil against me; but
God meant it for good, to bring to pass, as it is this day, to save
much people alive" (ASV). Whether this conclusion is valid depends ultimately not on Joseph's saying so but upon his experiences in the narrative. So the reader ponders the personalities
of Joseph and his brothers, their response to the incidents that
befell them, the sequence of those incidents, their nature and
outcome. Then, having concluded that all these attest beautifully to the truth of Joseph's statement, the reader concludes
that this statement is indeed part of the true meaning of the
story.

Or take the Book of Esther. Here the reader is favored with
no summarizing statement of theme. Yet all lovers of Scripture
agree that the story clearly teaches that a special providence of

God guards his people. What conveys this meaning, except all the various aspects of the form of the book? These work in remarkable harmony to establish this meaning in the readers' minds. The same sort of observation can be made of the Book of Jonah and other scriptural narratives, to say nothing of the parables of Christ.

And so in any novel: form indicates meaning. Much more needs to be said about the elements of form than can be said here. Let this suffice: only as the form of a novel attests to one's sense of the way things may happen—that is, one's sense of plausibility (cf. Aristotle's *Poetics*)—is the novel speaking truth. And when the elements of a story take the reader somewhat deeper, giving him new insights into the way things happen, showing him what he may have vaguely felt to be true but had never articulated, the reader may then be sure this story has a quality that makes for great literature. Thus literature clarifies life, helping us to interpret it. On the other hand, when a novel arouses a sense of improbability, and we feel that the author is missing the true qualities of reality, we are forced to conclude that his work fails as literary art.

In functioning as a critic of the novel, the Christian student rightly feels that, having examined the form and its relation to ideas, and thus determing literary worth, he is ready to confront his main task. He must now measure the validity of what this novel says, imaginatively, about life. He is equal to this task only if he brings to it a thorough knowledge of the Word of God, and has imbibed the spirit as well as the precepts of the Word. The fifth principle, then, is that the manner of Christ is the perfect model for making moral judgments. Christ's manner was incisive yet kind, always penetrating to the heart of a matter, invariably seeing value where more obtuse minds did not. He always put the value of an individual first. He patiently understood the unregenerate mind.

And no Christian critic can afford not to. The creative artist often evidences his fallen state primarily, it seems to me, in that he chooses not to have the true God consciously in his knowledge; the thrust of his energies is away from God. It is, therefore, in his speculations about the moral and spiritual aspects of experience and about the relation of man to God that a novelist must be most carefully examined.

Guided by an earnest talent, however, an unbelieving novelist may impressively penetrate the nature of human experience in its horizontal relations and in its effects upon the individual consciousness. In this lies his strongest claim to artistic achievement. And inasmuch as he accepts no supernatural revelation, he generally asks the hard questions of meaning more intensely than his Christian counterpart. He also scrutinizes life more closely, hoping it will give him some insights, some answers. The believing author is in danger of looking too quickly upward, thus failing to help us to see life from a more penetrating perspective. For the true novelist must, in the spirit of Job, insist on grappling inductively with experience itself for answers. He must reject solutions deductively conceived, no matter how logical, if they fail to fit the nature of things as he sees them.

As a critic of novels, then, the Christian takes the shape of his task from the Word of God. The Bible gives him at least the above five working principles. His task is to use them to evaluate the novel Christianly while not depreciating it as an art form valid in its own right. Performing his task, he finds that the novel can be a source not only of aesthetic delight but also of much indispensable instruction.

The Art of Poetry

Leland Ryken

How can Christians know that God intends them to understand and enjoy poetry? The answer to that question should be indisputable: because a major part of the Bible is written in the form of poetry. The list includes Job, Psalms, Proverbs, the Song of Solomon, and huge sections of the prophets. There are also passages of poetry embedded in the stories of the Bible. Furthermore, Jesus frequently spoke in poetic terms: "consider the lilies of the field"; "I am the light of the world"; "the kingdom of heaven is like. . . ."

In view of the Bible's emphasis on poetry as a means of expressing truth in a beautiful manner, it should be no surprise that Paul writes in Ephesians 2:10, "For we are his poem [Gr., poiēma, "work," "creation"], created in Christ for good works." Paul's metaphor should mean more to Christians in our culture than it appears to.

A Special Use of Language

> O my Love's like a red, red rose,
>   That's newly sprung in June;
> O my Love's like the melody
>   That's sweetly played in tune.

It is obvious that poetry is a special type of language. Poets use words in a way different from ordinary discourse. We should, in fact, speak of "the poetic idiom," meaning that poets speak a language all their own.

In our day we look upon poetry as a sophisticated and difficult and unnatural manner of speech. We usually encounter poetry first in literature courses and therefore tend to regard it as a peripheral use of language. This state of affairs is a recent phenomenon, however. Poetry developed before prose in virtually every culture that we know about, and until the eighteenth century most people expected even their stories and plays to be in poetic form.

In response to our customary attitude toward poetry as an unnatural way of talking, Northrop Frye comments, "In the history of literature we notice that developed techniques of verse normally precede, sometimes by centuries, developed techniques of prose. How could this happen if prose were really the language of ordinary speech?"[1] The first obstacle to enjoying poetry that a modern reader needs to overcome, therefore, is the misconception that poetry is an unnatural and obscure type of discourse.

Thinking in Images

One good way to overcome the obstacle is to recognize that the poetic idiom is, first of all, a language of images, that is, a language filled with sensory objects and vivid actions. In this regard the poetic idiom is a considerably *simpler* and more elementary language than the language we encounter in a textbook.

Poets think in images. In his classic essay entitled "The Making of a Poem," Stephen Spender writes that a poet "should be able to think in images. . . . Can I think out the logic of images?

---

1. Northrop Frye, *The Well-Tempered Critic* (Bloomington, Ind.: Indiana University Press, 1963), p. 18.

That is the terrifying challenge of poetry." Almost any poem
that you read will illustrate the tendency of poetry to be concrete and vivid. It is, of course, especially prominent in nature
poetry:

> Therefore all seasons shall be sweet to thee,
> Whether the summer clothe the general earth
> With greenness, or the redbreast sit and sing
> Betwixt the tufts of snow on the bare branch
> Of mossy apple-tree. . . .

> Praise the Lord from the earth,
>   you sea monsters and all deeps,
> fire and hail, snow and frost,
>   stormy wind fulfilling his command!
> Mountains and all hills,
>   fruit trees and all cedars!

> Sweet is the breath of morn, her rising sweet,
> With charm of earliest birds; pleasant the sun
> When first on this delightful land he spreads
> His orient beams, on herb, tree, fruit, and flower,
> Glistering with dew; fragrant the fertile earth
> After soft showers. . . .

But lest we think that poetry is concrete only when the poet
is describing nature, we can observe the same tendency when
the topic is an abstract idea. The subject of Psalm 23 is a theological doctrine—providence—but the poet approaches the
topic with concrete images:

> He makes me lie down in green pastures.
> He leads me beside still waters.

The psalmist elsewhere turns the abstraction "slander" into a
razor, a slab of butter, and a wild dog: "your tongue is like a
sharp razor" (52:2); "his speech was smoother than butter"
(55:21); "each evening they come back, howling like dogs, and

prowling about the city, . . . snarling with their lips" (59:6-7). What could be more abstract and "spiritual" than the law of God? Yet the writer of Psalm 19 turns it into something we can taste: "sweeter also than honey / and drippings of the honeycomb."

This, then, is one of the basic principles of poetry: it is overwhelmingly concrete and vivid in language. As C. S. Lewis comments, "From Homer, who never omits to tell us that the ships were black and the sea salt, or even wet. . . , poets are always telling us that grass is green, or thunder loud, or lips red. . . . To say that things were blue, or hard, or cool, or foul-smelling, or noisy, is to tell how they affected our senses."[2]

Why do poets use such a concrete vocabulary? They do it to capture the attention of the reader, to touch us where we live, and to elicit emotional responses. They also use concreteness to achieve universality; everyone has experienced sweet and sour and sharp and cold. Furthermore, we must remember that poetry is heightened speech, and in real life such intensity is often experienced as sensation. Most of all, though, we must realize that from start to finish the poet's aim is precision in his use of language. The poet is the enemy of vagueness. Nothing could be more inaccurate than the common assumption that scientific or technical language aims at precision, while poetry does not. Both types of discourse aim at precision, and the type of precision that poetry aims to convey is the very quality of experience as we live it.

Comparison

He is like a tree
    planted by streams of water,
that yields its fruit in its season.

The world is charged with the grandeur of God.
It will flame out, like shining from shook foil.

2. C. S. Lewis, *Christian Reflections* (Grand Rapids: Eerdmans, 1967), pp. 131-32.

Poets not only think in images; they also speak the language of comparison. The principle that A is like B underlies most figures of speech. The poet's most constant resource is to use one area of human experience to illuminate another area.

The poet's reliance on comparison places on the reader or listener the obligation of interpreting exactly *how* one thing is like the other. And the similarity is often multiple rather than single. To illustrate the frequency with which poets use comparison, I will look at the common figures of speech.

A *simile* is a comparison between two phenomena that uses the formula "like" or "as":

> I saw Eternity the other night,
> Like a great ring of pure and endless light.

> And we are here as on a darkling plain
> Swept with confused alarms of struggle and flight,
> Where ignorant armies clash by night.

In cases like this, we have no difficulty in seeing what things are being compared. The only burden placed on the reader is deciding how A is like B. In the first passage, by Henry Vaughan, the poet himself suggests the right interpretation: eternity is like a circle of light in being spiritually pure, endless, and a realm of glory. In the second passage, Matthew Arnold compares a world that no longer believes in God to a plain on which armies fight in darkness; both phenomena convey the feeling of confusion, chaos, ignorance, and terror.

A *metaphor* is an implied comparison; it is like a simile, except that it omits the formula "like" or "as." Milton, for example, described his blindness at the age of forty-three or forty-four thus:

> When I consider how my light is spent
> Ere half my days in this dark world and wide. . . .

Milton has not literally lost any "light." The eyesight that he had lost, however, was *like* light, because it is only in light that we see. Or consider Emily Dickinson's poetic description of the grief that occurs when a loved one dies: "This is the Hour of Lead." How is grief like lead? It is *emotionally* like the physical properities of lead: heavy, dull, cold, a load that drags one downward.

A *symbol* is an object or event that has, in addition to its literal meaning, a second (usually conceptual) meaning. A symbol is an image or event that stands for or represents something else, and it, too, is based on the principle of comparison. William Blake wrote a poem that begins,

> Tiger! Tiger! burning bright
> In the forests of the night,
> What immortal hand or eye
> Could frame thy fearful symmetry?

One of the things that alerts a reader that a poetic image is a symbol is if it cannot be interpreted literally. Blake's tiger is an example. Tigers do not literally burn, and there are no "forests of the night" as there are forests of Africa. As the poem itself makes clear, Blake has made the tiger a symbol for all that is evil and terrifying in human experience (just as the companion poem "The Lamb" makes the lamb a symbol for all that is innocent and gentle in human experience). Psalm 97:11 asserts, "Light dawns for the righteous." We know that the sun is no respecter of persons, and we therefore perceive at once that the poet is using light as a symbol. God's favor and blessing are *like* a sunrise.

An *allusion* is a reference to past history or literature. Although an allusion does not always compare one thing to another, it is remarkable how often it does. When Milton in his sonnet on his blindness speaks of his "one talent which is death to hide / Lodged with me useless," he alludes to Christ's parable of the talents. By means of this allusion, Milton compares himself to the slothful servant who received one talent and buried it in the ground; the point of the comparison is that Milton fears that in his new state of inactivity he cannot serve God acceptably. When Francis Thompson describes the closeness of God by asserting that he can see "Christ walking on the water/ Not of Genesareth, but Thames," he implies that Christ's presence in London is *like* his presence when he walked on the Sea of Galilee. Even when an allusion is not so obviously a comparison as in these examples, the poet who uses an allusion is almost always drawing a connection between his utterance and the "world" to which he alludes.

Personification consists of attributing human qualities to something nonhuman. Wordsworth imagined the city of London at daybreak to be a person wearing a garment:

> This city now doth, like a garment, wear
> The beauty of the morning.

The psalmist personifies nature when he calls the winds the messengers of God (Psalm 104:4). Personification, too, is based on the principle of comparison, for it pretends that something nonhuman is like a person.

The figures of speech I have cited do not exhaust the list, but they represent the most frequently used figures. The thing that they all have in common is the principle of comparison in which one thing is said to be like another.

Why do poets depend so heavily on the principle of comparison? Chiefly because they hate the approximate and the vague. The poet is not content to say that God's word is good and illuminating; he tells us *how* good and illuminating it is by comparing it to honey and a lamp.

It should now be evident, too, how the poetic imagination works. It is the great synthesizer and unifier inside us. Whereas the scientific intellect classifies and divides things and shows how they differ from each other, the imagination sees the connections among things and unifies our experience into a vast interlocking whole.

There is yet another reason why poets speak a language all their own. Poetry is the best way of overcoming the stereotyped nature of language and the cliché effect of the familiar. When compared to the way in which we usually talk, poetry is fresh and attention-getting. It has arresting strangeness (for more on the topic, see Owen Barfield's book, *Poetic Diction*). Poetry thereby rescues a statement from the indifference that we might otherwise show. This is what T. S. Eliot meant when he said that the poet is forced to "dislocate language into meaning" and Cleanth Brooks when he wrote that "the poet is continually forced to remake language." The poetic idiom is the poet's way of counteracting the principle that familiarity breeds contempt and indifference. Coleridge theorized that the greatest truths we know "are too often considered as *so* true, that they lost all the life and efficiency of truth"; the task of the poet is to state the truth in a fresh way. And such is the magic of poetry that even when it becomes familiar, it does not become a cliché but remains perpetually fresh, recongizably different from normal discourse.

Suitability

As the foregoing discussion has suggested, a main task of the poet is to find apt and accurate images and comparisons to express his idea. The principle of suitability, correspondence, or appropriateness is thus a prime feature of poetry. Poets themselves have described their task in various ways. Milton said that in writing poetry "decorum" is "the grand masterpiece to observe," and by "decorum" he meant partly the suitability of the imagery and figures of speech to the subject. T. S. Eliot spoke of "the objective correlative," by which he meant that the poet must discover "a set of objects, a situation, a chain of events" that will automatically or objectively correlate with (correspond to) the topic he is writing about.

It thus becomes a leading task of the reader of poetry to concentrate on the ways in which the images and figures of speech fit or suit the subject matter of the poem. To illustrate,

I wish to look at Shakespeare's Sonnet 116. The poem is a definition or description of true love or friendship:

> Let me not to the marriage of true minds
> Admit impediments. Love is not love
> Which alters when it alteration finds,
> Or bends with the remover to remove.
> Oh no! It is an ever-fixed mark
> That looks on tempests and is never shaken.
> It is the star to every wandering bark,
> Whose worth's unknown, although his height be taken.
> Love's not Time's fool, though rosy lips and cheeks
> Within his bending sickle's compass come.
> Love alters not with his brief hours and weeks,
> But bears it out even to the edge of doom.
>   If this be error and upon me proved,
>   I never writ, nor no man ever loved.

The opening statement in the poem, "Let me not to the marriage of true minds / Admit impediments," is hortatory in construction and has a formal, oratorial, even solemn cast to it. This, in turn, can be related to the fact that the opening statement echoes the language of the Anglican form of marriage in the *Book of Common Prayer*, which states, "If any of you know cause, or just impediment, why these two persons should not be joined together in holy matrimony, ye are to declare it." Given the subject of the poem (the nature of true love or friendship), Shakespeare has chosen words whose associations are appropriately romantic, emotional, and solemn. The same decorous choice of terminology can be seen in the word "marriage." The poet is not talking literally about a wedding ceremony. He is talking about the union or meeting of minds. By metaphorically calling this a "marriage," Shakespeare manages to introduce associations of permanent union and, if we view the subject of the poem as love rather than friendship, romantic love.

The next description of love or friendship is largely abstract:

> . . . love is not love
> Which alters when it alteration finds,
> Or bends with the remover to remove.

The only concrete image is "bends," which calls to mind the picture of a bent stick or bow. The suitability of this abstractness lies in the fact that the poem is a definition, which is necessarily abstract and generalized. The method of the poem is, like a definition always is, formal, detached, academic, universal. Furthermore, the two great concepts that are applied to love in this poem, time and space, are abstract in nature, as is love itself when regarded as a quality.

The navigation image of the second quatrain displays a similar skill in the poet's choice of imagery and metaphor:

> Oh no! it is an ever-fixed mark
> That looks on tempests and is never shaken;
> It is the star to every wandering bark,
> Whose worth's unknown, although his height be taken.

For one thing, the figure of the lover as a ship at sea was a conventional one in Renaissance love poetry, apparently based on the analogy between the tossing of a ship in a storm and the emotional turmoil of a person in love. The "ever-fixed mark" is a sea mark, defined by the dictionary as a conspicuous object distinguishable from sea which serves to guide or warn sailors in navigation. Its appropriateness to a definition of permanent love or friendship is that the mark is stable and reliable despite the agitation of the circumstances around it.

There is appropriateness, too, in Shakespeare's comparing true love to the North Star, which sailors use as a guide to their location and direction. The last line of the second quatrain ("Whose worth's unknown, although his height be taken") alludes to the practice of sailors' determining the altitude of the

North Star and thereby directing their own course. What is not known about the North Star, according to the poem, is its "worth," which might refer (say the commentators) to mineral riches, or astrological influence on people on earth, but most likely is a way of saying that it is impossible to estimate how many sailors it has helped. Applied to love and friendship, the image praises the reliability and permanence of such love, and also its mysteriousness, just as the true worth of the North Star remains a mystery. Furthermore, Shakespeare's subject is the meeting of true *minds*. He is praising a love or friendship that is intellectualized and spiritualized, rising above the merely physical or earthly. There is fitness, therefore, in comparing such love to a star, which is above the earth and is a celestial or supra-terrestrial phenomenon.

The next two lines declare the permanence of true love by using a harvest image:

> Love's not Time's fool, though rosy lips and cheeks
> Within his bending sickle's compass come.

By personifying time instead of leaving it an abstraction, the poet makes it more ominous and malicious, and also invests it with a mythical or primeval quality. Furthermore, since the poet is talking about love as the marriage of true minds, he needs a picture that will convey the idea that such love continues independent of the presence or absence of physical beauty. In contrasting this kind of true love to love that is subject to time, the poet chooses images for the latter type of love that are appropriately concrete, physical, and visual—rosy lips and cheeks.

The next line continues to personify Time: "Love alters not with his brief hours and weeks." This continued personification enhances the mythical "feel" of Old Man Time, wielding a scythe and carrying "hours and weeks" in his possession.

The next line, which declares that love does not alter "But bears it out even to the edge of doom," introduces a spatial metaphor for time into the poem. The journey is an archetypal image for time, since both unfold in linear fashion and lead to a destination. There is vividness in the picture of a journey that ends on the edge of a vast abyss. This image of a journey completed may also echo the earlier image of the ship at sea, sailing in a direct and purposeful direction toward a goal.

In the concluding couplet, the poet wishes to assert triumphantly the truth of his definition of love:

> If this be error and upon me proved,
> I never writ, nor no man ever loved.

Poetic decorum leads the poet to choose language that conveys the impression of airtight logic. Accordingly, the imagery of the next-to-last line comes from the legal world of trial, error, and proof. In the last line, the poet needs situations that are either obviously or universally valid. It is an obvious fact that the poet has written, and it is a universal fact that people love. We can reject the accuracy of the poet's definition of true love only by denying the obvious and the universal—only by saying that the poet "never writ" and that no one "ever loved."

This kind of analysis of imagery is something that a reader of poetry has to do, either consciously or intuitively. What such analysis reveals is the importance of poetic suitability—of the poet's discovering the images and words that maintain the logic of the theme and that inevitably convey the precise experience he is attempting to present to the reader.

Theme and Variation

The most universal principle of art is unity in variety, or theme and variation. C. S. Lewis explains the principle in this way:

> The principle of art has been defined as "the same in the other."
> Thus in a country dance you take three steps and then three

steps again. That is the same. But the first three are to the right and the second three to the left. That is the other. In a building there may be a wing on one side and a wing on the other, but both of the same shape. . . . Rhyme consists in putting together two syllables that have the same sound except for their initial consonants, which are other.[3]

No principle is more useful in seeing the overall organization of a short poem than this principle of theme and variation, or the same in the other. It is something that a reader should look for whenever reading a poem. To illustrate, observe the movement of John Donne's sonnet "Death, Be Not Proud." The theme of the poem, that death is ultimately powerless, is stated at the outset in the form of a taunting command addressed to death, personified:

> Death, be not proud, though some have called thee
> Mighty and dreadful, for thou art not so.

The variations on this theme consist of a series of reasons *why* death should not be proud. The first reason is the Christian belief in immortality:

> For those whom thou think'st thou dost overthrow
> Die not, poor Death; nor yet canst thou kill me.

A second reason why death should not be feared is that death, like sleep (to which it is compared), is a source of pleasure, another implied reference to the doctrine of immortality:

> From rest and sleep, which but thy pictures be,
> Much pleasure; then from thee much more must flow.

Then we get two one-line variations on the theme, the first an allusion to Socrates' comment that the virtuous person desires

3. C. S. Lewis, *Reflections on the Psalms* (New York: Harcourt, Brace and World, 1958), p. 4.

death and the second a pair of titles for death, both having positive connotations:

> And soonest our best men with thee do go,
> Rest of their bones, and soul's delivery.

A further variation on the theme of the ultimate powerlessness of death is a disparaging description of the ignoble things with which death is associated:

> Thou art slave to fate, chance, kings, and desperate men,
> And dost with poison, war, and sickness dwell.

A final item in the list of reasons why death should not be proud is a scornful assertion that drugs can produce the same effects as death:

> And poppy or charms can make us sleep as well
> And better than thy stroke; why swell'st thou then?

The final variation on the theme, placed climactically and with the weight of the whole preceding argument behind it, is the Christian consolation against death, the resurrection into eternal life:

> One short sleep past, we wake eternally,
> And death shall be no more; Death, thou shalt die.

This principle of unity in variety is discernible in any carefully constructed poem. It accounts for the time-honored idea of "the whole in every part." This means that a reader should look upon a poem as a series of restatements in different images of a single unifying theme. The principle of theme and variation imposes a double obligation on the reader: to find the theme (and to state it in such a way that it indeed covers the whole poem) and to discern how every part contributes to the overriding unity of the poem.

The Play's the Thing—
Or Is It?

Gordon C. Bennett

Of the three major literary forms —story, drama, and lyric —drama has fared the least well with the Christian church. Tertullian condemned plays as false, idolatrous, and immoral. Augustine, after his conversion, recoiled from the plays he had enjoyed as a youth. The English Puritans closed the theaters. Fifteen centuries of Christian attacks on the stage culminated in the seventeenth century with William Prynne's eleven-hundred-page Historio-Mastix.

Why this Christian opposition to the theater? There are many reasons. In classical antiquity plays were part of pagan religious worship and from a Christian viewpoint idolatrous. Drama, being a very communal form of literature, has throughout history tended to appeal to the lower rather than the higher moral strata of society. There have, in fact, been eras of alarmingly licentious and immoral drama. Professional actors, taken as a group and considered by the norms of Christian morality, have tended to be an unsavory lot. Because of the vividness with which the stage presents life, the portrayal of evil in drama has always run the risk of offending Christian sensibility, especially in such areas as profanity and sex. The emotional extravagance of the stage has given it the potential, according to many Christians, to sweep an audience into emotional acquiescence with immoral or untruthful view-

points. And with the advent of the erotic movie, the argument that drama can lead to immoral behavior has received new impetus.

The defense that Christians in drama make for the stage can be stated simply: do not the very things that give drama such a fearsome potential for evil when it is abused give it an unrivaled power for good when it is used well? Think of what happens positively, say Christian enthusiasts for drama, when the incarnational vividness, group dynamics, and emotional impact of a staged play come together in the service of truth.

The Religious Significance of Drama

Eighteen years ago, T. S. Eliot's *Murder in the Cathedral* awakened me to the use of drama as a means of modeling the gospel. I was on the student staff at the American Baptist Assembly in Green Lake, Wisconsin, and it was my first real involvement with Christian theater. I was stunned by the beauty and power of Eliot's verse and found the putting on of the role of Thomas Becket to be a personal challenge. It was a memorable experience. Since then I've spent a chunk of my life exploring the church-theater dimension, and I've worked out ways of using drama to convey a message about God and man, love, sacrifice, justice, redemption, and resurrection.

Many think that religious drama is a narrow, limited field, populated by saints and mystics, biblical characters in bathrobes, preachy clergy, and *dei ex machina*. But the field is really quite broad. Important playwrights from Sophocles to Arthur Miller have treated the basic questions of human identity and human destiny. Such questions are religious questions; therefore, while the plays may not talk about God, they are religious drama.

Roderick Robertson has said there are three basic areas of human experience that drama may treat: man's state as unrelated to God; man's search for ultimate reality, or God; and man acting in close fellowship with God, or as God's agent in the world. Plays of the third type generally treat matters of conscience and often martyrdom. To illustrate the Robertson scheme further, there seem to be these three categories: drama of alienation *(Rhinoceros; Death of a Salesman; Waiting for Godot)*, drama of religious experience or search *(The Cocktail Party; J.B.)*, and drama of religious heroism *(Murder in the Cathedral; St. Joan; The Cup of Trembling)*. Many plays, of course, combine elements of two or three categories.

We have, then, a lot of high-quality plays that treat religious questions. Granted, affirmative *Christian* drama of high quality is harder to come by. There is some, and we ought to be writing more. But we should also examine the plays written by non-Christians, for we need to know what modern artists are saying about life, though we may not agree with it. Unwillingness to do this is one of the complaints that as a Christian dramatist I have about some of my brothers and sisters in Christ. I find fault with my fellow Christians on some other counts as well. Let me explain.

The Problem with Some Christians . . .

1. They tend to confuse stage reality with life reality. Obviously, the stage is not the world, the play is not life reality. It is a subjective enlargement of an aspect of life. Confusing the two kinds of reality leads one to make mistakes like criticizing an actress for playing the part of a prostitute as if that real-life woman is somehow to be identified with the character she "puts on" while on the stage. The stage is a place of make-believe. Often it's necessary for Christians to play unbecoming roles so they may contribute to the play's total impact, which may be affirmative and highly spiritual.

2. They tend to mistake biblical pageantry for good art. The traditional Christmas play with Mary, Joseph, and the manger is not generally good art. It may well have a valid function in the life of the congregation of God's people; it may be a communal experience, a participatory act, an annual high time of inspiration as such plays were in the Middle Ages. But it is

seldom fine drama. People should be exposed to more provocative, profound, artistic Christian drama. Perhaps we should do something rich and profound like Ward's *The Holy Family* or Auden's *For the Time Being* next December instead of the simple pageant.

3. Christians often underreact or overreact to certain kinds of dramatic material. My experience with chancel drama has shown me that people aren't used to the idea of laughing in church, so it's very hard to "loosen up" a congregation and get them to respond to humorous material. In the plays I have published under the title *From Nineveh to Now*, I have tried to use satire as a method of provoking self-reflection and self-improvement. By striking the funny side of faith we can often have a back-door influence on people and do it without moralizing. I wish that church people would see humor as one of the facets or faces of God and respond better to its use in a religious context.

About overreacting: here I'm referring to how some Christians respond to some kinds of language. Drop one "damn" in a church play and you'll lose perhaps 60 percent of your congregation. After that they don't hear anything else. Although some of them will sit through a ton of swearing at the Locust Theatre downtown or in front of the TV, they won't accept a single four-letter word in a church drama. We did a college production of Ibsen's *An Enemy of the People* and two of our college administrators were aghast at hearing three "damns." I wonder if they caught the play's heavy message. The point is that if you overreact to certain words you may miss the message, and that message is a hundred times more important than the language in which it's expressed. To turn off a play because you're offended by a few words is like throwing out a dinner because there's too much salt on the spinach!

Some current plays are so full of filth and profanity that, while there may be some message in it all, it's not worth wading through the mud to find it. I deplore such drama; it offends both my aesthetic and my moral sensibilities. We must condemn such so-called art and at the same time write material with better language and more affirmative values.

4. Christians often require a very explicit message. Some don't think a play is religious unless there is a Christ-figure, or someone quotes Scripture, or it contains a heroic minister, or someone is converted in the traditional sense of the word. Some such plays are fine—many of them are inspirational—but the explicit gospel play may not provoke thought or change attitudes as well as cloudier, more subtle drama can do. There is a general rule (one that permits some exceptions) that the more obvious its message the less artistic the play. The trouble with much of the simplistic drama is that it's not true to life. So here's my conclusion, for what it's worth: If you can say it as well in a sermon, write a sermon—don't write a play. The sermon is a more explicit medium, more linear, unilateral, while the play is more abstract, multisensory, multilateral, and more involving. So don't demand simple plays with obvious conclusions. The drama may be somewhat ambiguous, the moral left unstated; you have to grapple with it, work out your own interpretation. It's a growing experience. I left a class of students recently feeling very "high" because while I was trying to help them understand MacLeish's *J. B.*, a rather ambiguous play, they had prodded my understanding and helped me to grow. MacLeish could have said it all more obviously, but we were glad he didn't!

On the Task of the Christian Dramatist

If we write plays for the church alone we're not doing much evangelizing, for most of the pagans are outside its walls. It's hard to write Christian drama, and even harder if it is to be performed in the theater as well as the church. The Christian writing for the theater must guard against moralizing—the critics will stomp on any play that seems preachy. The dramatist can preach in the sense of sharing his values, but the message must come through a logical development of action and authentic characters—not through *lines* so much as *lives* put on stage. Of course, that's the best kind of witness offstage as well. So Christian drama must be dramatically sound as well as spiritually uplifting. This is a hard task and has been done successfully only a few times in writing for the theater. Perhaps the best examples are to be found in the works of the British Christian playwrights T. S. Eliot and Christopher Fry.

The Christian dramatist may choose to work only a limited area of religious experience and omit other areas. Dale Rott develops this point in a fine essay in the volume *Christ and the Modern Mind*.[1] He doesn't have to tell the whole gospel at once. He may find insights coming from the negative dramatic work of people like Albee, Ionesco, and Samuel Beckett, who depict man's loneliness and hopelessness without God. But he will not stop there. He must do more than expose man's depravity, more than raise searing questions about human existence; he will start to work out some answers in terms of justice, love, reconciliation, and resurrection.

In an essay entitled "The Shrinking World of Christian Drama," Nancy Tischler wrote:

> The Christian artist . . . could also explore a Christian life that is not a series of sterile and confusing symbols but a pattern of grand emotions and real dignity. He could present (as Graham Greene has consistently striven to do) the reality of God's presence in life. He could end his plays, not in futility and despair, but with a recognition that there is a power that can save and heal man and guide him so that he need not live in chaos. He could show men of God as something more than nervous Nellies, organization men, seducers, perverts, egotists, and weak-minded exponents of a worn-out system. He could explore the possibility that sins against our fellow human beings are not the only sins, that we may also sin against ourselves and against

1. Robert Smith, ed., *Christ and the Modern Mind* (Downers Grove, Ill.: InterVarsity, 1972).

our God. . . . The Christian artist could emphasize salvation as well as sin, peace as well as turmoil, certainty as well as doubt.[2]

The task of the Christian dramatist is huge. It's more than just putting on pleasant Christmas pageants and finding plays with language safe enough to not offend anyone. The Christian dramatist will be careful in using language, of course, because he knows there is great power in words. And yet, to convey valid ideas he may have to offend people occasionally, just as any preacher worth his salary will sometimes administer spiritual shock therapy. The Christian dramatist will sometimes use plays to please and inspire only, but at other times his material will expose, disturb, awaken, or condemn. So be it. He too has a prophetic function.

2. *Christianity Today*, Oct. 13, 1967.

A Christian Perspective on Film

Mark Coppenger

Why is it important to know contemporary literature? Primarily because literature is an index to the attitudes that are prevalent in our society; as such, it increases our awareness of the world in which we live.

Nowhere is this more true than in the case of modern movies. Some analysts have gone so far as to claim (descriptively, not necessarily approvingly) that the movie has replaced the pulpit as the primary moral/spiritual influence in our society. The following essay explores the topics of why and how Christians should attend movies, and what elements make a movie good or bad.

The Promise of Film

Why should a Christian attend movies? What is there to warrant a variety of investments—of time, money, and energy? What gain can he expect from a medium whose sins are notorious in Christian circles? The answer has at least three parts.

First, he can find himself, his world, and others in film. Whether the discoveries be flattering, depressing, edifying, shocking, reassuring, amusing, or bewildering, they are valuable. Whatever ministry the Christian hopes to have, it is enhanced by a familiarity with the circumstances, images, passions, and perspectives which occupy him and his neighbor.

Second, he can find his way. While movies provide their share of error, they are not without wisdom. Nested among the lies and irrelevancies are dependable and life-important lessons. Indeed, a film experience can be so strikingly true and helpful as to assume benchmark status.

Third, he can lose himself for a time. Movies have the power to free him from his preoccupation with life's demands. While they cannot act as a substitute for spiritual renewal, they can provide the same sort of natural and healthy satisfaction found in sports, conversation, sightseeing, and music. The delights in receiving a well-crafted product of human ingenuity are considerable.

This, then, is the promise of film. The prospects are sufficiently gratifying to warrant the appreciative and hopeful remarks that follow.

Components and Contexts

Film is a hybrid medium; it demands of its artists a range of skills and sensitivities to match its component media. Because a film is narrative, it finds instruction in literature. Because it is visual, it learns from painting and still photography. And because it employs a score, it answers to the art of music. Ordinarily the literary interests take precedence; that is to say, the story is usually the heart of the film. The photography tells the story, and the music supports it. But now and then the supporting media match or surpass the literary aspects in importance. For example, the visual effects of *Days of Heaven* and *Barry Lyndon* rival the stories, while in *Fantasia* the animation serves to illustrate the music. But in the great majority of films, the story rules.

Since film does call so many skills and interests into play, there is an enormous body of pertinent knowledge. Aristotle's *Poetics*, a bassoon's timbre, the Rule of Thirds for pictorial composition, first person perspective, color complimentarity, instrumental improvisation—these are only a few of the things whose relevance to film is based upon its artistic synthesis.

Theology, history, sociology, military science, physics, and a host of other disciplines each contribute useful background understanding to the art of film. And since motion picture photography is so technologically sophisticated, there is room for valuable study on such things as variable shutters, focal length, depth of field, film emulsions, and anamorphic lenses. Film, of course, has its own fascinating history, including the formation of United Artists, the impact of television on the industry, and the transition from silent films to "talkies." And it has generated its own techniques—zoom freezes, jump cuts, cutaways, and dissolves. In short, the array of background information for film is bewilderingly extensive. The student of film will not run short on subject matter.

Focal Dexterity

What good, though, is all this information? The answer depends upon one's role. If you chose to direct a film, then you need to be familiar with a good deal of it. A director's literary, technological, or historical blind spots can undermine a film. The art demands a lot of its practitioners. But what about the viewer? What difference does this sort of study make to him?

The studious viewer, the viewer who is well-acquainted with contexts and concepts, enjoys the blessings of what can broadly be called *focus*. A focus is a way of seeing, a perspective, a manner of attending to this or that detail. In the presence of a newborn child, the proud father and the pediatrician see different things. Their interests and background knowledge differ. The former recognizes his father-in-law's nose while the latter detects a trace of jaundice in the skin tone.

The viewer who has done his homework has at his disposal a variety of foci. He can shift from one to another at his pleasure. He might, for example, compare this particular Paul

Schrader film to those others he's seen. He could scrutinize *Apocalypse Now* for its fit with Conrad's *Heart of Darkness*. He could focus on the efforts of a new actress, the screenwriters' mastery of dialogue, the pace of the narrative, or the use of symbol and metaphor.

This ability to alternate foci can serve his viewing experience in several ways. He can treat the film as something of a sampler, tasting first one and then another type of treat. He can seek out his favorite aspect and dwell upon it. He can retreat from a poorly fashioned component of the film to a more satisfying frame of reference. He is, so to speak, master of his cinematic experience. He has the know-how to adjust his attention for his advantage. He has the tools to mine whatever ore a film has to offer.

The benefits of background study extend, though, beyond the viewing experience to the discussion that follows. One familiar with the range of film structures, contexts, techniques, and purposes is in the best position to savor the film, to multiply his satisfactions through analysis and reflection. He is able to lead his audience through an imaginative reconstruction of the film, disclosing and high-lighting this or that juxtaposition, theme, or shift. He can direct his listeners to a new vision, an alternative focus, a novel insight. As cinematic tourguide, his pleasures equal those of the sightseers he serves.

When a film fails, the knowledgable viewer finds himself again at an advantage. John Stuart Mill is paraphrased, "Better Socrates dissatisfied than a pig satisfied." For purposes of this discussion, we will do better with, "Better Socrates dissatisfied than a pig dissatisfied." The pig is trapped in his discomfort until something better comes along. Socrates, on the other hand, can analyze his discomfort, come to terms with it, and thereby discover new things about himself and the world. He gains the upper hand on his difficulties by naming them. There is deep satisfaction in knowing exactly what's bothering you. But there is more than the peace of understanding here. Once the problems are identified, one's in a position to avoid them

in the future or to eliminate them. Socrates' discomfort is constructive in a way that the pig's is not. When a film fails or
stumbles, the viewer who has done his homework finds himself
in a favored position. For he is able, by means of concepts and
contexts, to deal with his pains. The pleasure he feels in putting
his finger on just what went wrong is almost as keen as the
pleasure he finds when things go right.

The blessings reserved for the viewer with focal dexterity are
substantial and plentiful; but it would be a mistake to overlook
the curse which can accompany these blessings, for the intrusion of background knowledge can skew the viewing experience. Each new fact about film can effect a corresponding loss
of innocence in our regard of films. Associations vie with the
film itself for our attention. But the same command of focus
we exercise in sorting through the film can be called upon to
exclude damaging irrelevancies. We can develop the capacity
to hold focus as well as the capacity to shift it. Both can serve
us admirably.

Invisible Movies

While the tools and skills of film analysis can be a great
help, there is a kind of movie which, while viewed, obviates
their use—the invisible movie. It's odd, of course, to speak as
though a movie could be invisible. After all, isn't camera work
an essential? What good is an unseen movie? In the ordinary
sense of the word *invisible* "invisible movie" is absurd. But there
is a way in which the expression makes better sense. Let us not
think of an invisible movie as an unseen one but as a movie
not seen as a movie. We are aware of all that is happening on
the screen except that something is happening on a screen. We
are oblivious to the facts of screen writing, editing, sound mix-
ing, and cinematography as we watch. This is not to say that
we do not know about these aspects of film production. Whether
we know about them or not, they are just not present in our

consciousness. The movie so thoroughly absorbs our attention that no room is left for technical reflections.

This whole affair is analogous to health; it too is invisible. Perhaps there is a popular image of good health as a combination of vibrant muscles, tingling sensations of vitality, and a sweet stomach. These are, of course, nice; but they are superfluous. Physical health is essentially the absence of physical distraction. When we are free to lose ourselves in the tasks at hand, when our bodies do not call themselves to our attention, then we are at our healthful best.

The application to movies should be clear. Good movies are those without distractions, those which permit us to enter fully into the matters at hand. When the "organs" of the film are in good working order, then they do not call attention to themselves. The film "organism" is so thoroughly integrated as to be a single thing instead of a collection of competing, self-important factions.

Distance

When we talk of a film's invisibility, we should not suppose that we come to regard what transpires on the screen as the actual course of events at present. It's not as though we take the movie as an occurrence which requires an ordinary life response. The legendary yokel in the balcony who actually shoots the villain on stage is not the model spectator. Good films don't need that kind of invisibility. It is enough that they fascinate us so thoroughly that we lose ourselves in their unfolding. In a sense to be explained, it is the truth and not the immanence of what we see that engages us. Of course, there is a variety of effects which can make us yell, jump, or duck as we watch—cinerama roller coaster rides, springing ogres, and low-flying airplanes. But these jolts which force us into an instantaneous real-world intimacy with the film are not central to the filmmaker's art.

Rather, the invisibility of a good film involves what is commonly called *distance*. Distance is not a feature of the film, something to be seen. It is a way of watching, a standpoint, a frame of mind. We don't need to worry about seeking it out and holding to it; a good film establishes its own distance for us. Indeed, as that distance breaks down, as we make real-life reactions, the film becomes visible. We catch and then reassure ourselves that it's only a movie, and so the spell is broken. In short, the film's invisibility depends in part upon the distance it sustains.

This is a paradox, since distance would seem to give the impression of distracting artifice. But it seems that a film can demand that we take it more seriously than it ought to for its own good. By driving us toward natural life responses, it gives away its special hold on us. Perhaps it would be better to say that it makes it so that we do not take it seriously enough. What began as a presentation of some truth deteriorates into a merely circumstantial event. The film then is merely one more thing to dodge in life and not a source of insight.

Accessibility

Now it might be objected that these invisible movies demand too little of the viewer. Their accessibility, their willingness to do the work, surely marks them as second rate. How can anything of value come forth without willful and studied attention? Don't invisible films accommodate flabby viewing, generate mass appeal, and supply merely pleasant diversion?

These remarks reflect a curious value structure. They seem to elevate the obscure, the difficult, the esoteric. Of course, experience teaches us that some of the finest things are available to only the diligent. And so we might insist that the viewer encounter a range of difficulties, for his own good. But surely this misses the point of the filmmaker's art. It is his task to appropriate the inaccessible, the obscure, and render it accessible and clear. He should eliminate obscurity, not transmit it.

And we, the viewers, should be the beneficiaries, not the victims, of his work.

Invisibility must not be confused with pleasure and ease. Some invisible films are, of course, quite enjoyable, but many are not. Those who saw *The Deerhunter* know how wrenching and exhausting a film can be in its invisibility. If we lose ourselves in comedy, we find delight. But if we lose ourselves in murky and desperate situations, we are drained and battered. Invisible films can teach us hard lessons as well as offer us pleasant reminders. Invisible films do not demand analytic work of us; rather, they work us over.

Film Truth

False films are visible. Our guard goes up, and we fall into critical review. We worry about whether other viewers are being duped. We resent the filmmaker's misconstrual and suspect his motives. Whether it is false through ignorance or deceit, a false film frustrates the viewer.

When we talk of truth and falsity in films, two misunderstandings naturally come forward. The first concerns fantasy and the second education. A film is not false simply because the characters or action is not to be found in the workaday world. The non-existence of dragons does not make *Sleeping Beauty* false. The portrayal of death as a chess player does not falsify *The Seventh Seal*. Truth can work perfectly well through such presentations as these. Secondly, an interest in the truth of a film is not the same as an interest in preachy or blatantly didactic films. A true film may be desultory. Although films make a statement of sorts, they don't need to be pushy about it. And, of course, this interest in truth does not excuse aesthetic failure. Falsity is just one way a film can fail.

To understand film falsehood, we should consider film truth. A film may be true or true *to* some vision of the world. The first sort of truth is philosophical, if you will. Both *The Green Berets* and *M.A.S.H.* had something to say about the nature of war, and both spoke falsely. *The Green Berets* made our men so thoroughly decent and competent, our cause so untouchably grand, our enemy so sinister, and our equipment and techniques so marvelous that one wonders how men of good conscience could object to the war in Vietnam. Whether or not the war was, on balance, just, the film was not, on balance, just. *M.A.S.H.* erred otherwise. War was portrayed strictly as institutionalized insanity; blasphemous, promiscuous, inebriated, disrespectful doctors were given a most honored status. It was simply *The Green Berets* for another group. No doubt there were truths to be found in these films—a good deal of the Vietnam effort was honorable and competent; there is plenty of futility and pretense in any war. But the films were not, finally, true.

The viewer who considers war to be sheer glory or sheer madness will likely find one of these war films true. He won't be plagued by the same reservations which surround the less sanguine or less cynical viewer. So the films could be invisible for some. This is why it's important to tie film quality to wisdom. Since surely truth is more worthy than falsehood, a film may be graded on the basis of its faithfulness to truth. The film which strikes the wise person as plausible has to be better than the one which impresses the fool as plausible.

Truth is not the same as edification, though truth may be edifying. Certainly the account of Thomas More's principled stand in *A Man for All Seasons* was edifying, as was the triumph of good over evil in *Cinderella*. But no less true are the plights of the sad characters played by Jon Voight in *Midnight Cowboy* and Gene Hackman in *The Conversation*. Truth can be bewildering and painful as well as edifying.

The Wise Christian Viewer

The best movies are invisible to wise Christians. Since some wise men are not Christians, and some Christians are not wise, both qualifications are important. Both groups suffer from blind spots. A person who is unable or unwilling to bring New Testament perspectives to bear upon movies is one who misses many truths. He will value some specious presentations and discount some of value. The Christian will always be judged, in some respects, a fool by the world's standards. And so there will be differences in evaluation between believers and non-believers. In many cases the Christian will join with the orthodox of other faiths in criticizing a film for falsehood. For example, both Christians and Jews will balk at *Same Time Next Year*'s rich portrayal of adultery as a workable and gratifying relationship.

But the Christian stands alone in his disdain for the frequently shabby treatment given to preachers. The film industry dwells upon Elmer Gantrys and besotted clergy with hellfire fixations. For every Christianly sensitive picture of a minister, there are scores of the other sort—the offensive joke of a team chaplain in *North Dallas Forty*, the slick, greedy evangelist in *Oh, God!* Of course, each of these images can be substantiated in the world, but the overall impression is unfair.

Among Christians, Roman Catholics seem to fare better in mainline commercial movies. One is hard-pressed to think of a set of Protestant clergy to match those found in *Going My Way, Lilies of the Field*, and *Boys' Town. A Man Called Peter* comes to mind, but then things get harder. Still, Catholics suffer their share of abuse; it is doubtful that many devout Catholics warmed to *Shoes of the Fisherman* or *The Exorcist*. But regardless of the proportion of abuse among Christian groups, it is clear that the moviemakers are quite insensitive to the fabric of orthodox Christian faith and practice. The offense is so pervasive that respectful treatment is surprising—consider, for example, George C. Scott's compassionate search for his daughter in *Hardcore*. As he tracks her through California's pornographic community, his single-minded devotion to the search and his indifference to the sordid attractions surprises us. We have been conditioned to expect a prompt breakdown in the veneer of piety. When the commitment of a Christian layman holds firm, we are filled with wonder. Here is, unfortunately, a case in which invisibility is lost either way. Misconstruals of Christianity are offensively visible but so frequent that fair portrayals are joltingly visible as well.

For the Christian viewer, a film is more or less invisible insofar as it is faithful to Christianity. That is not to say that a film must have a doctrinal or evangelistic theme to be worthwhile. It is enough that the film be consistent with the Christian account. Inconsistency can occur on several levels—the scene may be downright sacrilegious, e.g., the chorus-line-kick crucifixion in *Life of Brian* or the Last Supper parody in *M.A.S.H.*; its theology can be murky, e.g., the ambiguous version of the sheep/goats metaphor and the Resurrection in *Godspell* and George Burns' answers to the theologian's questions in *Oh, God!*; it can smile on a practice which Scripture rejects, e.g., robbery in *Butch Cassidy and the Sundance Kid* or adultery in *Cousin, Cousine*; it can fashion a world-view which is non-Christian in any of a range of ways, e.g., Woody Allen's engaging world-dismay in *Annie Hall* and *Manhattan* or Robert Altman's unrelieved but clever cynicism in *Nashville*. This is not to say that these films are less than extraordinary; many of them are remarkable. It is simply to say that they are less worthy than a film is capable of being.

It's not enough that the viewer be Christian, of course, for Christians can be foolish and blind in many ways. That's why it's important to stipulate that the assessing Christian be wise, to the exclusion of both naiveté and willful parochialism. The success of such whiz-bang productions as *In Search of Noah's Ark* and *The Late Great Planet Earth* should say enough to warrant the qualifying word "wise." For while these films involve both Christian perspective and Scriptural truth, their arguments are shabby displays of rhetorical expediency. This sort of thing should make a film painfully visible.

The counsels of wisdom assist the viewer not only in regards to truth but also in appreciating truth *to*. A film which is not true may be true to some view of the world or even some fantasy or psychological need. While *And Justice For All* is not a true slice of an attorney's life, it presents an engaging vision of the struggle between good and evil. Much the same can be said for Clint Eastwood's *Dirty Harry* and *Magnum Force*; they are true to certain of our emotional needs in a society beset by loathesome criminals. The treatment given them in these films as well as in *Death Wish* resonates with our psyches and answers our frustrations. They are true to something in us. So in their own way are *Rocky I* and *II*. Our dreams of simple, triumphant courage find genuine portrayal here, as do sexual fantasies in *10*. Our souls are called forward and stung in *The Heart Is a Lonely Hunter*; the juxtaposition of selfless care and selfish indifference is painfully right in this movie. A film then may be true in its faithfulness to our personal frames. It may answer to some dishonorable aspect of ourselves, but there is a sort of truthfulness in this encounter. We know when the film has found us out. And to the extent that the contact occurs, the film is invisible.

A movie may be true to the perspectives and values of others. Whether it be the "good ole boy" attitude of *Cool Hand Luke* or the fierce familial loyalty of *The Godfather*, there is a ring of truth. This, it strikes us, is fidelity to someone's mind or life. As we learn, the film vanishes.

In sum, a film can "get it right" or "get it wrong" in several ways; and so wisdom counts in viewing. Film truth or falsity is not, of course, an all-or-nothing thing. The work is more or less correct, more or less faithful. Aspects of the movie may ring true while the total picture is false, and vice versa.

Other Distractions

Falsity is just one of the many ways in which a movie can appear as a movie, can call attention to itself in a distracting fashion. In the made-for-television film series, *Roots*, Edward Asner's wig was sufficiently ill-conceived to undermine his role as ship's captain. And while the effects of a boxing match can be devastating, even lethal, Rocky's fight makeup was so lurid as to declare itself as makeup.

Camera technique can intrude as it does in the classic example of the carriage scene in the early German vampire movie, *Nosferatu*. Intending to create an eerie effect by undercranking the camera, the director made the stranger's ride in Dracula's coach funny. What was meant to be an unnaturally and so chilling upspeed trip to the castle turned out to be a mood-destroying Keystone Cops-style scamper. The high-speed pans in *The Good, the Bad, and the Ugly*'s graveyard scene was a forceful representation of a desperate man's search for the grave holding stolen gold. But the camera motion was not enough to capture the whole of perceptual frenzy; its simulation of the driven man's vision was impressive but retained the visibility of a simulation.

An unsuccessful media transplant can render a film visible. It is difficult for a stage play to work fully as a movie. Since plays stick to only a few scenes and so concentrate on dialogue rather than visuals, they ordinarily underuse the filmmaker's resources. The range and power of the camera is noticeably checked, and we get a sense of stuffiness. As engaging as dialogue in *Little Murders* and *Same Time Next Year* was, the viewer couldn't help but feel a bit cramped. Action which fills a Broadway stage can disappointingly occupy only a corner of the filmmaker's "stage." Some films fare better in the telling than in the seeing. A delicious cognitive or imaginative absurdity can go stale on film. The sympathetic viewer finds himself narrating or explaining the film to himself in order to get the full jolt. Whether it be the knights who go "Knee!" in *Monty Python and the Holy Grail* or Bernadette Peters' cornet serenade in *The Jerk*, something is lost in translation from the oral to the visual. What works on paper or in a gag writers' session can fall flat on the screen. Some scenes are best left to the imagination. They lack the direct charm of Cato's attacks on Inspector Clouseau in *The Pink Panther* and Marty Feldman's

"Walk this way" bit in the Transylvania train station in *Young Frankenstein*.

Film editors can destroy the invisibility of the movie in a variety of ways. Even such extraordinary films as *Apocalypse Now* and *Deerhunter* suffered stalls because of the editors' lack of will or judgment. We simply saw too much of Martin Sheen's captivity in the first movie and too much wedding party in the second.

The list of distractions could go on and on—vapor trails in a nineteenth-century sky, stagecoach wheels turning slowly backwards, deterioration of Eastman color resulting in loss of greens and yellows in aging films, mismatch between sound and action, superfluous cameo appearances by aging stars, gratuitous violence, excessive profanity, painfully obvious pretense, the cliché "cut" from sexual passion to exploding fireworks, the self-contradictory expression "Roger Willco Over and Out." These are simply a few of the thousands of ways a film can announce itself as just that, a film. When these distractions arise, the force of the movie ebbs. Our focus shifts from the film's focus to the film itself. And since there are so many ways in which this shift can occur, the art of the filmmaker is terribly difficult. The complexity of the medium defies amateur success.

Proper Christian Viewing

Considering all this talk of focus and invisibility, how should we approach a film? What sort of stance does the wise, Christian viewer take in the presence of a movie? Does he marshal his aesthetic and theological sensitivities for the encounter? Does he, so to speak, interrogate and grade the film as he watches? Is he on his guard? Does he search for soundness in form and content? Not at all. For this would be just so much wasted motion, somewhat analogous to studying for a blood test.

If you are wise, aesthetically sensitive, and Christianly informed, then the films' flaws will announce themselves. They will trip your critical mechanisms, calling them into play. If the errors are significant, then you won't miss them. If they take a good deal of scrutiny to detect, then your offense is as petty as that of the spinster who objects to indecencies she can see through her telescope.

The proper stance for viewing is, then, receptive and open. Either you are wise and sensitive by the time the film begins, or you are not. If you suspect that you are gullible or philistine, then you should fasten on "training wheels" in the form of critical friends. They can help you in spotting the flaws a mature viewer can see. But this kind of exercise is, at best, remedial and not paradigm. This is the sort of thing you want to outgrow. The perspectives should become so thoroughly a part of your perceptual and cognitive makeup that they can fend for themselves. When the mature and receptive viewer does spot flaws, when these difficulties show themselves so clearly that they cannot be ignored, then he should call upon whatever critical faculties he needs to analyze, salvage, or dismiss the film. He has the equipment, the flexibility, to handle the film in a variety of redemptive ways. He might even employ it as a study course in bad technique.

When the film is done, he has at his disposal the range of analytical instruments for illumination, evaluation, and persuasion. His critical capacities serve him well as he multiplies the effects of the film, drawing out its subtleties, assembling its parts, and underscoring its various statements and images. But none of this expertise should move him from the basic open viewing stance for which the stewardship of his life has prepared him.

The Weaker Brother

Something more should be said about the "weaker brother." It just is the case that one Christian's choice of films can influence another's. And that influence can have unfortunate consequences. Your decision to see a Clint Eastwood film might, for example, convince one of your admirers that you approve of all the film contains. And so he attends and is persuaded that violence is fairly glamorous. The danger of this sort of eventuality is real and ought not be lightly dismissed.

But our responsibility to the weaker brother is not absolute. For by honoring his frailties, we may cut ourselves off from a different sort of ministry. If we refrain from viewing misleading films, we remove ourselves from the critical discussion which surrounds them. We are unable to enter effectively into the conversation they generate. We are not rationally discursive with an aspect of our culture. And so we are forced to take pot shots from the perimeter. In conforming our behavior to the needs of those who don't attend, we cut ourselves off from persuasive work with the many who do attend. And so both choices have liabilities. The correct policy is, then, vocational. What needs and interests are you personally called to address? Are you servant of the weaker brother or missionary to the culturally captive? Do you attend to the weaker brothers who reject filmgoing or minister to the weaker brothers who embrace it? Do you mix it up with secular filmmakers or speak prophetically from the sidelines? Surely, this is a matter of calling.

This is not to argue that some of us need to become drunks so that we can more effectively work with drunks, or that some of us should murder so as to empathize with murderers. We should not willfully sin for the sake of our ministry to sinners. But it has never been a sin to listen to lies or to observe sin. The sin, rather, occurs in our response to what we see and hear. And that response is up to us. The analogy between drunkenness and film attendance, then, fails.

Christian Filmmaking

It is unfortunate that Christians have produced some of the most visible films to be found—shepherds in bathrobes marvel at an off-camera spotlight; Ozzie and Harriet types invite their acquaintances to the big Crusade; the post-rapture crowd tries to pick up the pieces. Subtlety escapes us. Our palette is meagre. We show more clumsiness than craft. We are all too hurried to make our point, teach the lesson, force the issue. We populate our films with ill-formed ideals rather than with Christians as we know them. We hide the pettiness in the best of us, for fear that carnal viewers will underestimate the power of conversion. Christian-made films are usually no fairer to Christians than those generated by secular filmmakers. Both trumpet their own artifice.

Too often short on candor, imagination, and technical skill, Christian filmmakers have failed to produce the world's most effective and invisible films. This is not to deny that there have been instances of Christian cinematic excellence. For example, portions of *The Hiding Place*, Johnny Cash's *Gospel Road*, and Franky Schaeffer's *Whatever Happened to the Human Race?* have worked beautifully. But the generalization stands. No doubt, though, a variety of artists will surface as the Christian community's regard for the medium grows. When Christians insist that their films be invisible, then the world will see its best films ever. Not the best Christian films ever, but the best films, because they are profoundly Christian.

With the best of intentions, Christian filmmakers have worked with the unsaved viewer in mind. Scenes of conversion and spiritual triumph are designed to bring unbelievers to a point of decision. This cinematic evangelism is valuable, as is evangelistic preaching. And there is in it some benefit for believers as well as non-believers. But the strategy in such films is obvious to the Christian, and so the richest viewing experience eludes him. He needs, instead, a "message" which illuminates the texture of normal Christian living. But these he cannot find. He finds, instead, breathless accounts of spiritual giants and repentant sinners. Where are sensitive Christian treatments of prayer, fellowship, sexuality, vocation, family life, ambition, material possessions, boredom, anxiety, illness, and courtship? Where are the invisible versions of marriage, death, reconciliation, and hope? In short, where are the best films? They have not yet been made.

In declaring Satan the master of the "silver screen" we have given him the leeway he needs to make it so. A generation of cinematic Luddites have retarded Christian work in films. It is our task to claim the medium for our own and to teach it its own best use.

part 5

The Christian Writer

Introduction

The writer's task is essentially three-fold. First, at the level of sheer form, writing is *a craft of words*. It is a skill, comparable to playing a musical instrument or painting a picture. The standards by which a writer is measured at this level would include aptness of expression, skill with words, inventiveness, and the ability to create a work possessing artistic form (unity, coherence, balance, and so on).

Second, at the level of content, the writer *presents human experience*. He is a sensitive observer of reality. At this point the writer is judged by his ability to see life steadily and whole, and to find the words, characters, dialogue, action, and settings that will adequately communicate the reality of human experience.

Third, also at the level of content, the writer *interprets reality*. Both consciously and subconsciously, a writer conveys a perspective on the experience that he or she presents. The writer gives us truth with a bias and a slant. The writer's task on this level is to reveal, exhort, teach, and serve as a catalyst on perception about the issues of life.

The following essays by Christian writers discuss these three aspects of literature.

305

The Advantages of the Christian Faith for a Writer

Chad Walsh

Is a Christian writer's faith a help or a hindrance to his craft? Chad Walsh answers that question with a refreshing affirmation. He believes that the Christian faith is the roomiest dwelling for a writer, because of the gifts conferred by Christianity: an ordered personal life; a conviction of the worth of one's work, coupled with a liberating awareness that this work is not the ultimate in life; a community from which to draw strength; an assurance of the value of sensory reality and human experience in this world; a devotion to the fulfillment of individual personality; and the right philosophic perspective from which to interpret reality.

Walsh also includes some speculations about the type of audience that a Christian writer might expect. And he concludes with some thoughts on whether there can be, in our day, "a hope for literature" (that phrase, incidentally, is the title of the essay from which the present selection is excerpted).

Although the focus of the essay is on what Christianity contributes to a writer, it is actually a discussion of what the faith can mean to a Christian in any walk of life. The essay is a small "classic" on the Christian

307

faith, filled with the wisdom of mature reflection and written with aphoristic beauty.

The Gifts Conferred by the Christian Faith

Some writers have discovered, and I think more will discover, that Christianity offers them the best pair of eyes. This is not the main reason for being a Christian—one should not worship Christ merely in order to write a *Hamlet*—but the discovery remains valid. To change the metaphor, the Christian lives in the roomiest house that seems to be available. The writer who becomes a Christian discovers that he has only his negations to lose. The affirmations that other faiths make, he can mostly second—with appropriate footnotes, of course. Their negations he must deny.

What advantages are there for a writer in being a Christian? I am speaking now of advantages to him *as writer*, not *as man*. In the first place, it gives him whereon to stand, an ordering of his own personal life that makes intellectual and emotional sense. It also gives him a perspective on his work as a writer. He can honestly see himself as a kind of earthly assistant to God (so can the carpenter), carrying on the delegated work of creation, making the fullness of creation fuller. At the same time, he is saved from the romantic tendency toward idolatry. Art is not religion. A writer is not a god or godling. There is wisdom and illumination but not salvation in a sonnet. Thus the work of any writer is set in proper proportion. Just as a husband and wife have a deeper marriage if they see their love as a human reflection of God's love, but do not make gods of each other, and do not equate the ceremonies of the marriage-bed with the love upon the Cross, so an author writes better (for the inner setting of his work is founded on true relationships) if he gives himself to his work in a spirit of deadly serious playfulness and does not pretend to himself and others that he is a temple builder and the high priest and divinity of the temple.

Christianity offers also to the writer, as it does to every man, a community. The old organic communities are visibly dissolving. I do not think this process can be reversed. Perhaps it should not be. In the organic communities, the individual was born into a world of inescapable relationships and duties. As the organic community crumbles into the vague society of the social contract and voluntary relationships, there is a gain in freedom. One must select, one must take the initiative to establish relationships, rather than merely inherit them. New dimensions of liberty—frightening, it is true—are opened up. In terror at their new freedom, men hastily erect clumsy substitutes for the old organic bonds: they invent ideologies and stage mass rallies; they organize interlocking committees and hire sociologists to create an ersatz togetherness. But a Communist rally or a community square dance planned by a committee with sociological goals in mind is not the same thing as the old organic community, which was like an extended family. One can be as lonely in a planned demonstration or a community-sponsored fun night as in a solitary cell.

Angels or demons with flaming swords bar the way back. The Church offers a way forward, beyond mere individualism, beyond mere organization. It is a voluntary community of those who have caught some glimmering of what God means in Christ and how Christ unites all who accept the Accepter. Thus in the Church, at its best, there is both the flowering of individuality and also the sense of belonging, of being accepted, of forgiving, of being forgiven, of loving and being loved.

Admittedly, the average parish church does not bear much visible resemblance to the community of voluntary love and acceptance and mutual responsibility that I have briefly sketched. It is too much like the world about it. It bears traces of the old organic society, now in decay; it is sometimes an anarchy of solitary individuals who come together and worship as though each were in a lonely, separate room; or at times it feverishly generates a synthetic sense of community by activities, activities, and activities. Those who have the peculiarly

Christian sense of community are likely to be a minority, a kind of third order or *ecclesia in ecclesia*. Thus it may be that the writer will find his "community" not so much in the parish church as in that "scattered brotherhood" of persons whom he meets here and there, comes to know, and in whom he finds a hint of what it means to be centered in Christ and therefore members one of another.

Any genuine community, whether localized or diffused, is a home. Living in it, drawing strength from it, the writer can move back and forth into the surrounding and interpenetrating world, and yet always have solid ground under his feet. Paradoxically, the firmer his sense of community, the less fearfully he will throw himself into society as a whole. He will be enabled to love it more, to study it with more compassion and interest, for he will not be afraid of absorption and destruction by it. And, yet another paradox, he will find strong evidence that in the apparently non-Christian or very vaguely Christian society, the secret Christ is at work. The scattered brotherhood will come to include, for him, men and women who do not recognize the Master they nevertheless serve.

What Christianity Offers to a Writer

Most of the gifts I have so far mentioned are those equally precious to the housewife, the business executive, and the writer. But there are some gifts that are especially valuable to the writer. The poet, for instance, is reassured that his preoccupation with sensory observations is not a frivolous study. Things are real; they are real because God made them; and, because he made them, they are important and worthy of study and even a proper portion of love. Not only did God make things. He built us so that we perceive them as much through our animal senses as our minds; the mind must turn to the senses to have something to feed upon. The color and smell of a rose are not irrelevant or illusory. We were constructed so that we come into communion with the rose through its color, fragrance, and the thorns that scratch. Compared to the rose that the senses perceive, the rose of the botanist—still more the rose of the physicist—is a construct or abstraction, true in its own way, but not the rose that we are built to admire and love.

The novelist and playwright receive the assurance that man's social and psychological life and his entire historical existence are meaningful. History becomes part of a cosmic drama, reaching backward to the moment outside of time when the command, "Let there be," was spoken into the void, leading forward toward a culmination that is destined but not compelled; a culmination that by some mysterious paradox lies both inside and outside history and calls forth man's deepest freedom in working with what will surely come to pass.

There is another gift that Christianity bestows. In some systems of thought, diversity dissolves into a totality of one kind or another. Sciences move steadily toward mathematics as the All. Hindu thought, so far as I understand it, has no meaningful place for diversity. The teeming variety of this earth is a strange and passing thing, eventually to be merged once more with the All. To Christian eyes, diversity is a good thing in itself, for God made diversity. He did not create "trees"; he created pines, oaks, and ginkoes. The animals are as fantastically varied as the impish drawings of a surrealist. The temperaments of men are as varied as the forms of animals. Christianity aims not at the bypassing of individuality and absorption back into the All, but at fulfillment and redemption of the individual. Salvation is not absorption but relationship. If Hamlet and Lear are both in heaven, it is not because they have become indistinguishable nor because they have lost individual consciousness and are now merged as raindrops in the ocean of God. No, each is more himself than ever, but each self is a redeemed self, oriented to turn with love to God and his creatures. In sum, Christianity is concerned with the fulfillment of personality, not its negation. We are called to be sons of God, and a son is not his father. A novelist is not being frivolous when he takes his characters seriously.

Another way in which Christian eyes aid the writer is simply that he can make greater sense of the towering heights and dizzy abysses of the human drama. He does not have to explain them away. He need not elucidate Hitler as a throwback to the anthropoids or St. Francis as a complex manifestation of the herd instinct. He sees in man both the angels and the demons at work, as well as the simpler imperatives of the animal nature. And he observes, and experiences, a drama with eternal stakes. The stakes are not merely the welfare or destruction of society, but the drama of individual damnation and salvation. It is a drama with no foregone conclusions. In real life, as in a good novel, the spectator is kept guessing up to the end.

So much for some of the special gifts and graces that a writer can receive when his eyes are baptized. His faith is no substitute for talent, for genius. But if he has that, the new eyes can aid him in seeing more, understanding more, saying more.

The Christian Writer's Audience

But to whom shall he say it? Is the Christian writer of the near future doomed to be an esoteric, coterie figure, speaking only to those who share his pair of eyes? It is possible that this is the case, but I am hopeful that he can reach many others. If it is true that the soul is *naturaliter christiana*, Christian insight should not be without response among non-Christians. Many an agnostic is deeply moved by Dante; there is Graham Greene, whose novels are meaningful to thousands who reject his theology. If the Christian faith provides the roomiest dwelling; if Christian eyes can see more and see it more exactly, it should follow that the truth a Christian writer can portray will somehow get through, because it will ring true even in men who consciously reject the faith that offers the new eyes.

I could be mistaken in this. It may be that for the next few generations the Christian writer is condemned to write for a coterie. This is more likely to happen with the playwright than anyone else. He requires a certain community of reaction. The people sitting in the theater need to have enough in common so that they will respond with some unanimity to the play. If their assumptions and ingrained attitudes are too different, it may be impossible to arouse the spontaneous symphony of individual responses that great plays call forth when there is common ground between playwright and audience. Conceivably, the Christian playwright may have to develop his own audience in Church circles. I do not believe this is the case, but it could be so.

The case of the novelist and the poet is more hopeful. Except for public readings of poetry (almost a form of drama) these two types of literature are read by individuals in their solitude. There is not the necessity to arouse a group response. A man reading a novel or a poem can mull it over, let it sink in, and respond to it at his own speed. If the soul is Christian by nature, it can take its time and slowly grasp whatever insight is offered.

At this point I have the uneasy feeling that some readers may assume I expect Christian writers to produce "Christian literature." If by that they mean books in which such words as God, Christ, soul, etc., frequently occur; or books dealing with Church life, ministers, devout souls, etc.—they are mistaken. The Christian writer does not necessarily deal directly with anything that would be labeled "Christian." His plots and characters may be precisely those one would find in a naturalistic or existentialist novel. The difference is much more subtle and more important. It is again the angle of vision, the nuances that a different pair of eyes can yield, a way of understanding, not subject matter.

A Hope for Literature

I have tried to state the "hope for literature" in modest and tentative terms. One must not claim too much nor hope too much. If there is to be a great literature, it will come about first of all because great talents arise. In the future, as in the past, many of these may be non-Christians. Their insights will often be more probing than those of devout but less gifted Christian authors. In a sense, a real sense, they may write books more radically "Christian" than many Christians have the skill to write.

But, for Christian and non-Christian alike, this is a world moving into a period when all foundations are increasingly shaken and new foundations are perhaps being built without our quite knowing the building material we are using. Science, for good or evil—that is our choice—is doubling and redoubling the wager. The old dream of world brotherhood is becoming a possibility, a mirage, an absolute necessity, all simultaneously. Mankind is called upon to achieve the impossible or perish. The nineteenth-century world order, as hierarchical with its distinction of "civilized" and "primitive" nations as the social hierarchy of the Middle Ages, is dissolving in fire, blood, and strident shouts for equality and dignity, in tongues only recently reduced to alphabetical form. Meanwhile, the space vehicles are probing the heavens, and who knows what adventures of the spirit lie barely beyond tomorrow's newspaper, when the first contact is made with intelligences independent of our parochial earth? Closer to home, all the advances of science make a human being more a marvel, more an impenetrable mystery, than ever before. The final frontier is ourselves.

It could be another Elizabethan age, a century of outer and inner explorations, while everywhere the relations among men and between men and whatever they call God are being reordered. Like the Elizabethan age, it is already a time dominated by voices of pessimism, at the very moment when men are acting with frantic energy and, for good or evil, are doing mighty deeds.

Writers will continue to write. They will have much to write about. It may be that the Christian faith will help some of them to see more, see it more truly. This is a hope, not a certainty, but when was hope ever the name for a sure thing?

Novelist and Believer

Flannery O'Connor

Flannery O'Connor once quipped, "When people have told me that because I am a Catholic, I cannot be an artist, I have had to reply, ruefully, that because I am a Catholic, I cannot afford to be less than an artist." No major Christian writer of our century has written more helpfully on the relationship between Christianity and the art of writing than O'Connor has in her book Mystery and Manners (from which the following essay is taken).

The essay reprinted here is a good summary of Flannery O'Connor's attitude toward the Christian as writer. The main topics include:

1. The task of the Christian writer, which begins by capturing concrete human experience and sees that experience in the light of Christian belief.
2. The direct influence a writer's world view has on his writing.
3. The spiritual climate of unbelief in which a Christian writer now writes, and how he must recognize the secular assumptions in his audience.
4. The sociological and pyschological biases of our time that have produced impoverished understandings of literature and life.

315

5. The specific Christian doctrines that are crucial for a Christian writer: sin, creation, the centrality and transcendence of God, redemption, judgment, Satan.
6. The respect that a Christian writer must show for the literary craft.

Being a novelist and not a philosopher or theologian, I shall have to enter this discussion at a much lower level and proceed along a much narrower course than that held up to us here as desirable. It has been suggested that for the purposes of this symposium,[1] we conceive religion broadly as an expression of man's ultimate concern rather than identify it with institutional Judaism or Christianity or with "going to church."

I see the utility of this. It's an attempt to enlarge your ideas of what religion is and of how the religious need may be expressed in the art of our time; but there is always the danger that in trying to enlarge the ideas of students, we will evaporate them instead, and I think nothing in this world lends itself to quick vaporization so much as the religious concern.

As a novelist, the major part of my task is to make everything, even an ultimate concern, as solid, as concrete, as specific as possible. The novelist begins his work where human knowledge begins—with the senses; he works through the limitations of matter, and unless he is writing fantasy, he has to stay within the concrete possibilities of his culture. He is bound by his particular past and by those institutions and traditions that this past has left to his society. The Judaeo-Christian tradition has formed us in the West; we are bound to it by ties which may often be invisible, but which are there nevertheless. It has formed the shape of our secularism; it has formed even the shape of modern atheism. For my part, I shall have to remain well within the Judaeo-Christian tradition. I shall have to speak, without apology, of the Church, even when the Church is absent; of Christ, even when Christ is not recognized.

1. At Sweetbriar College, Virginia, in March, 1963.

If one spoke as a scientist, I believe it would be possible to disregard large parts of the personality and speak simply as a scientist, but when one speaks as a novelist, he must speak as he writes—with the whole personality. Many contend that the job of the novelist is to show us how man feels, and they say that this is an operation in which his own commitments intrude not at all. The novelist, we are told, is looking for a symbol to express feeling, and whether he be a Jew or Christian or Buddhist or whatever makes no difference to the aptness of the symbol. Pain is pain, joy is joy, love is love, and these human emotions are stronger than any mere religious belief; they are what they are and the novelist shows them as they are. This is all well and good so far as it goes, but it just does not go as far as the novel goes. Great fiction involves the whole range of human judgment; it is not simply an imitation of feeling. The good novelist not only finds a symbol for feeling, he finds a symbol and a way of lodging it which tells the intelligent reader whether this feeling is adequate or inadequate, whether it is moral or immoral, whether it is good or evil. And his theology, even in its most remote reaches, will have a direct bearing on this.

It makes a great difference to the look of a novel whether its author believes that the world came late into being and continues to come by a creative act of God, or whether he believes that the world and ourselves are the product of a cosmic accident. It makes a great difference to his novel whether he believes that we are created in God's image, or whether he believes we create God in our own. It makes a great difference whether he believes that our wills are free, or bound like those of the other animals.

St. Augustine wrote that the things of the world pour forth from God in a double way: intellectually into the minds of the angels and physically into the world of things. To the person who believes this—as the Western world did up until a few centuries ago—this physical, sensible world is good because it proceeds from a divine source. The artist usually knows this by instinct; his senses, which are used to penetrating the concrete, tell him so. When Conrad said that his aim as an artist was to render the highest possible justice to the visible universe, he was speaking with the novelist's surest instinct. The artist penetrates the concrete world in order to find at its depths the image of its source, the image of ultimate reality. This in no way hinders his perception of evil but rather sharpens it, for only when the natural world is seen as good does evil become intelligible as a destructive force and a necessary result of our freedom.

For the last few centuries we have lived in a world which has been increasingly convinced that the reaches of reality end very close to the surface, that there is no ultimate divine source, that the things of the world do not pour forth from God in a double way, or at all. For nearly two centuries the popular spirit of each succeeding generation has tended more and more to the view that the mysteries of life will eventually fall before the mind of man. Many modern novelists have been more concerned with the processes of consciousness than with the objective world outside the mind. In twentieth-century fiction it increasingly happens that a meaningless, absurd world impinges upon the sacred consciousness of author or character; author and character seldom now go out to explore and penetrate a world in which the sacred is reflected.

Nevertheless, the novelist always has to create a world and a believable one. The virtues of art, like the virtues of faith, are such that they reach beyond the limitations of the intellect, beyond any mere theory that a writer may entertain. If the novelist is doing what as an artist he is bound to do, he will inevitably suggest that image of ultimate reality as it can be glimpsed in some aspect of the human situation. In this sense, art reveals, and the theologian has learned that he can't ignore it. In many universities, you will find departments of theology vigorously courting departments of English. The theologian is interested specifically in the modern novel because there he sees reflected the man of our time, the unbeliever, who is nevertheless grappling in a desperate and usually honest way with intense problems of the spirit.

We live in an unbelieving age but one which is markedly and lopsidedly spiritual. There is one type of modern man who recognizes spirit in himself but who fails to recognize a being outside himself whom he can adore as Creator and Lord; consequently he has become his own ultimate concern. He says with Swinburne, "Glory to man in the highest, for he is the master of things," or with Steinbeck, "In the end was the word and the word was with men." For him, man has his own natural spirit of courage and dignity and pride and must consider it a point of honor to be satisfied with this.

There is another type of modern man who recognizes a divine being not himself, but who does not believe that this being can be known anagogically or defined dogmatically or received sacramentally. Spirit and matter are separated for him. Man wanders about, caught in a maze of guilt he can't identify, trying to reach a God he can't approach, a God powerless to approach him.

And there is another type of modern man who can neither believe nor contain himself in unbelief and who searches desperately, feeling about in all experience for the lost God.

At its best our age is an age of searchers and discoverers, and at its worst, an age that has domesticated despair and learned to live with it happily. The fiction which celebrates this last state will be the least likely to transcend its limitations, for when the religious need is banished successfully, it usually atrophies, even in the novelist. The sense of mystery vanishes. A kind of reverse evolution takes place, and the whole range of feeling is dulled.

The searchers are another matter. Pascal wrote in his notebook, "If I had not known you, I would not have found you." These unbelieving searchers have their effect even upon those of us who do believe. We begin to examine our own religious notions, to sound them for genuineness, to purify them in the heat of our unbelieving neighbor's anguish. What Christian novelist could compare his concern to Camus'? We have to look in much of the fiction of our time for a kind of sub-religion which expresses its ultimate concern in images that have not yet broken through to show any recognition of a God who has revealed himself. As great as much of this fiction is, as much as it reveals a wholehearted effort to find the only true ultimate concern, as much as in many cases it represents religious values of a high order, I do not believe that it can adequately represent in fiction the central religious experience. That, after all, concerns a relationship with a supreme being recognized through faith. It is the experience of an encounter, of a kind of knowledge which affects the believer's every action. It is Pascal's experience after his conversion and not before.

What I say here would be much more in line with the spirit of our times if I could speak to you about the experience of such novelists as Hemingway and Kafka and Gide and Camus, but all my own experience has been that of the writer who believes, again in Pascal's words, in the "God of Abraham, Isaac, and Jacob and not of the philosophers and scholars." This is an unlimited God and one who has revealed himself specifically. It is one who became man and rose from the dead. It is one who confounds the senses and the sensibilities, one known early on as a stumbling block. There is no way to gloss over this specification or to make it more acceptable to modern thought. This God is the object of ultimate concern and he has a name.

The problem of the novelist who wishes to write about a man's encounter with this God is how he shall make the experience—which is both natural and supernatural—understandable, and credible, to his reader. In any age this would be a problem, but in our own, it is a well-nigh insurmountable one. Today's audience is one in which religious feeling has become, if not atrophied, at least vaporous and sentimental. When Emerson decided, in 1832, that he could no longer celebrate the Lord's Supper unless the bread and wine were removed, an important step in the vaporization of religion in America was taken, and the spirit of that step has continued apace. When the physical fact is separated from the spiritual reality, the dissolution of belief is eventually inevitable.

The novelist doesn't write to express himself, he doesn't write simply to render a vision he believes true, rather he renders his vision so that it can be transferred, as nearly whole as possible, to his reader. You can safely ignore the reader's taste, but you can't ignore his nature, you can't ignore his limited patience. Your problem is going to be difficult in direct proportion as your beliefs depart from his.

When I write a novel in which the central action is a baptism, I am very well aware that for a majority of my readers, baptism is a meaningless rite, and so in my novel I have to see that this baptism carries enough awe and mystery to jar the reader into some kind of emotional recognition of its significance. To this end I have to bend the whole novel—its language, its structure, its action. I have to make the reader feel, in his bones if nowhere else, that something is going on here that counts. Distortion in this case is an instrument; exaggeration has a purpose, and the whole structure of the story or novel has been made what it is because of belief. This is not the kind of distortion that destroys; it is the kind that reveals, or should reveal.

Students often have the idea that the process at work here is one which hinders honesty. They think that inevitably the writer, instead of seeing what is, will see only what he believes. It is perfectly possible, of course, that this will happen. Ever since there have been such things as novels, the world has been flooded with bad fiction for which the religious impulse has been responsible. The sorry religious novel comes about when the writer supposes that because of his belief, he is somehow dispensed from the obligation to penetrate concrete reality. He will think that the eyes of the Church or of the Bible or of his particular theology have already done the seeing for him, and that his business is to rearrange this essential vision into satisfying patterns, getting himself as little dirty in the process as possible. His feeling about this may have been made more definite by one of those Manichean-type theologies which sees the natural world as unworthy of penetration. But the real novelist, the one with an instinct for what he is about, knows that he cannot approach the infinite directly, that he must penetrate the natural human world as it is. The more sacramental his theology, the more encouragement he will get from it to do just that.

The supernatural is an embarrassment today even to many of the churches. The naturalistic bias has so well saturated our society that the reader doesn't realize that he has to shift his sights to read fiction which treats of an encounter with God. Let me leave the novelist and talk for a moment about his reader.

This reader has first to get rid of a purely sociological point of view. In the thirties we passed through a period in American letters when social criticism and social realism were considered by many to be the most important aspects of fiction. We still suffer with a hangover from that period. I launched a character, Hazel Motes, whose presiding passion was to rid himself of a conviction that Jesus had redeemed him. Southern degeneracy never entered my head, but Hazel said "I seen" and "I taken" and he was from East Tennessee, and so the general reader's explanation for him was that he must represent some social problem peculiar to that part of the benighted South.

Ten years, however, have made some difference in our attitude toward fiction. The sociological tendency has abated in that particular form and survived in another just as bad. This is the notion that the fiction writer is after the typical. I don't know how many letters I have received telling me that the South is not at all the way I depict it; some tell me that Protestantism in the South is not at all the way I portray it, that a Southern Protestant would never be concerned, as Hazel Motes is, with penitential practices. Of course, as a novelist I've never wanted to characterize the typical South or typical Protestantism. The South and the religion found there are extremely fluid and offer enough variety to give the novelist the widest range of possibilities imaginable, for the novelist is bound by the reasonable possibilities, not the probabilities, of his culture.

There is an even worse bias than these two, and that is the clinical bias, the prejudice that sees everything strange as a case study in the abnormal. Freud brought to light many truths, but his psychology is not an adequate instrument for understanding the religious encounter or the fiction that describes it. Any psychological or cultural or economic determination may be useful up to a point; indeed, such facts can't be ignored, but the novelist will be interested in them only as he is able to go through them to give us a sense of something beyond them. The more we learn about ourselves, the deeper into the unknown we push the frontiers of fiction.

I have observed that most of the best religious fiction of our time is most shocking precisely to those readers who claim to have an intense interest in finding more "spiritual purpose"— as they like to put it—in modern novels than they can at present detect in them. Today's reader, if he believes in grace at all, sees it as something which can be separated from nature and served to him raw as Instant Uplift. This reader's favorite word is compassion. I don't wish to defame the word. There is a better sense in which it can be used but seldom is—the sense of being in travail with and for creation in its subjection to vanity. This is a sense which implies a recognition of sin; this is a suffering-with, but one which blunts no edges and makes no excuses. When infused into novels, it is often forbidding. Our age doesn't go for it.

I have said a great deal about the religious sense that the modern audience lacks, and by way of objection to this, you may point out to me that there is a real return of intellectuals in our time to an interest in and a respect for religion. I believe that this is true. What this interest in religion will result in for the future remains to be seen. It may, together with the new spirit of ecumenism that we see everywhere around us, herald a new religious age, or it may simply be that religion will suffer the ultimate degradation and become, for a little time, fashionable. Whatever it means for the future, I don't believe that our present society is one whose basic beliefs are religious, except in the South. In any case, you can't have effective allegory in times when people are swept this way and that by momentary convictions, because everyone will read it differently. You can't indicate moral values when morality changes with what is being done, because there is no accepted basis for judgment. And you cannot show the operation of grace when grace is cut off from nature or when the very possibility of grace is denied, because no one will have the least idea of what you are about.

The serious writer has always taken the flaw in human nature for his starting point, usually the flaw in an otherwise admirable character. Drama usually bases itself on the bedrock of original sin, whether the writer thinks in theological terms or not. Then, too, any character in a serious novel is supposed to carry a burden of meaning larger than himself. The novelist doesn't write about people in a vacuum; he writes about people in a world where something is obviously lacking, where there is the general mystery of incompleteness and the particular tragedy of our own times to be demonstrated, and the novelist tries to give you, within the form of the book, a total experience of human nature at any time. For this reason the greatest dramas naturally involve the salvation or loss of the soul. Where there is no belief in the soul, there is very little drama. The Christian novelist is distinguished from his pagan colleagues by recognizing sin as sin. According to his heritage he sees it not as sickness or an accident of environment, but as a responsible choice of offense against God which involves his eternal future. Either one is serious about salvation or one is not. And it is well to realize that the maximum amount of seriousness admits the maximum amount of comedy. Only if we are secure in our beliefs can we see the comical side of the universe. One reason a great deal of our contemporary fiction is humorless is because so many of these writers are relativists and have to be continually justifying the actions of their characters on a sliding scale of values.

Our salvation is a drama played out with the devil, a devil who is not simply generalized evil, but an evil intelligence determined on its own supremacy. I think that if writers with a religious view of the world excel these days in the depiction of evil, it is because they have to make its nature unmistakable to their particular audience.

The novelist and the believer, when they are not the same man, yet have many traits in common—a distrust of the abstract, a respect for boundaries, a desire to penetrate the surface of reality and to find in each thing the spirit which makes it itself and holds the world together. But I don't believe that we shall have great religious fiction until we have again that happy combination of believing artist and believing society. Until that time, the novelist will have to do the best he can in travail with the world he has. He may find in the end that instead of reflecting the image at the heart of things, he has only reflected our broken condition and, through it, the face of the devil we are possessed by. This is a modest achievement, but perhaps a necessary one.

Poems Should Stay Across the Street from the Church

Rod Jellema

Christian writers have not generally agreed among themselves as to how their faith affects their writing. At one end of the spectrum is the comment of Graham Greene that "every creative writer worth our consideration [is] a man given to an obsession." Then there is Flannery O'Connor's claim that Christian "dogma is an instrument for penetrating reality," not excess baggage that needs to be discarded when a writer takes up a pen. Or note Milton's comment —"what religious, what glorious and magnificent use might be made of poetry, both in divine and human things."

Most Christian writers in our century have been uneasy with such comments, and with the prevailing expectations of Christian readers. The following essay is an eloquent elaboration of these reservations. Written by a creative artist, the essay is wary of the intrusion of Christian dogma into the writing process and distrustful of the designs that Christian readers have on writers.

The essay also makes some penetrating comments about the nature of poetry (and by extension about imaginative literature as a whole). Note the emphasis on poetry as a revelation of reality, on the imagi-

*nation as a means of truth, and on literature as something that sharpens
our perception of human experience.*

Are Christians Really Serious about Poetry?

Once or twice a year I notice the Church picking up its
binoculars and scanning the cluttered horizon, looking for
Christian poets. For the moment that the search is going on,
it is made to look almost urgent. Up until the time that I began
really writing poetry I used to busy myself periodically in the
same little ritual. Whack through the underbrush of the little
magazines, professor, and see if you can find some poets who
are on our side. But why? I confess that I understand less and
less what this search is all about.

Now that I'm out there in the underbrush with thousands
of other published poets, I want to get some focus on the flow
of energies among three troubled landscapes: poetry, the Church,
and the world in which we live.

I don't think the Church seriously wants "Christian poetry"—
except in the rather vain way in which it is pleased to display
a little Christian *anything* in a secular world. How can we
judge its sincerity? Well, look, if you say you want Japanese
food, you must first want food; if you want a three-power
microscope with oil-immersion lens, it is implied that you already have some working interest in microscopes and what
they can do. Likewise, if the Church wants Christian poets, it
should be apparent that the Church is tuned to the vision of
poetry generally, and finds poetry valuable in its rendering of
human experience. But it is not at all apparent to me that this
is so.

I know that poetry does have that kind of value. It broadens
and deepens human experience. I'm going to promote that
argument further along. Right now I only want to question
how seriously the Church is looking and longing for its poets.

There are isolated exceptions, but generally the Church gets
its data about the world from political machinery, the press,

and the social sciences—very little of it from the arts. This is expected; it is the way our culture is structured. We mistrust the creative imagination; if we deal with the products of the imagination at all, we deal with them as cultural ruffles, diversions, nice fancy desserts. Let's be honest: most Christians wouldn't know a good poem, not even a good "Christian poem," if they fell into it.

Actually, poems are hard, concrete things. It is our thinking about them that is misty and wistful. When church people say they want poems, they want poems destined at once to open up the heavens and bring down the house. They aren't going to get them.

Part of the reason why the Church looks for poetry is that poetry might be useful—in the liturgy, on printed programs, for sermon illustrations. That makes some sense. But it is not a pressing need at all. Over the past twenty centuries quite a few poems have been written that are "useful" in this very limited way. The good ones are seldom used. Slick but devout bad verse—which ought to be a contradiction—is probably more "useful" in this way than good poetry is. To commission such work from poets is equivalent to asking a composer (Elliott Carter, say, or Aaron Copland) to interrupt work on his symphonies so that he can compose "useful" singing commercials for General Motors. The Church would have nobler intentions than General Motors, but the degree of impropriety is about the same. Works of art are not useful in that quick and mechanical way.

What Is Poetry?

A big part of the problem is that most people in our world are huddled captive to so much else that they do not discover what poetry really is. I cannot break through that dark tangle in the single paragraph I'm allowing myself, but I will try to throw off, in one mad dash through rough terrain, whatever glints and flashes I can of what it is in poetry that tugs and dazzles and pricks and soothes human consciousness. Head down, and here goes:

You have to know right away that poetry is not eloquence or decoration or a nice way of saying things. It is a way of seeing, a way of discovering perceptions, moments of awareness that were not there before. The poem is the body of a different kind of "knowing," a kind of awareness that the conscious intellect by itself cannot get to. But the poem is also the process of its own little discovery: it leaves its footprints; the reader can follow the creative process step by step, feeling the swerves and leaps and undertones and soundings and strange connections in the language that got the poet's imagination into that unified awareness, that little incarnation, that poem. Its "message" was not there at the beginning (otherwise the poet could simply say the message and would have no reason to create the poem); if the poem has a "message" now, it is in any case inseparable from the process, the body of awareness, the incarnated poem. The above might help to explain why poets say all those spooky things about poetry: it "tells us . . . what cannot be said" (E. A. Robinson), helps me to remember "something I did not know I knew" (Frost); the poem "is what ideas feel like" (Karl Shapiro), "is the feel and body of the awareness it presents" (M. L. Rosenthal), "is a pheasant disappearing into the brush" (Wallace Stevens), contains "no ideas but in things" (W. C. Williams). Poems expand consciousness, deepen human awareness, get us beyond understanding into layer upon layer of the exact feel of "thingness," grief, exaltation, loneliness, love, fear, mystery, stabs of joy. The poem is a thousand times closer to the concerto or the painting than it is to the sermon, speech, article, editorial, or discussion. The imagination rides out the play that can exist among words and images until it makes a living body that shows and is but "cannot be said." What it embodies has little to do with the poet's opinions or even his beliefs, and almost everything to do with his growing creative vision. (Randall Jarrell says somewhere that the poem transcends, and sometimes even repudiates, the mind behind it.) In the vernacular of the kids, a poem is a trip. It's a trip for the poet, too; if he thinks it clarifies something or catches something worthwhile, and perhaps links to themes he has been seeing and developing elsewhere, he sends it out, invites us to ride along.

So what the poetry of our century is after is breakthrough perception. It does not draw us away from the world we live in and dream us off to some isolated place called the "poetic"; it pulls us into sharper and fuller encounters with our life in this world. It is a stirring of conscience. Most poems (modern poems especially) begin not with ideas but with things and their relationships. Imagination (image-making) begins its work with surfaces, with what the senses are in contact with. Art is fed by the experience (not very much by the social-science data) of the everyday world. The poet then feels obliged to earn his way, step by step or leap by leap, to what is beneath or beyond or mysteriously manifested in that surface.

I hope those last two paragraphs are somehow effective, because they have moved me into talking about poets and the world. Before I go back to matters of the Christian community and the poets, I want to say something about the significance that this stuff called poetry might have for the world.

Ezra Pound called poets "the antennae of the race." If you look at past masters or the good moderns, the poets who are really breaking through into experience-beyond-statement, I don't think you'll find Pound's claim exaggerated. Through a kind of double vision, they are looking at the things and lives and attitudes around all of us. They see specifically the same things that all of us can see but tend to generalize: guilt-ridden faces, our fascination with violence, "the inexorable sadness of pencils" (Roethke), the glow of young love, the fear of loneliness, cheap manufactures, the loyalty of dogs, the plumpness of ripe fruit, our helplessness, the good feeling of skipping down a busy street, the fear of death, Viet Nam, laughter from playgrounds behind a news report on the CIA, drugs, washing dishes. . . . This is everyone's world, and it is the world that modern poems spin off from and connect to.

When you encounter that world again in poems, you find that it is more terrible, more beautiful, more intense, more everything than it is on TV or in the newspapers or in your own memory of it. In the poems you ought to recognize moments that you have almost felt but could not quite get to. Strange connections have been made, unexpected patterns have clustered. Sympathy has deepened somehow, and the senses are more alive—more alive, even if sometimes to things you would rather not think about. Consciousness widens; conscience deepens. Though it might be painful at times, you feel more human. Sometimes you want to sing, or to cry, it doesn't matter which.

Not much of this is going to happen if you lunge at the poems, trying to rip out of them messages and meanings. But if you read poems as poems, the "meanings" of things and lives around you can sharpen and deepen in profoundly human ways—in ways that the social sciences cannot achieve.

Is There "Christian Poetry"?

The Church should have some interest in the signals and vibrations that the poets of our society are sending out since poets are "the antennae of our race." Poetry is intensified awareness. It is society's conscience. The Church is trying to address its compassion and love and reconciliation to an estranged world that seems dazed, numb, inarticulate about its deepest feelings. Well, some of those deepest feelings are caught in the anger or quiet or exaltation of poems in the little magazines.

The Church and the poets do not have much in common just now. But they probably do share one deep conviction: that our basic needs lie far, far beneath the search for the mere social machinery of problem-solving. Poets know, too, that men are not robots or computer-numbers—that they need purpose, can cry out, are puzzled by death, can ponder a beer-bottle cap and feel lost without being able to say it. This is that deep level which the Church calls the soul.

It's a cruel irony. Not many people read the poets, and yet anyone who does could make a strong case for the notion that the poets are indeed the antennae of our society and its most intense spokesmen. The Church should be tuning in, not for a summary "message" translated into flat words by a critic but for the embodied experience that poetry is.

So now I am recommending poetry to the Church. But I mean any poetry that can show us the significant (signifying) experience of life around us. I am not going to single out the "Christian poets" at all. Christians will be among the poets, and they might very well give us some additional pleasures or insights, but those would be secondary to the Church's getting itself focused on the imaginative vision of our times.

In fact, I am no longer certain that it is meaningful to talk about "Christian poets." W. H. Auden, who was classified as one of them, says this: "There is no more a Christian art than there is a Christian diet." This made no sense to me at all until I got far along into writing. It makes more sense to me now because I've learned under fire what poetry is. And remember, the Bible never uses "Christian" as an adjective. There is a profound difference between revealing what you make and saying what you believe. *As poet*, a poet can be a spokesman only for what he achieves, attains, embodies through the creative process of his poems.

To talk about "Christian poetry" is to suggest witnessing and didacticism and to get us away from what poetry is. I don't think it's healthy for poets to use words like *didactic*. That's for the reader to worry about. The poet's job is to catch, discover, reveal—and if the reader feels taught, as he very well may ("revelation," says Ezra Pound, "is always didactic"), that's fine—but the poet has to get on with his work, which is far more mysterious than teaching, and far more risky, and a wholly different kind of communication. The term "Christian poetry" not only lacks clear meaning but also tends to put the reader on the defensive, stiffened against the oncoming didactic message that shouldn't be consciously there.

There is another reason for uneasiness with the concept of "Christian poets." I know this from experience. It invites the poet who is a Christian into a frame of mind in which, proud of his humility, he can knock the tough commitment to art as being merely arty, shrug off the world's expected indifference to his work as the price he must pay for his martyrdom, and isolate himself in mutual-admiration groups of like-minded poets. Then they can all ignore the work of unredeemed poets and send their own Christian poems to Christian magazines. I know this is not the intention of the concept, but it is a danger. Instead of carrying his cross, he begins to drag it.

The poet who is a Christian needs Pound and Stevens and Williams the way a Christian physicist needs Einstein and Heisenberg and Planck; he needs the *American Poetry Review* the way a Christian physician needs his *AMA Journal*. He also needs give-and-take with working poets and editors who will judge his work by strictly literary standards, expecting him not to be sucked in by fads but to be alive to the discoveries that other poets are making. The principles that poets who are Christians follow should be the same as those followed by poets who do not profess Christianity.

Earning the Right to Speak

I do not mean to sound discouraging. I mean to broaden the horizon, not to narrow it. It is not yet time for Christians to go back to the catacombs.

I think that, unlike other kinds of communicators, the poet who is a Christian should not write for a particular audience. Such matters distract him from his work. "If you want to communicate," says poet-teacher Richard Hugo to young poets, "use the telephone." If you have something more general you want to say to the Church or the world, write an article. Then get back to the work of creating. If a poem really works, it may find its own miniscule audience. A poem becomes communication when it is read by persons who share or understand the vision revealed there. But first it has to be authentically born, and that's job enough for the writer. A Catholic critic says of the Catholic poet Francis Thompson, "his religion was a temptation instead of a discipline." It encouraged him into "fashionable religiosity." He stopped looking and listening. He stopped creating.

This is a kind of interim field-report from a poet who is learning. I am a Christian. I have been writing poems for about eight years, and I am not at all a poet who has "made it."

When I walk across the campus of the university at which I teach poetry to college kids, I can know with one kind of knowing that God is a father who loves us all. But when I am at my desk, working on a poem, trying to catch something from the students' faces and the lengthening shadows and, say, the pulsing blue light from a police cruiser, I have no right *as a poet* to say from inside this murderous world that God is a father who loves us all. I have to earn it by creating it out of those images and the words and sounds and echoes and forms that begin to move. I know with one kind of knowing that the bodily resurrected Christ is in the bodies of those students. He is that black girl stung by our insults, he is the mourned friend maimed or killed in our senseless wars, he is that imprisoned face I passed by which asks to be visited or given a cup of water. I "know" that, and it may be part of the general social conscience that's stirring, but if I cannot see it, make it, pull it through lines of light and shadow that create the love that struggles to be born, I have no right to say it in the poem. So the poem might very well go on growing toward another "secular" poem, as most of them do.

I need detachment only because poetry is what it is. I find that *as a poet* I have had to shake loose some of what I learned in church and catechism class. The problem with those heady doctrines is that I can mumble them. And what I can mumble, the poem cannot incorporate or believe. Maybe the poetry will catch up, maybe the working imagination will freshly rediscover those formulations up ahead, alive and useful and experiential. If not, there is no way *as a poet* that I can use them.

That's the way I have to work. Across the street from the church. Call it "the willing suspension of belief." Other Christians may very well find other ways to keep the imagination alive and the job true to the art. I got to my own position, not by reading all those ponderous works about the relations between art and Christianity, but by trying to keep the poems honestly poems. Only now, thinking it out on paper and dipping into those works, do I discover that it's pretty much the solution of others, too. Eliot and Auden, for example.

Although it is hazardous to think about it, there are and will be such things as "Christian poets" and "Christian poems." My point is simply that the Church tries to pull them in for the wrong reason and overlooks the real value it could draw from poetry—while poets who seek that designation probably confuse their jobs as poets.

T. S. Eliot was certainly a "Christian poet," but he earned every syllable of that triumph called the *Four Quartets* through growth of imagination. And then, significantly, he stopped writing poems, though his life went on for fifteen more years. He didn't start the poem with an affirmation of his faith; he won the faith all over again, deepened, this time as a symphony of the imagination wrung out of structural movements and difficult perceptions. He didn't start with the Christian vision; he ended there. That's worth thinking about. Eliot, the Christian and also the giant poet who discovered and taught us much about the use of archetypes and the collective unconscious in the creative process, said this: "What I want is a literature which should be *un*consciously, rather than deliberately and defiantly, Christian." Without meaning to follow, I think I have written my way into the same position.

The Christian Novel and the Evangelical Dilemma

James Wesley Ingles

Stories fall into several categories. Amos Wilder describes them thus:

> Some good stories ... turn upon the fortunes of men, the ups and downs of life, success and failure, surprise and disappointment. The appeal of such stories and of such wisdom as they have is identified especially with the plot and its surprises. Other good stories turn on the perennially interesting topic of character in men, their varying traits and types, and the consequences of these. Or a good story may have its chief appeal in the sheer surface delineation, the absorbing detail and concreteness of the portrayal.[1]

By themselves, however, stories that excel in plot, characterization, or description do not convey the sense of ultimacy that Christian narrative, especially as found in the Bible, conveys. The French novelist André Gide claimed it was Christianity that gave Western fiction the moral plane that alone does justice to the full scope of human destiny.

If the Christian faith is indeed what gives spiritual ultimacy to literature, we are left with an uncomfortable dilemma: why has the evan-

---

1. Amos Wilder, Early Christian Rhetoric (Boston: Harvard University Press, 1964), pp. 75-76.

gelical Christian community, with its high regard for the faith taught in the Bible, been unable to produce a flourishing tradition of great modern fiction? This is the "evangelical dilemma" that the following essay explores.

The Poverty of Evangelical Fiction

Why are so few significant novels produced within the evangelical tradition? Why is it increasingly difficult for the serious novelist to give expression to his view of life within the framework of this tradition? The answer is not simple.

Of course there are those who decry fiction as a whole, who either oppose it or neglect it, considering it unworthy of the concern of thoughtful people, particularly of Christians. Such indifference or hostility may be justified when one considers the annual flood of works which have no purpose beyond mere entertainment, and this sometimes of the lowest order, and the increasing number of novels that are morally defiling.

However, fiction may be and often is a significant vehicle of thought, a means of carrying truth alive into the heart by way of the imagination, and no one seriously interested in knowing the best that has been thought and written can afford to neglect completely this powerful force in the shaping of life. For serious fiction has had an extensive influence upon multitudes of readers, affecting, often subtly, their views of life, their moral ideas and attitudes, and thus their conduct.

And this shaping power of fiction is not confined to those novels which aim directly at social reform, or which are openly concerned with customs and manners. There is a pervasive spirit emanating from the general portrait of life revealed in an author's selection of his material, by what he includes or omits, by the slanting of his material toward a point of view.

Fiction and drama are closely related, and plays and cinemas are often drawn from works of fiction, and together they wield an influence beyond all calculation. Roman Catholics, realizing this, have made effective use of both media of communication, and they can list some of the great novelists, as well as many of the more popular. And the other liturgical branches of the Church, Anglican, Lutheran, Eastern Orthodox, have each produced their share of significant writers.

Evangelical churches have not fared well in the area of the novel. It would seem that our form of the Christian faith has either been the object of cynical and satirical attack in fiction, or it has been handled sympathetically by pious but artistically limited writers. The latter give either a shoddy two-dimensional picture of life or a prim and proper portrait, so emasculated, so colorless, or so obviously faked that the books say nothing about life of any significance, and can be read only by the already convinced who believe that they are keeping themselves "pure," "unspotted from the world," by reading an adulterated rather than an adulterous version of life.

What are the reasons for this sad state of affairs? Why have no recent novelists of stature arisen within the evangelical tradition to handle life within a religious context with the same sort of power and beauty one sometimes finds within the liturgical traditions? The reasons are many.

The Need for Symbols

There is first in the evangelical form of Christianity a tendency to eliminate wholly or at least to minimize the use of symbols, and thereby to reduce religious experience to an ethereal, completely spiritual relationship with the divine that does not adequately, if at all, clothe itself in the visible and the tangible. This decrying of the symbol is the product of a certain extreme reaction in the Protestant Reformation. So gross had become the dependence on the tangible in the medieval Church that it had often approached the idolatrous. In trying to sweep away this error, some of the more radical reformers actually fell into the opposite error, basically a denial of the meaning of the Incarnation, the Word made flesh, which is at the heart of the Christian faith.

And this sweeping denial of the function of symbols, of the importance of symbols, cuts at the very roots of any genuinely artistic representation of the Faith in life, for art deals in symbols. The symbolic is its language, its means of communication.

One cannot properly study the Bible, the supreme revelation, and at the same time the supreme achievement of literary art in the world's literature, and not observe the dependence of the biblical writers upon symbols, upon the tangible, the concrete in the communication of spiritual truth. Even at Pentecost, the most spiritual of experiences surely, there is the wind and there is the fire. Jesus does not merely speak a word to a blind beggar. He makes clay with spittle and lays it upon his eyes. And at the last hour of greatest intimacy with his disciples, He took bread and poured out wine. The mightiest books of the Bible in literary power are the most symbolic: Genesis, Job, the Psalms, Isaiah, the Apocalypse.

It may well be that the evangelical branch of the Church must recover a sense of the meaning and function of symbols (as it veritably seems to be doing) if it is to produce writers who can communicate the experience of the Faith with power and beauty. The church building that cannot be distinguished from a lecture hall in appearance is not functioning as a spiritual instrument, though spiritual activity may be going on within it unaided by the setting. It may shelter the congregation adequately from the elements, but it does nothing in itself to lift the spirit Godward. And the ministry of the Word in such a building receives no assistance from the stones that should cry out in praise to God.

One cannot deny that there may be, that there have been, great outpourings of spiritual power without the assistance of instruments, but one must admit the difficulty of its representation for the artist. Too often the creative writer within the evangelical tradition is left with the most meager, and sometimes even pitifully shoddy instruments with which to shadow forth the most holy faith in graphic and pictorial terms.

The Writer's Province: All of Life

But this is only one of his problems. There is further the pressure upon him to select subjects which are in "good taste" in the Victorian sense. He is required to shun any realistic probing into the basic and most vital problems confronting the individual and society. And yet all life, high and low, sordid and noble, vile and pure, is the province of art.

Surely if the Bible is to be our standard, we must admit that nothing lay outside the province of the inspired writers. There are passages in the Bible concerned with the grossest and sometimes the most shocking forms of evil. There are stories of Sodom, of the Benjaminite war, of Amnon and Tamar. And there are the less startling but no less realistic stories of Joseph and Potiphar's wife, of David and Bathsheba, of Hosea and his faithless wife.

It certainly is not necessary for the Christian writer to dwell on the portrayal of evil in human experience. Indeed he cannot be a Christian writer if he prefers to wallow in human perversity and sin, to titillate the perverted taste and the defiled imagination of the carnally-minded reader.

But, on the other hand, he cannot be a true artist, he cannot be a significant writer, if his vision does not include the whole of human life, the depths of depravity as well as the heights of aspiration. If Christian readers, and Christian editors and publishers, insist on imposing unbiblical restrictions on contemporary authors, they will continue to produce people of little power and less vision, incapable of stabbing awake the conscience of the unregenerate.

Ibsen, whose dramas often shocked the prudish of his day, was once compared to the naturalist, Zola. This aroused him to anger. "Zola," he said, "descends into the cesspool to take a bath; I, to cleanse it." Ibsen was there suggesting a profound difference in the handling of evil in fiction and drama. The portrayal of evil per se does not make an evil book. If that were true it would be necessary to cut out great portions, not only of the Bible, but of the works of Shakespeare as well. Unless there is a growing demand for Christian writers who will be free to write about the whole of life with compassionate honesty, the Christian faith cannot find any great expression in fiction.

"Let marriage be held in honor among all," wrote the author of the Epistle to the Hebrews, "and let the marriage bed be undefiled." But the Christian novelist seems almost as embarrassed in dealing with sex as is the non-Christian novelist in dealing with prayer. Surely there is an area between prudery and pruriency where the Christian view of sex may be handled honestly, forthrightly, and even beautifully, as in The Song of Songs.

So long as certain areas of life are handled only by the non-Christian writer, we will continue to advance a non-Christian view of life in its deepest recesses. We cannot combat the pagan view of sex in our time by ignoring its significance in human experience, or worse, by preserving in a realistic age the Victorian prudery and hypocrisy that made an ugliness of what God intended to be beautiful.

The sex relationship can be sacramental, an "outward and visible sign of an inward and invisible grace." But without the divine grace, without the spiritual aspiration infusing and inspiring the mutual love of two people, it tends to become merely the physical drive for personal gratification, which it is too often in fiction and in life. Surely the Christian novelist has a responsibility to reveal the distinction.

Of course, sex is only one area of life in which the realistic approach is needed in our time. Some of our great social problems cry out for a Christian treatment in fiction. Where is the great labor novel written from a Christian perspective? Where is the farm novel dealing honestly with that problem in our national life? Where is the missionary novel written with depth and power, recreating the whole milieu in which the transplanted Christian faith operates? Why does the popular denigration and disparagement of the missionary, as in Michener's

Hawaii, go unchallenged? Where is the novel dealing with the momentous ferment in Japan? Where is the Christian novel realistically and dramatically coming to grips with Communism?

The Need for Realism

But not only is the Christian novelist limited in his selection of material; he is forced to handle even the properly selected material in a prudish and unrealistic manner. And yet we are living in a realistic age, an age that is as earthy and frank in its diction as was the age of Shakespeare. And that was the age also of the King James Version of the Bible, published in the same year (1611) as Shakespeare's last play, *The Tempest*. And the same earthy Anglo-Saxon words provide the translation from the earthy and realistic Hebrew text.

Here again, if the Bible is to be our standard, the modern Christian prophet would be able to call a spade a shovel as well as his ancient prototypes. Why should "the prophetic voice in modern fiction" (as William R. Meuller suggests in his book under that title) be largely heard in writers that are non-Christian? It has not always been so. There have been great Christian voices in fiction: Dostoevski, Merezhkovski, and Sienkiewicz, to name a few.

Is the evangelical tradition then so artistically anemic that it can produce nothing full-blooded, full-bodied? Must the great writers of our time be intellectual rebels? Can the Great Acquiescence produce nothing worthy of our time, no mighty expression of our Faith's triumphant and transforming power?

Most of the so-called "Christian" novels are artistically reprehensible, however proper their morality or their message. Often their characters are paper puppets, mere mouthpieces for the author's pious propaganda. They have nothing of the vitality we seek in fiction of a genuine sort. They are cut to fit the moral, which is often as obvious as the message of Edgar Guest in verse. There is no subtlety in the handling, no sense of irony. The dialogue reads like written, not spoken English. There is little of idiom or idiosyncracy to identify one particular person from another. They all speak the speech of their author. There is no real understanding of all sorts and conditions of men. There is no all-embracing, Christ-like compassion.

Is it any wonder that these artificial representations of life say nothing to those outside of the fold, and very little to those of education and intelligence within it?

The Need for Excellence of Style

And finally, all of this papier-maché world of romantic illusion, often so far removed from the real, or so pale a representation of it as to be unrecognizable, is too frequently conveyed in a style so shabby, so literal, and so careless as to disgrace the Faith they would proclaim.

Hemingway is said to have gone over the manuscript of *The Old Man and the Sea* eighty times. By comparison, stylistically, some of the religious novels of our time resemble the first draft of a college composition. There is no sense of the poetic, no attempt to create the rhythms of effective prose, to shape the imagery that lifts the mind from the dull commonplace, that rising from sullen earth sings hymns at heaven's gate.

One novelist at least in our time has done the thing beautifully, and he is an Anglican, within a liturgical tradition. Alan Paton's *Cry, the Beloved Country* is not only a novel dealing realistically with one of the most serious problems of our time, but it is a thing of classic beauty, of poetic power and simple grandeur that lifts the spirit singing after the heart has been broken.

No sensitive spirit can come away from reading of such a novel untouched, unchanged. Here are the evil, the sordidness, the irony, the tragedy, and the pathos of life. But here also are love and joy and peace that pass understanding. Here the Christian message is given wings. But here also it speaks in a voice with the sound of many waters, a voice that is prophetic, that speaks to our condition and to our need.

Only as Christian editors and publishers, Christian ministers and laymen rally to encourage the writing of works of such power and beauty will the Message go forth persuasively as it should in fiction to the troubled hearts and the confused minds of people in our time.

We will continue to neglect or to inhibit this potentially great vehicle of truth to our own loss and to the limitation of the artistic expression of the Faith. An alerted and aroused ministry might help to create an educated and intelligent laity that could in turn raise the standard of creative writing within the evangelical tradition. Only as we see the necessity of the total penetration of our culture by the Gospel can we bring every thought into submission to the high and holy will of Christ.

Unwelcoming the Christian Poet

John Leax

The question of the Christian writer's audience has generally been a cause for tears rather than joy. Since the Christian writer does not look primarily for financial rewards, surely he is not asking too much to hope for an appreciative audience. Or is he?

John Milton's Poems of 1645 attracted almost no public attention in its day; for Paradise Lost Milton received a meager payment of five pounds. It is small wonder that in that poem Milton speaks of his "fit audience, though few." The Renaissance poet Edmund Spenser died in poverty, and according to tradition he may have actually died of hunger. George Herbert wrote his poems in private and handed over the finished manuscript on his death bed. The poems of Gerard Manley Hopkins were published thirty years after his death. And the Christian fiction of C. S. Lewis was an embarrassment to his Oxford colleagues and a leading reason why Lewis never received at Oxford the advancement he deserved.

In the following essay a contemporary evangelical poet takes a look at the Christian writer in relationship to the Christian community, to the secular world, and to himself as writer. The title of the piece captures some of the frustration that Christian writers have long felt.

The Christian Poet and the Problem of Priorities

The New Testament clearly proclaims that Christ taught a law of love. The world is to know we are Christians by our love, and yet in Luke 14:26 Christ makes a statement that takes the form of a contradiction of that law. He says to a multitude of would-be followers, "If any man come to me, and hate not his father, and mother, and wife, and children, and brothers, and sisters, yes, and his own life also, he cannot be my disciple."

This apparent contradiction troubles no one, for it is easily recognized as an overstatement used to make an important point. Our love for Christ is to be so great that the legitimate, and God-ordained love of a man for his family is to be as hate beside it. Also understood is the idea that only when such love for Christ exists can a proper love for the others exist.

On a very different scale, the Cavalier poet Richard Lovelace recognized a similar concept when he wrote, "I could not love thee, dear, so much / Loved I not honor more." In both cases the principle is clear. A meaningful love can thrive only when there is something beyond it giving it life. C. S. Lewis applies this principle to poetry. In "Christianity and Literature" he writes:

> It is not hard to argue that all the greatest poems have been made by men who valued something else more than poetry— even if that something else were only cutting down enemies in a cattle-raid or tumbling a girl in a bed.

The contemporary poet, however, finds this a difficult principle to remember. Consequently his art often suffers visions of grandeur and offers itself as a substitute for religion. It is, as Lewis points out, a poor substitute, not even measuring up to venery. It demands of its initiates a continual cycle of desperate and solemn attempts to create themselves in their own images. The possibility of joy is lost, for life itself ceases to exist in the instant of the poem.

The malaise is so common that even the Christian poet is subject to it, although for him it generally takes on a less obvious (but nonetheless fatal) form. It occurs when the Christian poet, thinking he is maintaining artistic standards, begins to compromise the content of his art. Struck down, like Paul, by the revelation of Jesus Christ, the Christian poet cannot help but see his art as something of little ultimate concern. Again C. S. Lewis speaks directly to the issue:

> The Christian knows from the outset that the salvation of a single soul is more important than the production or preservation of all the epics and tragedies in the world.

It is clear, then, that for the Christian artist, art is not of primary importance. How then can he justify his vocation?

The answer is simple: the same way a doctor or carpenter justifies his. The doctor must live for Christ, not healing; the carpenter must live for Christ, not building; and the artist must live for Christ, not art. But paradoxically, when a man lives in and for Christ, Christ makes him a gift of the possibilities of the creation. The doctor is freed to heal; the carpenter is freed to build; and the artist is freed to create. For the poet this freedom is the freedom to prophesy, to speak forth God's Word through the power of the Holy Spirit:

> The spirit must scream
> plummet down
> like a bird of prey
> and sit   fierce
> talons clenched
> in your bleeding lips
>
> and your words become
> his Word
> and his Word become
> your words
>
> that your speech
> dead in the agony of self
> might be resurrected
> in self-extinction.

It is the freedom to worship, to participate in the joy of creation; it is the freedom to praise:

> Glory be to God for dappled things—
> For skies of couple-colour as a brinded cow;
> For rose-moles all in stipple upon trout that swim.

The Christian Poet and the Christian Community

Probably no one will disagree that the poet has the freedom and even the responsibility to speak prophetically and to offer up worship in his art. Both functions are easily used by the Church. And as long as the poet's doctrine remains pure, he is welcomed into the fellowship.

But the poet is also free to look critically at himself and at society. Chad Walsh, for example, is able to write irreverent limericks. Eugene Warren is free to write the politically violent and obscene "Launching Apollo 12." With poems such as these the Christian community is uneasy, and the poet who insists on exercising his freedom to write them is likely to be regarded as a fellow to keep an eye on.

The cause for this is twofold. The first cause is obvious. We live in a society that is literate only in the sense that its members can march one word after another through a sentence. Few have actually learned to read. The second cause is more important and rises from a profound error in the very foundation of our thinking. Calling some things Christian and other things worldly, we have split God's creation into two incompatible parts.

The error, however grievous, is understandable. We are rightly concerned with living holy lives. We take Philippians 4:8 seriously:

> Finally, brethren, whatsoever things are true, whatsoever things are just, whatsoever things are pure, whatsoever things are lovely, whatsoever things are of good report; if there be any virtue, and if there be any praise, think on these things.

But in doing so we have stressed an ethical approach to life at the expense of a theological approach. Consequently we have ruled certain words, subjects, and literary forms immoral before we have even attempted to understand the creative process. Worse yet, we have tended to consider the process itself questionable. In all fairness, though, it must be said that this is true of the entire middle class, not just of Christians. Remember Ben Shahn's comment to the effect, "A Van Gogh on the wall is status, but one in the family is hell."

A theological approach to art probably should have as its starting point the creation narrative of Genesis. There we are told that man is made in God's image. Whatever else is included in that phrase, it is clear that man is made in the image of a creator. It can be assumed, then, that when man functions as a creator he is functioning as he was intended to. The difficulty arises immediately; man has fallen. And to my knowledge no one has completely diagnosed the effect the fall had on his creativity.

Fortunately, in Christ not only the soul is redeemed but the whole man, and substantial steps are taken toward restoration of the condition man was intended to enjoy. The various relationships of man to the creation are also substantially restored. This restoration makes it possible for the Christian, when he functions as a creator, to function in the image of God. But it does not guarantee that he will. The restoration is substantial, not total.

It can be seen, then, that a theological approach, while of prime importance, is necessary as a foundation for the ethical approach. The two must be employed simultaneously. Neither in itself is adequate.

The Christian Poet and the Secular World

The Christian writer faces another difficulty when he attempts to address an audience outside his subculture. No matter how up to date or how skillful his technique, if the content of the Gospel is present, he is charged with writing propaganda. Were the results less disheartening, the charge would be laughable. We live in an age of propaganda.

Gary Snyder is a propagandist for Buddhism; Allen Ginsberg is a propagandist for Hinduism and pederasty; Alta is a propagandist for lesbianism; Denise Levertov is a propagandist for the peace movement; and Robert Bly is a propagandist for the Great Mother.

The reason those writers are accepted by critics, who supposedly reject propaganda, and Christian writers are rejected is not hard to find. The critics realize full well that the Christian message is unique. The Christian work cannot be discussed as an object in isolation. It is constructed in relation to eternal truths and demands from a reader either a commitment to or a rejection of those truths.

This can be illustrated by the discussion of Eugene Warren's *Christographia* and Bill Butler's *A Cheyenne Legend* that appeared in a review magazine. One paragraph is particularly enlightening:

The story of Falling Star's birth, fruit of the union of a woman and a star, when his mother fell from the tree,

> all the way home
> bones broken
> dead from the fall
>   not her kid
> born from the shock
> half-star
> he was hard like stone
> Meadowlark flying by
> heard the bawling
> took him up to her nest
> stuffed him on grubs
>   all spring
>   summer

is as fantastical as any story of virgin birth. And yet, because the narrator here is removed from his material, because this legend needs no personal logic and demands no personal commitment from us, and because the language, the imagery, and what symbolism there is, are fresh, we can accept this telling.

The criterion for evaluation has been reduced to fresh language. The poem is praised precisely because it is extraneous.

Of these three major problems, keeping his priorities in order, distrust from fellow Christians, and rejection by the secular literary world, the third is probably the easiest for the Christian poet to handle. Because of his faith and his pursuit of holiness, the Christian poet is not success-oriented. He realizes from the beginning that financial gain, prizes, and fame are not meaningful goals. He knows also that, for him, they are unlikely. Recent literary history tells him that the prizes go to those who represent the age. Even the objection that W. H. Auden and T. S. Eliot are Christian poets is irrelevant. Auden made his reputation as a socialist and Eliot as a prophet of despair. The influence of each declined after his conversion. No, the Christian artist learns very quickly that he is unwelcome.

But wisely accepted, the rejection by the world can become the source of his success. For that rejection is freedom from the bondage of fashion.

part 6

Christian Perspectives
on the Visual Arts

Introduction

Like literature, the visual arts are one of the means by which the human race has grappled with and assimilated reality. Painting and sculpture are an expression of human values, and a visit to an art gallery will reveal how the human race has viewed its experience in the world. At this level the visual arts, like literature, record what people have most valued and longed for, as well as what people have feared and abhorred. As Northrop Frye writes in *The Stubborn Structure*, the arts show us "man's views of the world he wants to live in, of the world he does not want to live in, of his situation and destiny and heritage, of the world he is trying to make and of the world that resists his efforts."[1]

Visual art is a revelation. It aims to rescue us from inattentiveness and half-awareness—the normal state of most of us—and to reveal things as they really are. With colors and shapes on a canvas or chiseled lines cut in stone, artists attempt to take us by the hand and say, "Look!" John Ruskin paid a great tribute to the power of art when he said the paintings of Joseph Turner alerted him to the true colors of the sky. The visual arts

1. (Ithaca: Cornell University Press, 1970), p. 18.

are preeminently a revelation at the level of our sensory perceptions, but artists also make significant comments about human values and meaning at a more interpretative level.

Part of the message of art is its concern with form. Every visit to an art gallery leaves one with an overpowering awareness that the human race, no matter how physically impoverished it has been, has always affirmed the importance of beauty and craftsmanship. It has known in its heart that people do not live by functional utilitarianism alone. G. K. Chesterton has said that "art is the signature of man." Art declares the unique identity of people as creatures made in the image of God.

How the Few and the Many Use Pictures

C. S. Lewis

It is customary to divide the arts into two categories — the useful arts and the fine arts. The useful arts, like ceramics, architecture, and furniture making, are those that attempt to add artistry to something whose main purpose is to serve a practical, physical function. The fine arts, like music, painting, sculpture, and literature, are those whose primary purpose is artistic joy.

To confuse these two types of art is to distort a work of art. One such confusion is particularly common: the attempt to "use" a work of fine art rather than recognize that its beauty and craftsmanship are their own reason for being. In the following excerpt from his book, An Experiment in Criticism (Cambridge University Press, 1961), C. S. Lewis explores what happens when we try to make fine art "useful."

I grew up in a place where there were no good pictures to see, so that my earliest acquaintance with the draughtsman's or the painter's art was wholly through the illustrations to books. Those to Beatrix Potter's *Tales* were the delight of my childhood; Arthur Rackham's to *The Ring*, that of my school-days. I have all these books still. When I now turn their pages

I by no means say 'How did I ever enjoy such bad work?' What surprises me is that I drew no distinctions in a collection where the work varied so vastly in merit. It now stares me in the face that in some of Beatrix Potter's plates you find witty drawing and pure colour, while others are ugly, ill-composed, and even perfunctory. (The classic economy and finality of her writing is far more evenly maintained.) In Rackham I now see admirable skies, trees, and grotesques, but observe that the human figures are often like dummies. How could I ever have failed to see this? I believe I can remember accurately enough to give the answer.

I liked Beatrix Potter's illustrations at a time when the idea of humanised animals fascinated me perhaps even more than it fascinates most children; and I liked Rackham's at a time when Norse mythology was the chief interest of my life. Clearly, the pictures of both artists appealed to me because of what was represented. They were substitutes. If (at one age) I could really have seen humanised animals or (at another) could really have seen Valkyries, I should greatly have preferred it. Similarly, I admired the picture of a landscape only if, and only because, it represented country such as I would have liked to walk through in reality. A little later I admired a picture of a woman only if, and only because, it represented a woman who would have attracted me if she were really present.

The result, as I now see, was that I attended very inadequately to what was actually before me. It mattered intensely what the picture was 'of'; hardly at all what the picture was. It acted almost as a hieroglyph. Once it had set my emotions and imagination to work on the things depicted, it had done what I wanted. Prolonged and careful observation of the picture itself was not necessary. It might even have hindered the subjective activity.

All the evidence suggests to me that my own experience of pictures then was very much what that of the majority always remains.

Nearly all those pictures which, in reproduction, are widely popular are of things which in one way or another would in reality please or amuse or excite or move those who admire them—*The Monarch of the Glen, The Old Shepherd's Chief Mourner, Bubbles*; hunting scenes and battles; death-beds and dinner parties; children, dogs, cats, and kittens; pensive young women (draped) to arouse sentiment, and cheerful young women (less draped) to arouse appetite.

The approving comments which those who buy such pictures make on them are all of one sort: 'That's the loveliest face I ever saw'—'Notice the old man's Bible on the table'—'You can see they're all listening'—'What a beautiful old house!' The emphasis is on what may be called the narrative qualities of the picture. Line or colour (as such) or composition are hardly mentioned. The skill of the artist sometimes is ('Look at the way he's got the effect of the candlelight on the wine glasses'). But what is admired is the realism—even with an approximation to *trompe-l'-oeil*—and the difficulty, real or supposed, of producing it.

But all these comments, and nearly all attention to the picture, cease soon after it has been bought. It soon dies for its owners; becomes like the once-read novel for the corresponding class of reader. It has been used and its work is done.

This attitude, which was once my own, might almost be defined as 'using' pictures. While you retain this attitude you treat the picture—or rather a hasty and unconscious selection of elements in the picture—as a self-starter for certain imaginative and emotional activities of your own. In other words, you 'do things with it.' You don't lay yourself open to what it, by being in its totality precisely the thing it is, can do to you.

You are thus offering to the picture the treatment which would be exactly right for two other sorts of representational object; namely the ikon and the toy. (I am not here using the word *ikon* in the strict sense given it by the Eastern Church; I mean any representational object, whether in two dimensions or three, which is intended as an aid to devotion.)

A particular toy or a particular ikon may be itself a work of art, but that is logically accidental; its artistic merits will not make it a better toy or a better ikon. They may make it a worse one. For its purpose is not to fix attention upon itself, but to stimulate and liberate certain activities in the child or the worshiper. The Teddy-bear exists in order that the child may endow it with imaginary life and personality and enter into a quasi-social relationship with it. That is what 'playing with it' means. The better this activity succeeds the less the actual appearance of the object will matter. Too close or prolonged attention to its changeless and expressionless face impedes the play. A crucifix exists in order to direct the worshiper's thought and affections to the Passion. It had better not have any excellencies, subtleties, or originalities which will fix attention upon itself. Hence devout people may, for this purpose, prefer the crudest and emptiest ikon. The emptier, the more permeable; and they want, as it were, to pass through the material image and go beyond. For the same reason it is often not the costliest and most lifelike toy that wins the child's love.

If this is how the many use pictures, we must reject at once the haughty notion that their use is always and necessarily a vulgar and silly one. It may or may not be. The subjective activities of which they make pictures the occasion may be on all sorts of levels. To one such spectator Tintoretto's *Three Graces* may be merely an assistance in prurient imagination; he has used it as pornography. To another, it may be the starting-point for a meditation on Greek myth which, in its own right, is of value. It might conceivably, in its own different way, lead to something as good as the picture itself. This may be what happened when Keats looked at a Grecian urn. If so, his use of the vase was admirable. But admirable in its own way; not admirable as an appreciation of ceramic art. The corresponding uses of pictures are extremely various and there is much to be said for many of them. There is only one thing we can say with confidence against all of them without exception: they are not essentially appreciations of pictures.

Real appreciation demands the opposite process. We must not let loose our own subjectivity upon the pictures and make them its vehicles. We must begin by laying aside as completely as we can all our own preconceptions, interests, and associations. We must make room for Botticelli's Mars and Venus, or Cimabue's Crucifixion, by emptying out our own. After the negative effort, the positive. We must use our eyes. We must look, and go on looking till we have certainly seen exactly what is there. We sit down before the picture in order to have something done to us, not that we may do things with it. The first demand any work of any art makes upon us is surrender. Look. Listen. Receive. Get yourself out of the way. (There is no good asking first whether the work before you deserves such a surrender, for until you have surrendered you cannot possibly find out.)

It is not only our own 'ideas' about, say, Mars and Venus which must be set aside. That will make room only for Botticelli's 'ideas,' in the same sense of the word. We shall thus receive only those elements in his invention which he shares with the poet. And since he is after all a painter and not a poet, this is inadequate. What we must receive is his specifically pictorial invention: that which makes out of many masses, colours, and lines the complex harmony of the whole canvas.

The distinction can hardly be better expressed than by saying that the many *use* art and the few *receive* it. The many behave in this like a man who talks when he should listen or gives when he should take. I do not mean by this that the right spectator is passive. His also is an imaginative activity; but an obedient one. He seems passive at first because he is making sure of his orders. If, when they have been fully grasped, he decides that they are not worth obeying—in other words, that this is a bad picture—he turns away altogether.

From the example of the man who uses Tintoretto as pornography it is apparent that a good work of art may be used in the wrong way. But it will seldom yield to this treatment so easily as a bad one. Such a man will gladly turn from Tintoretto to Kirchner or photographs if no moral or cultural hypocrisy prevents him. They contain fewer irrelevancies; more ham and less frill.

But the reverse is, I believe, impossible. A bad picture cannot be enjoyed with that full and disciplined 'reception' which the few give to a good one. This was borne in upon me lately when I was waiting at a bus stop near a hoarding and found myself, for a minute or so, really looking at a poster—a picture of a man and a girl drinking beer in a public house. It would not endure the treatment. Whatever merits it had seemed to have at the first glance diminished with every second of attention. The smiles became waxwork grins. The colour was, or seemed to me, tolerably realistic, but it was in no way delightful. There was nothing in the composition to satisfy the eye. The whole poster, besides being 'of' something, was not also a pleasing *object*. And this, I think, is what must happen to any bad picture if it is really examined.

If so, it is inaccurate to say that the majority 'enjoy bad pictures ' They enjoy the ideas suggested to them by bad pictures. They do not really see the pictures as they are. If they did, they could not live with them. There is a sense in which bad work never is nor can be enjoyed by anyone. The people do not like the bad picture *because* the faces in them are like those of puppets and there is no real mobility in the lines that are meant to be moving and no energy or grace in the whole design. These faults are simply invisible to them; as the actual face of the Teddy-bear is invisible to an imaginative and warm-hearted child when it is absorbed in its play. It no longer notices that the eyes are only beads.

If bad taste in art means a taste for badness as such, I have still to be convinced that any such thing exists. We assume that it does because we apply to all these popular enjoyments in the gross the adjective 'sentimental.' If we mean by this that they consist in the activity of what might be called 'sentiments', then (though I think some better word might be found) we are not far wrong. If we mean that these activities are all alike mawkish, flaccid, unreasonable, and generally disreputable, that is more than we know. To be moved by the thought of a solitary old shepherd's death and the fidelity of his dog is, in itself and apart from the present topic, not in the least a sign of inferiority. The real objection to that way of enjoying pictures is that you never get beyond yourself. The picture, so used, can call out of you only what is already there. You do not cross the frontier into that new region which the pictorial art as such has added to the world.

Letter to a Christian Artist

H. R. Rookmaaker

It seems like a long jump from a painting to the doctrines of the Christian faith. What does the Christian faith have to say about the concrete colors and shapes and textures on the canvas?

As the following "letter to a Christian artist" suggests, the Christian faith speaks to the visual artist, in artistic terms, just as it speaks to the poet, novelist, or musician. Because Christians serve God as stewards in the world He made, they are sanctioned to cultivate their artistic talent, to immerse themselves in the created realities of the world about them, and to learn the norms or principles inherent in the visual arts as a human discipline.

Within this perspective of the arts as an arena for a Christian's activity, Professor Rookmaaker suggests general answers to the following questions: What is appropriate subject matter for Christian artists? Is beauty of form significant in its own right? Is art more than color, line,

For illustrations of how Professor Rookmaaker applies the principles he briefly states in this letter, consult his Modern Art and the Death of a Culture (Downers Grove, Ill.: InterVarsity, 1970).

and texture? Must its subject matter be tied to human life and thought? Must the form suggest a meaning? Does art embody a world view or express an identifiable spirit? Is there such a thing as Christian art?

DIEMEN, THE NETHERLANDS
August 23, 1966

Dear Miss Stephenson:

Your letter reached me yesterday after its trans-Atlantic voyage, and I propose to answer you directly. Your request touches on a problem I have been thinking about for a long time. Maybe what follows can be of help to you. I'd like to approach the matter in a schematic way, pointing out some principles.

Your questions concern your wish to paint—that is, to work as an artist—as a Christian. It really is remarkable that you decided to do this when you were just converted. Many times new Christians just drop their artistic careers because they think painting and art today are incompatible with being a real Christian. I'm glad you made this decision and hope to help you by suggesting the following principles for Christian artists:

1. If God has given us *talents* we may use them creatively—or rather, we *must* use them creatively. A Christian artist is not different from, say, a Christian teacher, minister, scholar, merchant, housewife, or anybody else who has been called by the Lord to specific work in line with his or her talents. There are no specific rules for artists, nor do they have specific exemptions to the norms of good conduct God laid down for man. An artist is simply a person whose God-given talents ask him to follow the specific vocation of art. There may be circumstances when love toward God would forbid certain artistic activities or make them impossible, but the present moment in history does not ask for such a sacrifice. Quite the contrary. We—the Christian world and the world at large—desperately need artists.

2. To be God's child means to be offered *freedom*—the Christian freedom Christ himself and Paul in his letters say much about. This freedom is most important for anybody who wants to do artistic work. Without freedom there is no creativity, without freedom no originality, without freedom no art, without freedom even no Christianity. This freedom can exist only if it is based on love toward God and our neighbors, and if we become new men through the finished work of Christ and the Holy Spirit is given to us. Without this base, freedom may easily mean being free from God and consequently free to indulge all the cravings of the sinful heart of unredeemed man. (For more on this matter of freedom, see Paul's letter to the Galatians).

Christian freedom is different from humanistic freedom, the freedom man gives himself to build a world after his own devising (as was tried by the Enlightenment and the humanist development after that time in the Western world). Humanistic freedom leads to all kinds of problems, as our Western world is now learning from experience. Freedom in the biblical sense is in no way negative—shun this, don't do that, you must leave that alone, keep away from this. Christian freedom has nothing to do with a set of rules by which you must bind yourself; indeed, such rules may easily be pseudo-Christian. Freedom is the necessary basis for creativity, for creativity is impossible when there is timidity, when you allow yourself to be bound by narrow rules. Do not think the modern art world is free— but we will turn to that later.

Freedom is positive. It means being free from tradition, from the feeling that everything you do has to be original, from certain fixed rules said to be necessary in art—but also from the thought that to be creative you must break all kinds of rules and standards.

Freedom means also that there are no prescriptions for subject-matter. There is no need for a Christian to illustrate biblical stories or biblical truth, though he may of course choose to do that. An artist has the right to choose a subject that he thinks worthwhile. But non-representational art provides no more freedom than the most involved allegorical or storytelling art.

Freedom includes the right to choose your own style, to be free from tradition but also from modernity, from fashion, from today and tomorrow as well as from yesterday. Yet there is no need to slap the contemporary in the face, as some streams of art nowadays deem necessary. Christian freedom also is freedom from the sinful lust for money, from seeking man's praise, from the search for celebrity. It is the freedom to help a neighbor out and give him something to delight in.

3. There are *norms for art* that are a part of God's creation. Without them art would be an empty name without sense. To say a person has been given a feeling for art and beauty (everybody has, to a certain extent), that he has been granted a strong subjective sense of artistic rightness, is but another way to say that he has been given an understanding of certain norms God laid down in his creation, the world in which we live. We call this *taste*, a feeling for design and color, the ability to grasp the inner harmony of a complex of forms and colors, the understanding of the inner relationship among elements of the subject-matter, the ability to recognize the indefinable dividing lines between poor and good art, between worn-out symbols and fresh ways of saying things that are important to man.

These norms do not stand in the way when we want to live in Christian freedom; they are a part of our world and our nature. Only when man revolts and does not want to be a creature, when he wants to be God and not man, does he feel bound by these norms. For those who love the Lord and rejoice in his good and beautiful creation, these norms provide the opportunity to live in freedom and to create. As one cannot act and live free as a woman if one is not a woman and has not the possibilities of a woman, so the norms for beauty and art are at the same time the opportunities to see beauty and create art.

4. When God created—and in that way made the perception of beauty and the human creation of art possible—he gave art

(or any artistic endeavor) a place in this world in which we live; and that world he called good. (I added artistic endeavor because we have to think not only of the rarefied museum type of art called Art with a capital *A* today but also of all other types, including ceramics, dance-music, pictures used in Sunday schools, and so on. We shall come back to this.) Art is here because God meant it to be here.

So art has its own task and meaning. There is no need to try to justify one's artistic activity by making works with a moralistic message, even if one is free to emphasize moral values. Nor is there any need to think one has to serve as a critic of culture, or always provide eye-openers to the non-artists, or teach, or evangelize, or do whatever other lofty things one can think of. Art has done its task when it provides the neighbor with things of beauty, a joy forever. Art has direct ties with life, living, joy, the depth of our being human, just by being art, and therefore it needs no external justification. That is so because God, who created the possibility of art and who laid beauty in his creation, is the God of the living and wants man to live. God is the God of life, the lifegiver. The Bible is full of this.

Art is not autonomous. "Art for art's sake" was an invention of the last century to loosen the ties between art and morality, that is, to give art the freedom to depict all kinds of sins as if they were not sinful but simply human. The human understanding of depravity, of morality, of good and bad was thereby undermined or erased. We are seeing the results today, in our century. The meaning of art is its being art, but it is not autonomous, and it has thousands of ties with human life and thought. When artists cease to consider the world in its manifold forms outside the artistic domain, their art withers into nothingness, because it no longer has anything to say.

Much abstract art today is art, yes; but it has little meaning because it is *only* art. All its ties with reality have been cut. This applies as much to a ceramic product as to a painting. Art has its own meaning and needs no excuse. But it loses its meaning if it does not want to be anything but art and there-fore cuts its ties with life and reality, just as scholarly work loses its importance and interest if learning is sought for its own sake. Art and science become aestheticism and scholas-ticism if made autonomous. They become meaningless idols.

The artist's work can have meaning for the society God put him in if he does not go to live in the ivory tower, or try to play the prophet or priest, or—turning in the other direction—in false modesty consider himself only a craftsman. He has to make art while thinking of his neighbors in love, helping them, and using his talents in their behalf.

5. Most art today expresses a spirit, *the spirit of our age*, which is not Christian. In some ways it is post-Christian, in others anti-Christian, in still others humanistic. Here and there there are Christian artists who try to do their work in a godly spirit. But often their brethren leave them alone, distrusting their creativeness or doubting that they are Christians. False art theories that have pervaded the Christian world—the artist as an asocial being, a non-conformist in the wrong sense, a dan-gerous prophet, an abnormal being who lives in an alien world—are often responsible for this attitude. But some Chris-tian artists themselves hold these false views and look down with contempt at their fellow Christians. There is a lot of confusion.

That the art of the world at large is also in a deep crisis does not make things easier. We live in a society where there is a break manifest between the mass of men and the elite, and another break between the natural sciences and technical reali-ties on one side and religion (most of the time rather mystical) of a completely subjectivistic and irrationalistic type on the other. We who live in this world cannot act as if these deep problems did not exist.

There is *no real Christian tradition* in the arts today to turn to. If an artist wants to work as a Christian and do something that he can stand for and bear responsibility for, he has to start with the freedom based in a true faith in the living God of

Scripture. He has to make art that is relevant to our day. Therefore he has to understand our day. And, in order to gain from all that is good and fine today and yet avoid being caught by the spirit of our age and its false art principles, he must study modern art in all its different aspects deeply and widely. He must try to analyze the language modern artists use, their syntax and grammar, in order to be able to hear correctly the message they profess to speak. To analyze, understand, and criticize lovingly, loving man but hating sin, in order to avoid their mistakes but gain from their achievements—that is the Christian artist's task. A new Christian tradition, as a fruit of faith, can grow only if artists who understand their work and task, their world and its problems, really set to work.

6. But what has the Christian artist to offer the world? He has *a freedom to do something*, not just the freedom for freedom's sake. What should he aim at? Let's be careful not to lay down new rules—there are no biblical laws that art must be realistic or symbolic or sentimental, or must seek only idealized beauty.

The artist as a Christian is free, but not with a purposeless freedom. He is free in order to praise God and love his neighbors.

These are basic laws. What do they mean in practice? May I refer, this time without comment, to Philippians 4:8—"Finally, brethren, whatsoever things are true, whatsoever things are honest, whatsoever things are just, whatsoever things are pure, whatsoever things are lovely, whatsoever things are of good report; if there be any virtue, and if there be any praise, think on these things." Here we read what a Christian standing in freedom as a new man, in God's strength and with the help of the Holy Spirit, must search for. This also applies to the Christian as an artist. It is up to him to work, to pray, and to study, in order that he may realize as much as he possibly can of these truly human and life-promoting principles.

In the Lord,

H. R. ROOKMAAKER

On Praising God with Our Senses

Virginia Stem Owens

William Wordsworth held that the quality of our mental and spiritual life depends on the quality of the sensations that we encounter. A person who believes as Wordsworth did will obviously pay careful attention to fostering the sensory experiences of his life. No wonder Wordsworth calls the mind "a mansion for all lovely forms" and the memory "a dwelling place for all sweet sounds and harmonies."

Wordsworth's attitude toward the senses has important implications for the arts. All the arts, and especially the visual arts, feed upon the senses. To appreciate the arts fully requires the attentiveness of our eyes and ears. The first step to enjoying a visit to an art gallery or improving the artistic quality of our home is not to master the principles of art but to learn truly to see with our eyes.

With their minds full of theological ideas, Christians have tended to slight the quality of their sensory experience. In our century, the frantic pace of life and the omnipresence of the popular media have led us to open ourselves uncritically to images that are cheap, tawdry, artificial, drab, and ugly. Not realizing that we become the sum of our sensory indulgences, we have paid little attention to protecting our sensory life from decay. How unfortunate —and how telling —that the words sensuous and sensual have become lumped together in a single pejorative *category.* Sensuous, *meaning "sensory," "having to do with the senses,"* ought to be one of the great positive words in a Christian's vocabulary. God gave us our senses and the materials to make them a doorway to glory. The following article explores how our senses can become what God intended them to be.

The Two Ways of Approaching God

I have a friend, an artist, who says the first thing she notices about a person is the colored splotch on the inner part of the eye socket where it curves upward to become a part of the nose, whether it is blue or purple or maybe slightly green. When she told me this, it startled me, and I was glad I was wearing glasses that hid my own little spot of color until I could go home and check it out for myself. If she had said that the first thing she noticed was the firmness of a person's hand-shake or the warmth of his smile or any of a dozen other characteristics by which we are admonished to judge people, I would not have felt self-conscious. But the inside of one's eye socket? That suddenly seemed a naked, vulnerable spot.

Charles Williams, in *Descent of the Dove*, says people have sought God in two seemingly contradictory ways; through the senses (that is, by apprehending his creation) and through the suppression of the senses, what is called the *via negativa*. "The Way of Affirmation was to develop great art and romantic love and marriage and philosophy and social justice," he says; "the Way of Rejection was to break out continually in the profound mystical documents of the soul, the records of the great psychological masters of Christendom."

But the way of rejection is one that few have followed. Williams cites an ancient canon, dating from the second or third century, to illustrate the church's official attitude toward the material world: "If any bishop or priest or deacon, or any cleric whatsoever, shall refrain from marriage and from meat and from wine, *not for the sake of discipline but with contempt*, and, forgetful that all things are very good and that God made man male and female, blasphemously inveighs against the creation, let him either be corrected or deposed and turned out of the Church. And so with a layman" (italics mine).

Now in no way would I want to undermine the validity of the *via negativa*. It has had little enough honor, especially in the Protestant tradition, where deprivation of the senses is usually "for your own good" rather than for God's good. Indeed, how *any* good could derive from fasting, retreat, silence, or celibacy (despite our Lord's practice of them all) has often escaped our notice as we clucked our tongues over the Roman monastic tradition. At least part of the success of the recent rapproachement between Protestants and Catholics can be attributed to the changes by which nuns dress like "normal people" and priests insist on matrimonial rights.

The Importance of Sensory Experience

However, our defense of the former way, access to God through the full use of our senses, has of late been truncated and confused. The reasons are numerous and tiresome. For a start, most of the population is surrounded not by primary creation—the things that only God can make, such as trees—but by secondary or even tertiary creation—the things that God's creatures can make or the things that God's creatures' creations, i.e., machines, can make. And those secondary and tertiary products are often shoddy enough to merit only the cursory attention they get.

So that when my friend speaks of the subtle colors on human faces, it strikes us as extraordinary, a little odd, even faintly amusing, but not of the earth-shaking importance it truly is. For how are we to give thanks for something we've never noticed? How shall we praise God for the world we've not paid proper attention to? Our practice of pigeonholing our praise into broad categories—family, friends, country, health, and the like—reminds me of the all-purpose five-second prayer I devised as a child for use on cold nights: "God bless everybody in the world. Amen." When we pray in terms of everybody-in-the-world, we imagine ourselves to be dealing with a divine, omniscient bureaucracy. But God doesn't love everybody-in-the-world. He loves each of us singly, knowing the hairs of our heads and the shadows of our eye sockets.

One of the chief champions of this way of the senses in the Protestant tradition is, surprisingly, Jonathan Edwards, whose reputation as a dour example of asceticism is due to his overly anthologized and journalistically interpreted sermon, "Sinners in the Hands of an Angry God." On the contrary, Edwards's early attention was absorbed by the natural sciences, the careful observation of spiders being his speciality. But natural science was not a mere sideline to his theological thought. His scrutiny of creation provided the full heart out of which he wrote his doctrine of creation, with which physics is only now catching up. "God not only created all things, and gave them being at first, but continually upholds them in being," he says. "It will certainly follow from these things, that God's *preserving* created things in being is perfectly equivalent to a *continued creation*, or to his creating those things out of nothing at each moment of their existence" (*Works*, II, 487 ff.).

Think of it. With each breath we take, God is again pumping into our lungs his exhalation of the breath of life, just as he did for Adam. If he withdrew his breath from the bubble of our world, it would instantly collapse. We are not a clock, once wound, running down. Developing this sense of continuous creation pulls the mask from our eyes, enables us to see creation hanging on God's breath, dependent, contingent. And the precariousness makes it all the more precious.

The world's existence hangs on God's continuing to pay attention to it, and to be properly thankful we in turn must pay rapt attention to his crafting. But there are dangers. In *Pilgrim at Tinker Creek*, Annie Dillard tells of her meticulous search of her surroundings in rural Virginia, from the single-cell algae in her pond to the view of Alpha Centauri from her backyard. Sometimes the evidence is devastating: nature is wasteful, extravagant, cruel, predatory. Never does the evidence point to chance, mere random agitation of atoms; and sometimes it points to the universe as the creation of a madman, a sadist. Yet it is beauty itself that is ultimately the answer to her questions, the fact that we desire and seek our beauty, that we separate the beautiful from the broken in creation. "No, I've gone through this a million times, beauty is not a hoax," she testifies. "Beauty is real. I would never deny it. The appalling thing is that I forget it."[1] It takes attention, rapt attention, to keep the reality before us. But our attention span is limited. Is this not perhaps the meaning of sleep, that dark bed of mystery in which our consciousness must rest in order to be restored to its task of thanksgiving?

When Jesus instructed us to "consider" the lilies of the field and the fowls of the air, he wasn't making some moralistic point, as in the dreadful fable of the ant and the grasshopper that was used to goad earlier generations into productive activity. The point of considering lilies is just the opposite: they are lazy lilies, occupying space amid the common field grasses for no reason other than that it pleases God. Can we appreciate God's creative prodigality? The idea of trillions of stars and cells offends our sense of proportion, especially as they keep exploding and dying. How can we praise such a wastrel, we who now are sweating out every barrel of oil and ton of coal? It's all very well for *him* to frivol about with wildflowers, but what about us—what shall we eat, what shall we drink, where shall we find fuel for the morrow?

Yet our business is not to be anxious about these matters but to praise God, to exult in him. And the most accessible way for most of us is through God's creation. What we call nature—flowers and trees and birds and bees, scorpions and hail and sharks—this is primary creation and reveals the "nature" of its Creator, the way he is. We know what steadfastness

1. Annie Dillard, *Pilgrim at Tinker Creek* (New York: Bantam, 1974), p. 273.

is because we see eons of predictability in the physical world. We know what surprise is because of sudden storms.

Andrew Wyeth once told an interviewer, "I love to study the many things that grow below the corn stalks and bring them back into the studio to study the color. If one could only catch that true color of nature—the very thought of it drives me mad." *That* is considering the lilies of the field. And it effectively drives out utilitarian anxiety.

Or take for an example Rachel Peden, a woman of uncommon considering power, who in her book *Speak to the Earth* describes the exploration of a hound's-tongue seed: "The dime-sized seed pod is enclosed by five sepals and marked off into four parts with a single spike rising at the center. I pinched open one yellow-green, burry section of this fruitlet and saw the watery unripe seed inside. The brown stalk gave out an uninviting smell, sometimes compared to mouse smell. . . . I like it because it is pretty and interesting and we were having a good time fishing when I first saw hound's-tongue."[2] On God's scale of knowledge, which weighs heavier: knowing the market value of Nielsen ratings or knowing that a broken stalk of hound's-tongue smells mouselike?

Unfortunately, there is unrelenting pressure not to pay very close attention to creation but instead to consume oneself with anxiety about survival. A bizarre example of such pressure comes from a recent book called *Language and Woman's Place*: the author cautions women not to make fine color distinctions—not to speak of mauve and lavender, for instance, because powerful people in our society lump them all together as purple. (While Andrew Wyeth meticulously studies the various shades of snow.)

The demonic line of reasoning runs like this: If human senses, often employed to subvert the spirit, can also be a primary access to God in this world, then humanity must be harassed into not using them. "You see one mountain, you've

---

2. Rachel Peden, *Speak to the Earth* (New York: Alfred A. Knopf, 1974), p. 82.

seen them all," a friend once said to me. I felt the cold wind of blasphemy on my face. Really seeing a mountain would take a lifetime, I protested silently. Or longer than that if we are to believe Dante, who pictured purgatory as mountain-shaped.

Now Is the Time to Behold

When Thornton Wilder wrote *Our Town*, his notion of purgatory was attention paid too late, misplaced in an afterlife of awareness devoid of action. When Emily dies in childbirth and joins the dead in the hillside cemetery, she wants to go back and observe just one day of her short life. "Choose the least important day in your life," the dead advise her. "It will be important enough." Emily's final soliloquies echo the lament of the psalmist who dreads to go down into the pit where there is no longer the possibility of praise. "I love you all—everything," she cries out to the world that can no longer hear her. "I can't look at everything hard enough. . . . Wait! One more look. Good-by, Good-by, world. Good-by, Grover's Corners . . . Mama and Papa. Good-by to clock's ticking . . . and Mama's sunflowers. And food and coffee. And new-ironed dresses and hot baths . . . and sleeping and waking up. Oh, earth, you're too wonderful for anybody to realize you. Do any human beings ever realize life while they live it?—every, every minute?"

And the Stage Manager replies: "No. The saints and poets maybe—they do some."[3]

My friend the artist, the observer of eye sockets, consented to give me drawing lessons. "It's simple eye-hand coordination." she insists impatiently. Although I learned to excel in only two areas, long-haired sleeping dogs and aspen bark, I learned concomitantly to give thanks for a great many aspects of creation I had never known existed before. The great gaping holes in my universe were suddenly filled with such intricate detail that

3. *Treasury of the Theatre*, ed. John Gasser (New York: Simon and Schuster, 1960), p. 948.

my eyes began to grow bulgy from looking. They felt too small to admit all the things there suddenly were to see: Where the whiskers grow on a cat's nose and how exceptionally long they are, the receding ridges within a sandstone cave, the rounding slope of my daughter's upper lip.

"Divinity is not playful," Annie Dillard warns us. "The universe was not made in jest but in solemn incomprehensible earnest. By a power that is unfathomably secret, and holy, and fleet. There is nothing to be done about it, but ignore it or see."[4] Sometimes when I have been focusing overlong on the miniscule world of leafhoppers hatched in mold still damp from snowmelt, or when I feel physically assaulted by the bombardment of stimuli from a supposedly dead, silent winter day at my back door, I think it costs too much. The whole human race is not enough to search out each cunning device of its untiring Creator. But attention is the price we must pay for awareness—without which there is no thanksgiving.

---

4. Dillard, *Pilgrim*, p. 278.

Christian Art

Calvin Seerveld

What is Christian art? Is it a matter of form, or of vision, or both? What makes an artist's view of reality "Christian"? Must art be explicitly Christian in order to be considered Christian art? What do Christian and non-Christian art share with each other? Is Christian art known by its subject matter? Or, if it is a matter of perspective on the subject, how does a Christian artist build that perspective into his work?

Such questions will always be crucial to Christians who want their production and viewing of art to be a distinctly Christian experience. The following essay provides some convincing answers to those questions.

Toward a Definition of Art

Christian art has to be *art* to be Christian art. You cannot get by with shoddy work or propaganda and say, "But I did it for Christ's sake!" and then make believe shoddy work and propaganda done for Christ's sake is "Christian art." Christian art has to be art, competently crafted work, obeying the norm that distinguishes art products from other kinds of things, if it is going to be Christian art.

Art must not be understood as if it were photographic reproduction of things. All the talk about "mirroring reality" and making "images" of other things is wrong. Such a misconception of art is born out of a godless theory of knowledge that supposes "true knowledge" is getting an exact mental copy in your head or on paper of exactly what is "out there" in the world. The better the likeness, the better the product—so goes the *wrong* idea.

But music does not imitate other sounds. The modulated tones of horns and strings in concert, the tempo and rhythm of their harmony does not "correspond" to everyday noises you can recognize. A Mozart or Haydn minuet brings to your consciousness a world of precise and dainty elegance, a society of leisure and decorum, but it does not get you to know about it by reproducing exactly something Mozart or Haydn saw or heard for twenty minutes one day.

It is the same with painting. Rembrandt's "Night Watch" is not a colorful presentation of what he actually saw on an Amsterdam street, and he did not get the captain, attendants, and whole crowd to pose for him long enough to paint it, the way news photographers say, "Once more, please, Mr. President," or the way Hollywood studios stage performances till they get the right shot. Rembrandt used rich colors with deep hues, graceful shadows and light, a canvas of massed figures moving slowly forward, to express a powerful celebration, measured jubilance, a glorious, weighty pageantry. It gets us to understand something of life, all right, but it is not a photographic reproduction or "image." That is not the nature of art.

Rather, by its very nature, art is elusively symbolical, "suggestive," or metaphorical. Art gets at the meaning of certain affairs by condensing, in a surprisingly compact way, all kinds of dissimilar things, into specially controlled tones and colors or bodily movements, and then it focuses your attention on those *suggesting forms*. That is what becoming "symbolical" is all about: taking a word or a gesture or a line and charging it with different, many-sided, often unnoticed, rich nuances of meaning.

For example, you could tell somebody, "I love you; I love you, even though you are getting old and pot-bellied." While that is an honest, straightforward statement of affection, and may even have the laughter that love often has percolating just below the surface of speech, it is not art. But:

> . . . Love is not love
> Which alters when it alteration finds,
> Or bends with the remover to remove

is art, because it indirectly, elliptically *suggests*. With its parabola of alliterated words, by the firm cadence and measured rest to its expression, it suggests the stern, reflected wisdom going deeply into the vowed character of love—that love is no surface passion but a committed betrothal, enduring through change.

Likewise with sculpture. Take, for example, Zadkine's statue of an oversized man rising up toward the sky, arms warding off blows, massively stirring toward life, with a jagged hole in place of its belly. That piece of formed metal captures symbolically the people of Rotterdam whose industrial heart was bombed to nothing by the Nazi bombers, and which now, after the war, is rising, writhing, strongly up from the ruins, scarred but massive again, the greatest port of Europe.

Art is form charged with metaphorical meaning. Like enriched bread, art is enriched form, suggesting form: poetry comes by way of symbolically enriched sentences; painting becomes art when the composition of colored shapes is charged with symbolical quality; music is art when the architectonic of sound relates meanings symbolically.

Toward a Definition of Christian Art

Christian art is art with a certain spirit in the suggestive form. Christian art has a certain kind of blood in its veins, you might say. *Christian art makes room for, and intimates, the glory of the Lord, how his blessing and judgment rest upon creation.*

Consider the statue by Ernst Barlach entitled "Hovering God the Father" (see Figure A on p. 387). It pictures a sculptured, robed figure hovering, as it were, suspended over everyone below. It has a venerable, patriarchal, grand distance to it that commands respect. Yet the arms are stiffly forward—no, better—stretched out in those sleeves, straining to reach, the hands simultaneously blessing and wanting to touch. While the visage is stern, forehead and eyes concentrated in prayer, the ancient

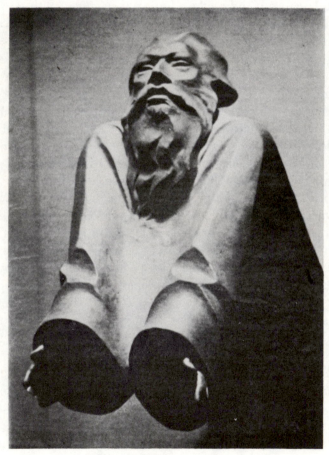

Figure A

beard is alive, like strong flames of fire that are steady but could consume. The round holes of the two sleeves could be trumpets. The chips are missing on the top fold of the robed arms, as if the majestic figure is hurt, nicked, grieved while loving, waiting and wanting to embrace.

This art product is Barlach's attempt to make known the *meaning* of our Father who is in heaven, God of the Old Testament who showed Himself in Jesus Christ.

Or consider Georges Rouault's painting of two prostitutes

Figure B

entitled "Women for Pleasure" (Figure B). It pictures two mis-shapen figures seated naked on a bench. The black shoulder-lines slump down. The belly is a tub of fat and sunken flesh; the ugly breasts have been wrestled and mauled. The jaw is set, the thick neck coarse, ringed ironically with baubles. The blue-brown, sunken colors reinforce the heavy-hearted lines: these bodies have been bruised, wasted, ruined from any glory. There is a kind of hurt horror and sorrowing compassion in the smeared, stolid, pitiful composition of these two old pros-titutes, gross, socially discarded, enslaved.

This art product is the way Rouault tried to express the truth that the wages of sin is death and that the wiles of the "strange woman" are an evil full of heartbreaking and heartbroken misery.

Do you see the spring-clean, outdoor world of kite-flying boys and girls in Figure C? There is space on the green and lightness in the sky, and their simple stylized bodies show how fresh, uncomplicated, and easy it is to be very young. Those

Figure C

are a child's hands. And the figures dance in pantomime, as it were, a ballet of balanced joy *toward* one another. The one to the left, with a modest bow of the head, proudly displays its kite—which looks like a mask, enigmatically serious. Yet the same kite is wagging its orange ribboned tail like a happy puppy, impatiently ready for the flying adventure.

The painting suggests there is certainty, simplicity, gentleness, air to breathe, and order in this world we inhabit. Creation is the playground of God where He lets His kids fly kites together, in happiness, when they stay close to Him. Henk Krijger puts symbolically to canvas here a modern beatitude: Blessed are the children who fly kites, in peace, for they are benefiting from the redeeming mercy of our creator God.

Do you get the point? Christian art is not a matter of pretty pictures. It is also not a matter of taking biblical topics, like angels, Gethsemane, or Samson and Delilah for one's "inspiration." Art with such themes can be very superficial and secular.

You also do not determine what is Christian art by checking whether the artist was an orthodox, church-going believer who lived an impeccable, moral life. Sometimes a believer's right hand does not know what his left hand is doing.

To recognize Christian art you must study the product, and test its spirit. What kind of allegiance penetrates its symbolical form? Does it show the majestic holiness of God, covenanting and judging His creatures (as Barlach's statue does)? Does the art product reveal, with a compassionate cry, the wasting devastation and emptiness of sin (as Rouault's painting does)? Does the sculpture or painting or poem or music or architecture or dance, or whatever kind of art piece it be, witness with laughter and hope to the goodly rich, earthy creation our Lord made for us to be obedient in (as Krijger's painting does)?

If genuine art breathes moments of this holy spirit, then you may carefully tell one another: this is the direction human craftsmanship must take to deserve the name of biblically *Christian* art.

Genuine art will not be didactic, teaching little lessons to the observer; genuinely Christian art will not be sentimental, recalling the good old days; it will not be prudish, Victorian, and a host of other negatives. Christian art will plumb especially the meaning of sin, instead of staying as far away from it as possible. It will handle the ugly, the cursed, the tragic, not with sympathetic understanding so much as with awe at the terribleness of sin and the soft play of forgiveness when it falls.

A Christian style will be honest, self-effacing, serious in its gaiety; fresh, candid, and confident in its naive immediacy. Perhaps, at times, exhilarating. Christian artists can let a certain gentle hope of life show through in the troubled ways of men. An artist will, with his painting or sculpture or music or writing, bring to human acts some such touch of light, when he does it in the grip of a reforming Christian faith. Such art will not be made to entertain or to stupefy. Yet it will have a popular, parable level to it because it is necessarily *diakonia*, a ministering.

That the earth is the Lord's and everything filling it is His, is a recognition missing in non-Christian art, an insight twisted in post-Christian secular art. It is a commitment that cannot be satisfactorily appended, circumscribed, or applied like varnish to an object conceived without it. It is a regrettable mistake to think that because our gracious God's cosmic theater allows all men to act coherently, this absolves the Christian community from its special calling to praise God wholly, unreservedly, in the bonds-bursting power of the Holy Spirit.

In short, art tells what lies in a man's heart and with what vision he views the world. Art always tell-tales in whose service a person stands, because art itself is always a consecrated offering, a disconcertingly undogmatic yet terribly moving attempt to bring honor and glory and power to something. Christian art is a form of worship.

Would Augustine Have Enjoyed Picasso?

Mark Marchak

The distinction between form and content is basic to all the arts. It is true, of course, that form and message are inseparable; you cannot have one without the other. There can be no meaning without the form that expresses it and in this sense form is meaning. But if the two are interrelated, they are also distinct. The classical scholar Werner Jaeger writes in Paideia, "It was the Christians who finally taught men to appraise poetry by a purely aesthetic standard — a standard which enabled them to reject most of the moral and religious teaching of the classical poets as false and ungodly, while accepting the formal elements in their work as instructive and aesthetically delightful."

The following essay traces such a philosophy to Augustine and applies it to modern abstract art, though what the author says is relevant to all the arts. This perspective allows Christians to avoid both provinciality, for they feel no need for a wholesale condemnation of the art of non-Christians, and an indiscriminate latitude, for they feel no need to agree with the ideas of works whose form they admire.

The Christian and Art

Beware the local movie house! Satan lurks there! At least my mother thought so. As a child she was careful not to walk near the neighborhood theater for fear the Devil would snatch her right off the street.

Many Christians, when confronted with "modern" abstract painting, remind me of my mother. Afraid of being caught in the clutches of some obscene philosophy, they refuse their senses the rich feast of a painting by a master like Picasso. His philosophy may be lost and despairing, but his paintings as paintings—their colors, their lines—are simply magnificent. And praise God I can enjoy them!

Many of the great artists of the twentieth century, while being slaves to godless philosophies, were masters of composition. Reject their philosophies, yes, but only after savoring their achievements as painters.

"Modern" Art

Just what is meant by "modern art"? Actually "modern" is misleading. What is usually referred to as modern art is abstract art as it evolved in the twentieth century, beginning with the impressionists at the turn of the century and culminating with the abstract expressionists in the 1950s. Usually it is distinguished from "contemporary art," that is, what is happening in the art world now.

More generally, most people label any abstract painting "modern." I will use the term in this broader sense, while not forgetting the historical context.

As we stopped before a painting by Paul Klee at the Denver Art Museum recently, a friend asked me, "What do you think he was trying to say with *that*?" The question is a good one in its place, but to ask it before one examines the painting as a painting is the quickest way to become puzzled and bored at an art museum. We should encounter a painting as a message only *after* we have encountered it as a painting.

Anna Pavlova, asked to explain her dancing, snapped at her interviewer, "If I could say it I wouldn't have danced it!" Painters are painters first, philosophers second. Don't rob the artist of his distinctive function by reversing his roles.

But if the message of a painting reflects an unchristian world view, does the believer have any business enjoying it at all? St. Augustine suggests some answers to this question.

St. Augustine on Art

Augustine was a poet before his conversion. He had tasted the sweet wine of sensuous pleasures in the various arts. Yet he struggled to find something deeper. Could sensory enjoyment be the only goal of art? Augustine recalls this inner tension in his *Confessions*: "My mind carefully examined the different qualities of the sensory impressions that were dinning at the ears of my heart; and all the while I was straining to catch your inner melody, beloved Truth."

Augustine answered his own question with a resounding no: art is not merely sensuous pleasure. The eternal God was the "inner melody" he begged to hear, the sound he finally captured when he became a Christian. After his conversion, though, Augustine did not shut off his senses. Nor did he wish to. Instead he discovered in God a reason for enjoying the sensuous pleasures of art.

To begin with, Augustine placed the Creator God at the center of aesthetics. All of creation bears the marks of His hand. And since God is not chaos, an underlying harmony characterizes nature. This harmony, manifested in the art object, is what appeals to man's senses.

Possibly drawing from Paul's remarks in the first chapter of Romans, especially verse 20, Augustine realized that this fundamental harmony could be perceived by Christian and non-Christian alike. Of course, if this is true, the unconverted artist can pay homage to the principle of harmony in his paintings while not recognizing the source of this beauty.

The tragedy of twentieth-century art is that it forgot its source. For Augustine, the work of art must aid the Christian in his ascent to God, or else it has failed. Yet he does not repudiate the first level of art, the sensuous. Great art is both sensuously satisfying and intellectually edifying. To demonstrate his point, Augustine tells us of a dancer whose graceful movements afforded his senses the greatest pleasure but whose message, conveyed through the senses, was less than Christian. He enjoyed the sensuous level while rejecting the suggested message.

A certain painting in the Museum of Modern Art in New York evokes a similar tension in me whenever I see it. The painting is Picasso's "Girl Before a Mirror." I often spend a great deal of time before it, enthralled by Picasso's masterly use of line and color. When I search for the underlying meaning I am disappointed, just as Augustine was with his dancer. Yet I have thoroughly enjoyed—and, as an artist, learned a great deal from—this painting.

A Christian Approach to Modern Painting

Given this two-pronged concept of art, how should a Christian approach a painting? Before a painting can be enjoyed as a painting its components must be observed. Basically a painting is nothing more than a stretched piece of canvas cloth covered with paint. This simple observation is one of the most profound discoveries of twentieth-century art. Artists began to take an interest in the materials they were using. They began to study the elements of composition apart from their purely pictorial function. In short, many artists became more concerned with *how* they painted than with *what* they painted. As a result, the subjects of "modern art" changed from recognizable objects to the actual compositional elements themselves.

Francis Schaeffer thinks that the inherent difficulty with abstract art is in this shift in subject matter. "The viewer," he claims, "is completely alienated from the painter." Certainly many people do throw up their hands in confusion or alarm at the first sight of an abstract painting. Al Capp, creator of "Li'l Abner," once complained that abstract art is "produced by the talentless, sold by the unscrupulous, and bought by the bewildered."

But is this really fair? In surveying God's creation do we not find the abstract? I have often been tempted to photograph a sunset, cut off the horizon, frame the picture, hang it in a gallery—and then listen to the ridicule it receives because it is abstract. People enjoy sunsets because of the brilliant colors. Drawing on this sensuous pleasure sparked by God's good creation, might not the artist make color the subject of his painting?

Or look at one of the pinnacles of God's creation, the tree. The beauty of branches cutting sharp patterns against the autumn sky of a brisk October morning is always satisfying. What evokes this response in the observer? The rhythm of the branches, of lines. Line is a legitimate subject for a painting.

Abstract art is not always destructive of nature. Rather, it often looks more deeply into the building blocks of God's harmonious creation. Observing line and color in nature is the best way to begin to enjoy abstract painting.

In a painting of mine called "La Raza," my intention was simple: to convey an appreciation for the Mexican culture I had encountered in Denver. Using lines and shapes suggested by designs I had seen repeatedly in Mexican art, I composed a painting in which the lines gaily play off each other to suggest the Mexican spirit. The "message" is not at all profound. The painting is simply an attempt to relay the feelings and pleasures I have had through an encounter with a different culture. It has no recognizable subject matter. The message is conveyed through the use of line, color, and form.

The next time you are in an art gallery or museum, take the time to look at the modern paintings. See them as an occasion for sensuous enrichment as well as an exercise in philosophy. Don't ignore the message, but do enjoy the painting as a painting. You are likely to find a whole new realm of pleasure waiting for you.

part 7

Christian Perspectives on Music

Introduction

Music is the most paradoxical of the arts. It is at once the most
elusive and the most universal.

On the one hand, music is more abstract and technical than
literature and painting, and is therefore more threatening to
the uninitiated. Literature, for example, is made from words;
nearly everyone feels comfortable talking about characters and
plot and settings. Similarly, we have learned to trust our eyes,
and when we stand in front of a painting we generally know
how to assimilate it. But how do we make sense of an art form
made from such intangibles as melody and rhythm and tone?

Yet history attests to the universality of music's appeal. There
are more listeners in our culture than there are readers or
viewers. If music is more easily vulgarized than the other arts,
it is also capable of the most spiritual effects of any art form.
It is the purest form of artistic beauty, and its beauty, moreover,
has the highest potential to be transformed into a religious
experience.

There are three levels at which we assimilate music. One is
the sensory level of sound. Another is the level of meaning or
expression; even when music is not accompanied by words it

399

can convey emotions or moods. The third level is musical technique, including awareness of melody, rhythm, harmony, tone color, theme, and musical form (such as the sonata or fugue).

Like literature and the visual arts, there are two perspectives of music that concern Christians. First, what is their response to music that is religious in nature and use? Second, what is their response to the whole canon of music beyond the realm of religious music? The essays that follow point out that both branches of music can be claimed by the Christian for God's glory and human enjoyment.

Christian Responsibility in Music

Harold M. Best

When God created the world, the morning stars sang together (Job 38:7). When King David brought the ark of the covenant to Jerusalem, he appointed "singers who should play loudly on musical instruments, on harps and lyres and cymbals, to raise sounds of joy" (I Chron. 15:16). The throne of God in heaven is surrounded by ceaseless song (Rev. 4:8). The worship of God has always poured forth into music. Music belongs to the Christian faith. Indeed, it is something that the Bible repeatedly commands.

Yet there are numerous unresolved questions concerning the relationship between music and the Christian life. In the following essay, Harold Best discusses a number of these questions, such as: What forms should music take within the church? What constitutes authentic music in the modern Christian community? What combination of the familiar and the new should we expect from Christian composers and performers? Is the musician's creativity itself valuable? Is music its own justification? What is the true role of music in worship? When or how does music become an act of worship? How can music become a part of Christian witness?

Music and the Church Today

In recent decades, the evangelical Christian community has made notable advances in education and scholarship, in missions, and in awareness of its social responsibilities. There is among evangelicals a new sense of the responsibility of every Christian to represent, as a living epistle, the incarnational aspect of his faith.

But in the arts and particularly in church music the development of a scriptural aesthetic lags behind. Beauty and truth continue to be confused, as do quality and results. Contentment with mediocrity as a would-be carrier of truth looms as a major hindrance to true creative vision among evangelicals.

Contrary to the statements of many publishers and leaders, there has been no recent revolution in church music. There has been a variety of imitations of a true secular radicalism, but no intrinsic upheaval. Church music continues its round of habituating listeners to the comforts of the past and the third-handedness of the present. Just enough vestiges of classicism remain to impart a sense of history, and our borrowings are controversial enough to titillate our sense of contemporaneity. In confusing relevance with immediacy and communication with imitation, we have reduced Christianity and what we mistakenly call Christian music to the level of market research and audience response.

Ironically, there is no lack of fine composers in the ranks of evangelicalism. They reflect a new outlook in refusing to view their art as merely a "come-on" to worship; they strive to avoid the use of art as a decoration for the gospel. They have chosen to remain true to the surrender of their creative abilities to God through imagination and disciplined workmanship. But their work is unwelcome in the stereotypes of worship and witness. They are forced to articulate their music in predominantly secular contexts. They become known more to their professional colleagues than to their brothers in Christ. In short, the church has secularized them and the creative integrity they possess—this in the face of the church's claim of being a new creation.

Scripture does not contain a set of rules for making art. It lays down life principles to which everything must answer, principles that call us all together. In this essay I shall try to view Christian responsibility in music in the light of biblical principles of creativity, worship, and witness.

Creativity

Our human creativity comes from the living God, who dwells in his transcendent advantage as the uncreated One and the inexhaustible Originator. He is the first while being the last, and in the eternal present of his vigor and imagination he is always creating. That he is maker of heaven and earth does not limit him to one time, mode, or means. It simply means that there is no other agency, purpose, or lack of it outside himself to dilute his sole prerogative. His work is the work of omnipotence—having created the unsearchable he still infinitely imagines. God is the first one to be unconcerned with replication or representation, for when he created there was nothing to replicate or represent. Instead, he imagined the most fascinating and bewildering assortment of creatures, and he made them. To him, everything has a priceless commonality—the blade of grass and the galaxy. What we walk on he loves; what we cannot measure he holds in the palm of his hand. The common is a mystery and the mysterious is common. There is pattern but not repetition. God's creation is a oneness; in its parts, unimaginable complexity. All is summed up historically, redemptively, and eschatologically, in the wisdom and purpose of the Triune God.

Man is God's unique creation. Made in the image of God, he reflects in his finite way his Maker's creativity. God alone creates out of nothing, and he does so without models or precedents. Man's creativity is always dependent and relational. He is part of the length of history and the width of individuality. He needs raw material and models. Culture is his handiwork, his fingerprint on the creation, and it is in the realm of his imagination that he comes closest to the godly prerogative of *ex nihilo*. He yearns for mastery over materials, to create shapes and articulate relationships amid a welter of options and disciplines.

The creation is at once God's handiwork and the resource for all of man's creativity. For the artist there is light, within which lies every possible nuance of color. For the musician, there is the over-tone series, within which lies every possible tonal resource. There is space, within which the visual arts seek their shape; and time, within which the musical arts seek theirs. Whatever man does creatively, he cannot step outside of the creation.

Though God called his creation good as it issued from his sovereign purpose, he did not intrinsically empower it, nor delegate authority to it. Man's responsibility is to be its steward and to apply to it the stewardship of his creativity. The essence of the cultural mandate rests on man's ability to act purposefully in contrast to the inability of the non-human natural creation to cause. There is, then, an important distinction between the moral neutrality of creation and its intrinsic worth. Created things are to be cherished for what they are in themselves. They are never to be worshiped. For idolatry is a confusion of intrinsic worth with intrinsic power. It is the corruption in which man worships the creature rather than the Creator. Man is not to fall down before chords, textures, or rhythms, to be shaped by them, any more than before trees, rocks, or totems.

Through his medium, the artist or musician tries to express his existence, to say *I am*. His imagination and skill endeavor to bring significance to the stuff of his art. He pushes against his temporality to substantiate what does not yet, even to him, exist. He lives in a world of models and precedents, knowing that he must take the further step. He thrives on nextness, hence mystery. Whatever the medium, his art is, as the painter Hans Hofmann said, "a created reality." Therefore it has its own integrity and speaks its own language. The artist, as any-one else, must avoid the temptation to clone, to repeat. Merely to represent anything that already exists without infusing the artist's own unique imagination is to deny the intrinsic worth of what exists and to degrade the artist's work to nothing but imitation.

In music, the same applies. Although music does not "rep-resent" in exactly the same sense that the visual arts do, it is faced with analogous problems. Just as a painter is suspect if his work is "abstract," so a composer is suspect if his work is dissonant, or lacks a traditional tonal center, or pushes toward new formal concepts. Inferior art and inferior music are simply those attempts that try to duplicate something that, whatever its quality, already is. Realism in any art form is a misnomer unless it is suffused with creative, and therefore individual, imagination.

Essentially, the excitement in artistic creativity is excitement about the mystery of existence itself. It comes from encounter-ing another person's creative imagination in doing something we cannot do. Even when disturbed, we can celebrate the gift-ing of another *I am* and participate in that which we cannot yet understand. Every time we hear or see something truly creative, truly imaginative, we should applaud God, more than each other—God, the giver of "every good and perfect gift," who is the source of the tremendous surge and urge within each of us. Let art and music disturb; let them amaze, even raise our hackles. Let them stretch unused muscles. And in so doing, let them take us back to the first days of creation when all was new, all was "for the first time" the issue of a vast imagination.

To be sure, man is a fallen creature. Sin leads to deviation in what he does. His ideas are often at cross purposes. What he creates is often bent in its content, purpose, and direction. And his ability to criticize and judge art is just as fallen as his other faculties. But the glory of the Christian Gospel is that, however fallen man is, however distorted and bent his characteristics, his life and gifts are redeemable. They may be rightly directed and used in the service of God. There is no telling how or whether his gifts will increase. But there is the promise for a radical perspective—Scripture calls it wisdom. And there is a demand that his gifts be exhausted in the pursuit of excellence.

Worship

Worship is intimately related to the chief end of man, which, as the catechism declares, is "to glorify God and enjoy him forever." Worship is God-centered and is a joyful celebration on man's part.

But the basic concept of Christian worship has often been limited to the way Christians conduct themselves during the few hours they spend in church. Various Sunday activities, churchly symbols, and aids to worship alternate with other activities: prayer meetings, Bible studies, "informal" services. And within the Sunday worship service itself there are lead-ins, interludes, and asides, which depending upon the kind of church, may include anything up to the sermon or the Eucharist.

But there is more to worship than these localized expressions. Redemption is so radical that it calls for a new totality, hence a total worship. In this sense, a theology of worship assumes the creational ideas expressed earlier and continues with those references found in Scripture which describe worship as a continuing state: the *beauty of holiness* of the Psalm, *spirit and truth* as spoken of by Jesus, and Romans 12:1 in particular. Worship, according to the latter, is the reasonable issue of being a sacrifice as long as one lives. Worship does not stop and start. Instead, it is highly translatable from one circumstance to another. One does not go to church to worship, but as a *continuing worshiper*; one goes to church to worship corporately, to be in league with his brothers and sisters, at one time, in one place, and with one accord. The essential call to worship, then, comes at conversion. If worship is our continuing state, and since, in Christ, being and action are inseparable, it follows that worship can only be seen to be one act after another. Our acts are only to be seen as offerings, in that all of our life is to be given over to our Creator.

Music and art have traditionally been seen as aids to worship. Through no inherent fault they have been considered suspect, even pagan, in their role as empowerers, or secular diversions away from true worship. To be sure, art does move us. But the problem in worship lies deeper. It has to do with whether we are moved because the repetition of something familiar in a familiar place conduces to worship, or whether we can worship with the same intensity in the face of change and newness. If the former is the whole function of music in worship, then music can be nothing more than a part of a complex system of conditioning and reflex. Errors in our theology of worship have led to the impression that music is more an agent than an offering. There are preludes, postludes, and interludes, implying preparation, cessation, and waiting. Rarely, if ever, is the worshiper faced with the necessity of music as an action, an offering, free of determinism, dependent on faith for its validity.

The problem lies in our attitude about music and the *way* it is used, not in the type of music used. Newness and true creativity imply more than a continuous venture into the avant-garde. When it comes to creating, newness is the opposite of sameness. The whole history of excellent music, including that of the present, is ours to celebrate. One should be no more impressed with group "x" preferring great music than appalled by group "y" preferring bad music, as long as both are stretching and yearning for the unexpected. Taste by itself, no matter how refined it is, is useless. If God senses faith at work, faith which makes us free of conditioned reflexes, he smiles, whatever the supposed level of achievement *at the time*. And the important words are *at the time*, because he ever expects us to be on the move. The question to us is not, "What have you achieved?" but, "What is your next move?" Only when we are in this restless attitude is the Spirit free to work a newness.

Whatever that newness is, it must first be seen as such and celebrated as such, before it is subjected to criteria which might be out of date or useless. It is not enough to love Bach or Stravinsky; we must be educated to love the quest for beyondness.

It is the preference for sameness which turns our acts into idolatrous aids. Winston Churchill once said that we shape our buildings and our buildings shape us. Isaiah said of man:

> He plants a cedar and the rain nourishes it. Then it becomes fuel for a man; he takes a part of it and warms himself, he kindles a fire and bakes bread; also he makes a god and worships it. . . . Half of it he burns in the fire. . . . and the rest of it he makes into a god, his idol; and falls down to it. . . . and says, "Deliver me for thou art my god!" (Isaiah 44:14-17).

There is more idolatry in us than we like to admit, as long as we relocate cause in the created order, equate content with context, and depend on the repetition of our shapings to shape us. Once this happens, change is precluded and our capability to act in the unknown is preempted. It is in this sense that church music has been imprisoned. Corporate worship can be turned on or off with chords, colors, rhythms, and textures; in short, by cultural devices. Creative expression that goes beyond what we are used to is suspect because it prods our sense of containment and security.

But there is a better way. When we hear a new piece of music, carrying no associative power for us, our scriptural role is to make in faith an offering even of our hearing. Thus, we worship the divine Recipient of the offering instead of depending upon the offering to cause us to worship. Thus God is free to act. Newness and strangeness can be celebrated, not as a cause of worship, but as an act of worship. No matter whether one or many voices are raised, the sacrifices of praise are always corporate. And there is no better place to experience the most profound and varied art for the first time than in corporate worship, where the Christian is knit to his fellow believers in "the communion of the saints." The faith that this takes is the faith that hopes for and substantiates that which has not yet been seen or heard. It is the faith that reaches beyond the gift to the giver.

Of course, the musician cannot expect the layman to go it alone. He must examine his own motives as to why he is doing what he is doing. He must not be on a perpetual "new music" binge. He must be able to move gracefully from simplicity to complexity and to share the problems and experiences of the layman in art. Excellence is not a matter of constant complexity and befuddlement. It is a matter of utter simplicity as well. There is no embarrassment in the kind of simplicity which issues from the most refined creative insight and technical mastery. This is the "kenosis," the emptying, for the composer as well as the performer. His work, like Christ's, lies in the putting aside for awhile of certain glories in order to become a servant to the needy. Just as Jesus, in his emptying, did not lose his excellence, neither does art. But the simplicity is discernible only to the highly trained. It must stand the test, not of simple audience research, but the best of the creative community.

Flexible creativity, the ability of the musician to move from excellent simplicity to excellent complexity, the gift which is best called functional integrity, is to be sought out and applauded at all costs. As with all specialities, it is not to be determined by the layman. Functional integrity is the ability to act in the context of need, for the vantage point of artistic excellence. It is reforming, innovative, and redemptive. Above this, it is totally honest.

An offering is costly. It is not a means, because it cannot earn anything. It is not an end, because it cannot be worshiped. The essence of a sacrifice, and its only glory, is that it can be surrendered. In a fullness that is uniquely right, God is both means and end. The Christian musician, like his Christian colleagues in the other arts, is responsible to live and work in accord with the biblical, God-centered world view. In offering his art to God, he is offering himself as best he knows how. So he worships and so through his music he serves and witnesses to the God who gave him his abilities.

Witness

The Christian is to spend his life knowing that the two words *Jesus saves* mean that nothing is beyond the scrutiny of redemption. Witness is not complete unless it demonstrates that every creaturely gift and response is capable of its longest reach when regenerated.

Today we are inundated by an unprecedented quantity of music, literature, films, and art. In music the market overflows with anthems, folk music, cantatas, and that unscrupulous aggregate of pseudo-rock-folk-pop called "Christian contemporary." Among these, the ratio of quantity to quality is appalling. And it is all supposed to support a so-called radicalizing Gospel. Its advertising abounds with superlatives and "with it" slogans, as if to repeat back to the world what it already knows—that the value of a thing is determined by what it is called, not what it intrinsically is. So we mix entertainment with the crucial task of exposing a person to the whole force and weight of the Gospel. We shy away from innovation and from matching the far reaches of truth with creativity. Instead we use borrowed materials as we talk about a new creation. We find out what people are musically used to— what they hear in the supermarkets, on easy listening stations, in restaurants, and so forth. We use this to carry the words of the Gospel—words which, if biblically correct, will tell the world that they can become new creations, radically redone. But we sing a lie. While the words tell of the radical rebirth, the music tells of artistic cloning.

It would, of course, be incorrect to denounce borrowing completely. Since man cannot create out of nothing, he must borrow as a catalyst for his imagination. But the error begins when borrowing becomes the mainstay instead of a point of departure. When this occurs, we produce flattened, redundant versions of what was once vital. A good example is rock, the best of which is indigenous to the secular counter-culture. For a good many the Church's answer is a kind of "chicken" rock, which is neither reformed nor transformed but merely diluted and institutionalized with just enough imitativeness to give a feeling of adventure and "relevance." Such a violation of integrity has driven a good many people of artistic sensitivity back to the world in search of greater honesty of expression. The implication is that authenticity, the consistency between being and doing, can exist only outside the Church. They are forced to conclude that Christianity is naive, even dishonest.

A misuse of history has overemphasized borrowing. A case in point is Luther's comment (when he was criticized for borrowing a drinking song) that the devil should not have all the good tunes. But Luther's position must be seen in the fuller context of his convictions about music. Borrowing to him was only a small part of a rich means of expression. When he borrowed, he borrowed excellence only and left mediocrity to the devil. A skilled musician and a composer, he looked with the greatest admiration to the best music of his time, that of the composer Josquin des Prez. If Luther's total position were injected into the contemporary discussion of church music, it would make him very unpopular.

And if he were here today, he would have to reckon with new factors. He would have to examine the practice of borrowing in the light of a distance between the Church and secular culture unlike anything he had to face. He would have to confront an unprecedented proliferation of musical styles from both within and without Western culture, and he would have to face the Church with its preference for a provincial witness. He would undoubtedly recognize that a large part of our musical experience is depersonalized, issuing electronically from walls, ceilings, and earphones as a background for everything from shopping to worshiping. Yet we continue to worship the

Lord of all and witness to his gospel in artistic forms that are provincial and tepid.

Of course, though in our witness some of our music must be direct and simple, this does not mean that it all must be so. Ironically, it is the borrowing of simple music that has been troublesome to the Church, because even though it is easiest to assimilate, it is also the most difficult to dissociate from its prior and often questionable contexts. This is largely why we wait for time to pass before we borrow. The longer we wait, the greater the detachment from the original context. This allows us to see the borrowed material for what it is intrinsically. Consequently, the baroque dance suite today is considered totally harmless, the Viennese waltz probably harmless, the panoply of jazz questionable, and rock highly controversial. But why must we commit ourselves so largely to retrograde creativity? If there is to be controversy, let it be generated by a stunning authenticity.

The concept of music as "act-of" and "aid-to" pertains to witness as much as it does to worship. For if art is used primarily for its associative powers and perceived only as a tool by which people can be moved, we must then ask, to what extent can art and music carry an extrinsic message, and to what extent does the message subordinate the medium? There is a difference between the concept of medium as a carrier and medium as a message. The ideal situation is when both "media" agree.

Unfortunately, this is not always the case with those who stress mass communication in the spread of the Gospel. If communication is described as the success with which a maximum audience is attracted and held to get a message across, and if art forms are the supporting means (the carriers surrounding the "word"), then the blunt question must be asked: "Given today's preference for shallow entertainment and instant pleasure, how does the Church reconcile the Nielsen ratings with the scandal of the cross?" The kind of mass communication on which the media subsist depends on two things: a minimal creative element and a perspective that sees music only as conveying a message rather than being a message. Viewed as a carrier, music tends to be reduced to a format equated with entertainment. The greater the exposure desired, the lower the common denominator. So the distance increases between the radical authenticity of the Christian message and the vulgarity of the means.

This is a peril, because in the very presentation of Christianity, a union of evangelical truth and methodological falsity may result. Christian witness may play into the hands of the very cultural determinism it sets itself against. Thus the new creation and the old may be confused. This is the ultimate consequence of a series of mistakes issuing from an honest desire to save souls without fully understanding the complete integrity that must mark any activity done in the name of the sovereign God. After all, it is God who saves souls, not a fawning musical "package."

It is impossible to escape the paradoxical nature of the gospel. It is both the power of God unto salvation and a stumbling block. Primarily because salvation is God's doing, it cannot be separated from the fullness of grace perceived outside the constraining power of Christ's love. A stumbling block has nothing to do with sneaking up on the world or tricking it. A stumbling block is out in front, far ahead, and the world stumbles over it in its own rush to save itself. If redemption affects man's whole being and doing, if it is the final benediction on his identity in Christ, then the life style of the redeemed must lead in opening new ways and developing new forms for worship.

If there is ever a truly authentic church music, it will come through a relocation of priorities in a flow of excellence celebrated creatively, by faith, as worship. The aesthetic faculties of each person can find complete expression in the service of God in the world. Church music can then be the place where excellence is born and where it is continuously welcome. It is church music only because it is heard there first. Then the world will have to face the necessity of borrowing from the

Church because Christianity offers more creative options than any other life. The best witness will see the world overhearing the Church at worship. We need never invert our priorities and violate our artistic integrity for Jesus' sake. The Gospel is too great for this kind of compromise. In reconciling the world to God, our Lord Jesus Christ did not compromise his integrity to gain maximum results. And he is the true model for a redeemed artist.

The story of Joshua and Jericho can be interpreted in two ways, each representing a pattern for the use of music in worship and witness: Men, blowing their trumpets, brought the walls down; or, as men blew their trumpets to the Lord, he brought the walls down. Only according to the latter pattern can we use music to the glory of God.

Christian Hymnody

E. Margaret Clarkson

It is no secret that people with a refined musical taste are often distressed by the music that is preferred in most evangelical churches today. This consensus among the people best qualified to judge should make Christians willing to listen.

The areas of concern regarding the hymns commonly sung today include unbiblical doctrine, thinness of doctrinal content, mindless or hypnotic repetition of phrases or lines as a substitute for solid and well-developed content, sentimental or juvenile verse, phrases or ejaculations (such as "hallelujah") sung without a surrounding context to explain them or give them depth, weak rhythm (evident when the text is scanned as poetry), poor melody or harmony, a strong beat or loud sound (especially in performed music) that overpowers the words, poor matching of the rhythm of the words to the rhythm of the music, "showmanship" of performers who imitate popular secular musicians, and failure of contemporary popular Christian hymnody to find its own language of integrity instead of imitating the harmony, beat, and syntax of the popular secular culture.

The following essay touches upon three important areas of hymnody: the history of hymns, the ingredients of a good hymn, and the assess-

ment of contemporary Christian hymns. Whoever has ears to hear, let him hear.

Christian Hymns: A Brief Overview

Hymns are expressions of worship—man's glad and grateful acknowledgment of the "worth-ship" of Almighty God, his confession of his own creatureliness before his Creator, his bowing before the transcendence of God. Hymns are a celebration of what God is and what He has done, songs of praise, thanksgiving and joy in God. Christians sing hymns because God is worthy to be praised.

From Genesis to Revelation the Bible rings with praise. The morning stars sang together and the sons of God shouted for joy in creation. In Old Testament and New, men and angels praised God in song. Psalms of Moses, David, Asaph and other singers formed part of the Temple worship. Fragrant buds of song appear in writings of prophets and historians. Personal praises are recorded—the songs of Hannah and Deborah, the "evangelical canticles" of Mary, Zecharias and Simeon. The Apocalyptic Vision echoes with the song of the redeemed: "Worthy is the Lamb!" and "Hallelujah!"

At first the early Christians expressed their joy in Old Testament terms. But soon they were driven to transcend these; their experience of God in Christ surpassed anything Old Testament saints had known. Their spontaneous expressions of joy and belief were the first Christian hymns. They used them as an integral part of Christian worship and for instruction in the faith.

Here and there we find fragments of these early songs. Some are doctrinal: Ephesians 5:14; Philippians 2:6-11; I Timothy 3:16; II Timothy 2:11-13. Others are doxological: Revelation 1:4-8; 4:11; 5:9-10, 12-13; 11:15, 17, 18; 15:3-4. Most appear as poetry in modern translations of the New Testament.

In a letter of Pliny the Younger written to Trajan in 112 A.D., we read of the Christians meeting for worship before dawn on the first day of the week and "singing antiphonally a hymn of praise to Christ as God." Among their hymns were the *Ter Sanctus* of Isaiah 6; the *Gloria In Excelsis* of Luke 2:14 (which became the morning hymn of the Church); the *Trisagion* ("Holy God, holy and mighty, holy and immortal, have mercy upon us"); the *Te Decet Laus* ("To Thee belongeth praise, to Thee belongeth laud, to Thee belongeth glory, Father, Son, and Holy Spirit, for ever and ever, Amen"); and a candlelighting hymn, *Hail, Gladdening Light*, which is still the evening hymn of the Greek Orthodox Church. That these hymns were sung when Christianity was a proscribed religion and discovery might mean immediate death shows the serious view of worship held by the first believers.

As the Church formulated its creeds, its leaders wrote hymns to help the people articulate their faith. By the fourth century the magnificent anonymous *Te Deum Laudamus* had assumed its present form. Every heresy that endangered the Church gave birth to a group of hymns as orthodox believers sought to counteract falsehood by hymns embodying truth. Some of these enrich our worship to this day.

From the first, hymnody followed the rise and fall of the history of the Church. As God's people worshiped, searched the Scriptures, grew in knowledge and grace and proclaimed the Gospel in a diversity of ways, they recorded their songs. In the hymns they left us we can trace their spiritual pilgrimage, and ours.

At first hymns were sung congregationally. But with the rise of monasticism in the Middle Ages music became the province of clergy and choir; the people no longer had a voice in Christian praise. Today we treasure many hymns from those years, but they were not sung by the people of their day. Only centuries later, and in translation, did they come into congregational use.

Martin Luther (1483–1546) was the pioneer of congregational singing. Newly touched by the Word of God, he wanted to make psalms for his people by which that Word could be kept alive among them, psalms of simplicity and plain speech which the people could sing to familiar tunes in their own tongue. Gathering a small creative group about him, he set about his task. His first hymn book appeared in 1524, the first of a steady stream of hymnals continuing into the present.

Luther's hymns succeeded beyond his highest hopes. The hearts of the people thrilled with surprise and joy as vast numbers sang themselves into a knowledge of the creeds of the Protestant Reformation. "By his songs he has conquered us!" mourned the ravaged Church of Rome, aware too late of the power of congregational song.

Calvin's *Genevan Psalter* had a similar effect on the French-speaking church. His psalms were strict paraphrases of the psalms of David, while Luther had not hesitated to look beyond David to praise "great David's greater Son." Lutheran hymns spread throughout Europe; Genevan psalms spread to Britain, then America. Many years were to pass before the two streams of song united.

Though Isaac Watts (1647–1748) is called the Father of the English hymn, he was not the first to envisage the Christian hymn as opposed to the metricized psalms. George Morison and others had paraphrased a few other portions of Scripture. George Wither, Thomas Ken and Richard Baxter had written hymns for their personal use. But from the time that the sixteen-year-old Watts hymned the Savior's praise in his *Behold the Glories of the Lamb* a tide of "Christianized psalms" swept across England. Watts' hymns eventually broke the exclusive domination of the psalms and vindicated the place of the Gospel in Christian praise.

Like Luther, the Wesley brothers recognized the teaching power of hymns, and the strength of their revivals lay as much in their hymns as in their preaching. Charles writing, John editing, they crystallized each day's message into a hymn and so taught doctrine to the people. They also gave rise to two new hymn forms, the hymn of Christian experience and the invitational or gospel hymn, thus enshrining in the common mind not only biblical truth but the reality of personal Christian experience. Every revival and new Christian movement since has used some form of hymnody to reinforce its message.

What Constitutes a Good Hymn?

If a hymn is an expression of the worth-ship of God, a statement of Christian belief, a means of teaching biblical truth and a witness to personal Christian experience, it follows that its words are of utmost importance. Good music must accompany them, but its highest office is to provide suitable expression for its words. For the words, rather than the music, decide the worth of a hymn. The music is merely the setting against which the words will be experienced. Important as it is, it has no function apart from the words. Its purpose is to strengthen and enhance their message. The best hymn tunes are those that best illuminate their text. With this by way of background, I would suggest six characteristics of a good hymn.

1. *Good hymns are God-centered, not man-centered.* Good hymns adore the Eternal Godhead for what He is, worshiping Him for His holiness, wisdom, power, justice, goodness, mercy and truth. They praise Him for His mighty acts—for creation, preservation, redemption; for guidance, provision, protection; for the hope of glory. They offer petition suitable to their theme. Good hymns are free from introspection, focused on God, not man. When man enters the picture it is to acknowledge the darkness of his sinful nature in the light of such a God, to seek His mercy and to marvel and rejoice in His redeeming grace.

2. *Good hymns are theologically sound.* Many hymns in common use today contain theological untruths. Yet they are sung by congregations who would root theological error from the sermon in short order, and who are quick to label other believers as liberal.

The Old Rugged Cross is an example. Waxing sentimental over an old rugged cross will never save anyone; our faith must be in the Christ of the Cross, in His death, resurrection, exaltation and present ministry for us, and our hymns must say so. Yet how many Christians sing this and similar songs, complacently certain they are praising God.

Today's church should be more aware of this than it is. As Erik Routley states in *Hymns Today and Tomorrow*, a hymn is a persuasive thing; it makes us feel that this is what *we* think, not just what the writer thinks:

> The reason in a hymn is underlying, and may not be noticed by many singers. Hence an unreason, a nonsense, an error in doctrine, may easily slip into a congregation's singing and eventually into its living. A congregation's disposition towards right belief or away from it is subtly influenced by the habitual use of hymns. No single influence in public worship can so surely condition a congregation to self-deception, to fugitive follies, to religious perversities, as thoughtlessly-chosen hymns. The singing congregation is uncritical; but it matters very much what it sings, for *it comes to believe its hymns*. Wrong doctrine in preaching would be noticed; in hymns, it may come to be believed.[1]

This needs to be heeded today. Satan has made great inroads into our hymn books. We should take a long, sober look at the theology of our songs and hymns and use only those that are true to the Scriptures. There is no shortage of theologically-sound hymns. Let us seek them out and use them.

3. Good hymns are doctrinal in content. So inseparable is true worship from the foundation-truths of our faith that most good hymns, in measure at least, are expositional in nature.

This is a good thing. Some preachers are evangelists or pastors rather than expositors or teachers. Some stress certain doctrines and neglect others. But the worshiping congregation with a good and wisely-used hymn book is constantly instructed and blessed as the great doctrines of the faith are brought before it in review. Truth is thus kept vernal.

1. Erik Routley, *Hymns Today and Tomorrow* (Nashville: Abingdon, 1964).

The doctrine of good hymns is true to Christian experience as well as to the Scriptures. It does not claim as everyday fare certain emotional, mountaintop experiences that for most Christians occur but rarely, if at all. Good hymns express the religious thought and feelings of the average believer, not some super-saint. The doctrine they express is not only biblical, but down-to-earth and practical; it helps the worshipers live as Christians should.

Good hymns are not myopic, but full-orbed in their view and expression of Christian doctrine. Thus good missionary hymns encompass the whole spectrum of evangelism. They are not content to chant "Bring them in!" or "Send the light!" again and again, nor to rely on man and his feeble though necessary labors for missionary fulfillment. Rather they embrace God's great redemptive purpose, lay hold on His promises of ultimate triumph, and give themselves unsparingly to work in coopera-tion with Him who alone can build His Church. Similarly, good hymns on prayer do not wallow in the sweetness of the hour spent in some mythical garden, but set forth the true nature of prayer and encourage us to give ourselves to the sacrificial warfare it demands.

4. *Good hymns have words of beauty, dignity, reverence and simplicity*. Whether their theme is one of lofty exultation or a simple expression of trust, good hymns are chaste, precise and lovely in their utterance. Their language is clear and concise. They are never glib, never pat, never extravagant, never senti-mental, never trite; they are always true. They speak beauti-fully, feelingly, compellingly and with restraint of the things of God. They do not transgress the limits of good taste in concept, word or setting. They cannot give offense.

Good hymns are adult in word and tone. They do not insult intelligence by requiring us to sing immortal truths in childish or unsuitable modes of expression. While remaining true to the gospel, they contain nothing to bewilder or embarrass an un-believer, but will speak to him of a deep, sincere, vital experi-ence of God. Their figures of speech will be in keeping with the worth-ship of God and have meaning for the contemporary worshiper.

5. *Good hymns display preciseness and finesse of poetic technique and expression*. Good hymns have a single theme and organic unity. They move from a bold attack in the opening line through a definite progression of thought to a clear and decisive climax. Rhymes and rhythms are interesting, original, and correct. The declamation (union of words and music) is accurate. Meters may be varied but will be conservative enough that good tunes, capable of being well sung by average congregations, may be written for them. Good hymns should be short enough to be sung in their entirety, that the full impact of their sequence may be felt. They should be free of irrelevant refrains which detract from the main thought.

6. *Good hymns turn heavenwards*. Good hymns rejoice in the unity of believers and the communion of saints. The best hymnwriters have recognized more than most of us that the people of God are one. They take their place with the warring, suffering and triumphing Church Universal, identifying with the saints of long ago as readily as with those of today. The hymns of such writers sing often, and with deep delight and longing, of the soul's true home.

What constitutes a good hymn? Good hymns are not the result of desire or ambition, but are an outgrowth of spiritual life. They are not based on feeling but eternal verities, not centered on man but on God.

Writing a hymn is more than using certain techniques correctly. It is a matter of looking on the face of God; of worshiping in His presence, embracing His will, accepting His cross, living daily under its obedience; then, having learned the disciplines of good writing, of singing God's grace. True hymnwriters have not primarily sought to write hymns, but to know God; knowing Him, they could not but sing. Theirs are the hymns that have lived through the ages and will live into the future. It is this kind of hymnwriting that we need today if our generation is to contribute anything real to the Church's treasury of worship and praise.

The Contemporary Scene

What is the state of hymnody today? What legacy are we leaving to future generations?

Good hymnody today is found largely in mainstream denominations, particularly liturgical ones. New hymnals show a high degree of scholarship. Texts of early Christian writers, still relevant, enrich our devotion; ancient melodies and folk airs blend with historic hymn tunes to enrich our worship, along with the best of contemporary writing.

Some gospel-song books are improving along similar lines, though the ratio of quality new material to traditional gospel song is still low. But introits and responses are being added. Devotional readings from past and present Christian writings are given alongside Scripture readings, most of which are in modern language. Better indices and cross-references are being added; tunes are being named and compositions dated. Accompanying handbooks may provide background material. Higher editorial standards are evident, along with broader and more creative scholarship.

But this is no guarantee of better worship. Old habits and sentiments die hard and all too many Christians resist new worship experiences. Despite the visibility of evangelical Christianity today and our increased educational advantages, perceptive leadership is sadly lacking. Theological discernment is at a pitiful level among us, not only among congregations but also among all too many leaders and pastors.

Yet never has spiritual discernment in Christian praise been more needed. In all our hymn books today there are theological errors and deceptions which must be discerned, identified, understood and avoided.

Particularly in North America, the standard hymnal is including more and more of what is known as the "literary hymn" as opposed to earlier hymns of evangelical truth and fervor. The "literary hymn" is a finely-crafted and highly polished form of hymn text that began in England in the nineteenth century and reached its zenith among the Boston Unitarians. Biblical and nourishing at first, the literary quality of the words gradually took precedence over their theological integrity. Eventually the "literary hymns" came to be a beautiful embodiment of little more than humanism. But the excellence of their expression is alluringly deceptive. Despite their biblical infidelity, they appear increasingly in our books. The same editors who are enriching us with the treasures of early Christianity seem heedless of the poverty of the modern literary hymns. Meanwhile, as Routley points out, Christians everywhere are singing themselves into believing them.

The danger in gospel-song books is different. Their pages are relatively free of "literary hymns," but the great bulk of their songs are of another variety, whose peril lies in a sentimentalism and an excess of religious expression often divorced both from the Scriptures and from reality. Frequently this is coupled with an imprecise use of language and a greater emphasis on emotional experience than on the Word of God.

Such songs distort Christian truth as surely as the "literary hymns" and even more subtly, since they use the "right" words while often making them say the wrong things. Every day hundreds of distortions, half-truths or downright untruths are sung and accepted as biblical by well-intentioned but undiscerning believers. The easy, rather hypnotic qualities of our contemporary gospel music tend to lull into unreason any critical faculties we might bring to bear on the words we sing.

Not that gospel music is necessarily poor; rather, it is a special genre, bright, light, facile. Gospel songs came into being at the turn of the century as first Moody and Sankey, then other evangelists, sought to reach the unchurched, illiterate masses of unskilled workers in crowded industrial cities in England and America. They presented elementary gospel truths in an easily-remembered manner to people who had never heard them. Words and tunes were simplicity itself, with repeated phrases and catchy refrains. The songs accomplished their purposes. As with the songs of Luther and Wesley, thousands were swept into the Kingdom by their power.

But while such songs do give the gospel, they do not present other biblical truth. They are not hymns of worship centered on the being of God; they tend to be songs of human experience. They neither nurture nor instruct. To use them as a means of worship is spiritual poverty. For several decades many evangelicals have done this, and thousands now know no true depths of worship. This may be the single greatest reason for our shallowness and lack of spiritual discernment today.

For gospel music now is big business. When businessman Moody copyrighted his first song book, a new element entered Christian hymnody. Earlier hymnwriters wrote from hearts burning with love of God, often publishing at their own cost to enrich Christian worship. Today's gospel writers face the pull of other motives. This is not to say there are no true worshipers among them or that the laborer is not worthy of his hire; but great rewards can give rise to great temptations. That all too many writers have fallen prey to them is evident in many of the "Christian" songs of today.

Yet a trickle of worthy hymns continues to be produced by evangelicals, particularly in Britain. They are contemporary, creative and biblical, and they are welcomed in discerning circles; the Church needs more such writers and publishers. But even in the shrinking field of hymnody such hymns are in the minority. For while most of the evangelical world is engrossed in gospel music of whatever type, in wider circles the ecumenical hymn, the "literary hymn," and other hymns of little spiritual worth are in the ascendency.

A recent arrival on the gospel-song scene is the so-called "Scripture song," usually accompanied by earnestly uplifted hands or vigorous clapping. Arising in charismatic circles, these have spread rapidly to become favorite "worship songs" of young people everywhere.

At first the words were purely Scriptural; and many well-chosen and well-set texts do indeed provide true worship experience. But not all tunes are good or even adequate for the Scriptures they profess. Some are almost unsingable, the well-intentioned but utterly unworthy work of music illiterates, a hindrance rather than a help to worship.

Eventually the base of the texts broadened. Oft-repeated bits of Scripture have come to be interspersed with commentary, as in a Greek chorus. Though supposedly related to the biblical theme, irrelevant interjections have crept in, as in some Negro spirituals. Some are meaningless; others are incomprehensible; some are even biblically untrue. Lines are long and irregular, making them hard to remember, and making declamation almost impossible. Hence their "tunes" are singularly tuneless, long-drawn-out and chantlike. Rather than being vehicles of worship, such songs are little more than mindless ditties to be chanted over and over as if in a hypnotic trance, a few voices carrying the stanzas while the rest merely join in the refrain.

A song may be a mindless ditty either because it is intrinsically mindless or because it is sung in a mindless manner. Even good hymns can be mindless ditties under certain leadership; so can bits of Scripture sung without reference to context or interspersed with irrelevancies or half-truths. What is needed is discerning and spiritual leadership. "I will sing with the Spirit; I will sing with the understanding also." Where are such leaders to be found?

We do not merely read the Scriptures when we gather for public worship; we expound them. Many Scripture songs require some exposition if they are to be truly meaningful. Good leadership can provide this. Leaders can use Scripture songs only in context, or tie them in with a good hymn whose words provide commentary on the text and expand and deepen its meaning. They can integrate into suitable places in public worship songs whose Scripture text provides a complete worship experience, blending the old and the new together with discernment. They can see that songs that are inherently mindless ditties are not used in Christian worship at all.

Why has Christian praise sunk to such low levels in America today? We have rightly replaced the legalistic "separation" of an earlier era with an awareness that Christians are meant to be involved with the world in which we live. But we have not matched this with discernment as to what such involvement really means. Most evangelicals today not only are "in" the world, the world is very much "in" us. Knowingly or unknowingly, we have made its values our own. This is not the teaching of Scripture concerning the Christian and the world.

Nowhere is the world's infiltration of our thinking more evident than in our frenetic need for entertainment. Older generations thought of church music, whether hymns or gospel songs, as worship. Today, if we think of worship at all, we see its components as entertainment; and we want our entertainment to be indistinguishable from that of the world, usually in its most mindless forms. We see no dichotomy between the truths about which we sing and the ways in which we sing them; in fact, we are gradually watering down the truth until no dichotomy exists.

Increasingly we tend to assess our songs not by their ability to draw out our hearts in worship of Almighty God, but by their success in the marketplace. If a song is a commercial success we assume it to be a spiritual success. If "everyone is singing it," it must be "good." Actually the opposite is more likely to be true. How can we measure the worth of Christian praise by the world's criteria?

We have brought the world's standards into God's sanctuary and called the result worship. Need we wonder if we no longer know the Spirit's presence with us?

We must learn that we do not have to embrace the world's values in order to be contemporary. We must discover that it is possible to express our historic faith in the language of today, both verbally and musically, and to produce hymns that are contemporary without being conformed to the spirit of the world. Who will rise to the challenge of creating such worthy hymns of praise for our generation?

The Place of Music in Christian Life

Robert Elmore

Aesthetically, as well as morally, we become the sum of our indulgences. What we habitually take into our minds and imaginations becomes a permanent part of us. If we consistently immerse ourselves in mediocre literature or painting or music, we become, in that sphere of our lives, mediocre people.

Perhaps the threat of mediocrity is greater in music than in any other art. The ease with which a flip of the switch fills the room with music, combined with the syndrome of mindlessly absorbing "background music," has conspired against good musical taste.

But Christians are obligated to excellence because of who God is. The doctrine of stewardship, moreover, teaches us that there is an obligation to develop every talent or capacity that we possess.

How, then, does one develop good musical taste? Music is the art of the ear. Good listening requires concentrated attention. It also requires listening to excellent rather than mediocre artistic form. The way to develop excellence in musical taste, the following essay suggests, is simple: it requires only that we keep listening to music that is excellent.

Music: The Neglected Art

Music is the Christian art par excellence. From that awe-inspiring moment in the past when the morning stars sang together and the sons of God shouted for joy, to that wondrous time in the future when Christians will join in the song of the redeemed, the Bible is full of references to music. Our Lord himself, in the Epistle to the Hebrews, speaks of joining in praise "in the midst of the congregation."

With this in mind, it is little short of amazing that the art of music should be so lightly esteemed among many evangelical Christians. Often in our churches music is approached and used almost as entertainment, and light entertainment at that. Some may be inclined to deny this statement or to take offense at it. But before you stop reading, consider a moment. What is the ordinary gospel hymn? Is it a noble melody, well harmonized, wedded to a text expressed in words of beauty and power? To ask the question is to answer it, regretfully, in the negative. Worthy hymns are, like everything that is worthy, in the minority. I have the distinct impression that a good many of our popular hymns are written to sell, not to save; for their bounce, not their blessing.

There seems to be a feeling in some Christian circles that if music is truly deep, it is suspect and perhaps subversive and therefore not to be used in church. There are even ministers who feed their congregations with the strong meat of the Word and at the same time surround their preaching with only the skimmed milk of music.

Leaving, for the moment, the place and use of music in our church services, what about its place and use in our personal lives? It is my conviction that many Christians are missing much blessing and inspiration by leaving great music out of their scheme of living. The deprivation may well be more significant today than in the past, for most of us have more leisure time than ever before.

Some may have the notion that to appreciate great music one must understand its technicalities. This is simply not true. To appreciate, enjoy, and benefit from music all you have to do is listen to it. A musical friend may give you advice about what to listen for, or you may find a good book on music appreciation that will help you. Yet these aids, while pleasant, are not at all essential. What I say is literally true: all you have to do is listen.

But the word *listen* needs clarification. In these days when our ears are assailed, whether we like it or not, with canned music (usually mediocre) in restaurants, stores, and even airplanes, we tend to push music aside without really paying attention to it. Thus listening has become, for many, a lost art. But when I suggest that you listen to music, I do not mean that, after putting a record on the turntable, you will then begin to read the paper, do the dishes, or converse with a friend. Instead I mean that you will sit quietly, and with every bit of mental energy you possess concentrate entirely on the music. This will not be easy at first. In fact, listening can be just as tiring as any other mental activity. But if you desire the rewards, you must pay the price in honest, intense concentration.

Learning to Love the Best

If your musical diet has largely consisted of the light, sugary, sentimental kind of music, typified by certain of the popular gospel-hymn arrangements or by the prevalent secular "mood" music so often heard today, you will find the going, temporarily at least, all uphill. One of the great virtues of the good gospel hymn is the immediacy of its appeal. This is not in itself a bad thing. Straightforward appeal is indeed the virtue of the popular song. And there are also pieces of great music that speak so very simply and directly that their message is at once grasped and enjoyed. Yet unlike lesser music, these pieces are wonderfully durable; repeated hearing year after year does not wear them out.

Let us not, however, deny ourselves the enrichment of much of the greatest music merely on the basis of its seeming obscurity. In general, the music of immediate appeal is somewhat like a handkerchief box: all the beauty is on the surface, and there is no depth. Very often music that on first hearing seemed strange and uninteresting will become more and more beautiful with each hearing as you further penetrate its beauty. Great and good music is part of God's truth, and is to be enjoyed among his gracious gifts to us. Without question, music is one of the "things [that] are true . . . honest . . . just . . . pure . . . lovely . . . and of good report" of which the Apostle speaks in Philippians 4:8. On repeated hearing, the layman can get a great deal from Bach, Brahms, Mozart, and even from contemporary composers whose idiom may at first seem strange.

After all, what does any artist, musical or otherwise, do? He tries to communicate some aspect of his own experience. If this is a deeply felt experience, sharing it can be helpful and moving to the rest of us. Some men are very great composers because they felt deeply, lived intensely, and had the technical expertise to express in music some of the inmost life of the soul and spirit. Every time I play the *Sonata on the 94th Psalm* by Reubke (a little-known composer whose principal legacy is this one masterpiece, since he died at the age of twenty-four), I am aware that he is expressing in tone the spiritual state that the old mystics called "the dark night of the soul." Through music he is saying things that are incredibly deep and moving and that could not be put in words.

What has just been said of Reubke brings us close to the very *raison d'être* of music. There would be no need for music if it did not go beyond, above, and beneath words in its communication. This applies to vocal as well as to instrumental music, for if a composer chooses to set a text to music, the reason must be that he feels he can intensify its meaning and deepen its significance. Great music, then, is simply the deep thought of the composer expressed in tone. It may be a composition for organ, for piano, or for any other instrument or combination of instruments. It may be a piece for solo voice or for a large chorus. The composer sets his music in the medium he thinks will best serve it. And we as hearers have the privilege and responsibility to listen to what he has to say.

Coming back to the place and use of music in worship, let me observe that we are missing much blessing if we do not seek to use the best, for who can deny that only the best is good enough for God? There is, of course, variety in respect to the best. Granted that there are some "best" gospel hymns that speak with integrity to the heart, do not the profound utterances of, say, a Johann Sebastian Bach, who expressed out of his heart the deep things of God, also have a place? The one is very easily grasped. And nobody should condemn a true but simple hymn because even a child can understand its message. The other is not so easily grasped. Dare we condemn it merely because of this? Are we to deny ourselves the rich experience of entering into the spiritual insights of Bach's great Christian mind simply because to do this takes time and effort?

Music in evangelical Christian circles is in something of a predicament. We hear third-rate music in church; therefore we tend to enjoy the same music in the home. Our children are raised hearing in church and home only this kind of music, and the cycle perpetuates itself. But this could be changed.

Stop at a record store today and buy, for example, a good recording of the Brahm's *First Symphony*. If you are timid, do not even listen to it all at once. Try the slow movement first. This is not deep; it is merely heavenly. Oh, it may not seem quite so accessible as "In the Garden" or "Ivory Palaces," but I promise that after two or three hearings you will be humming bits of it. Or try the last movement. You will find a tune there so vigorous and so ennobling that you will wonder why nobody ever put words to it and made it a hymn, as has indeed been done to tunes of other of the masters. Its very virility may spoil you for some of the lesser stuff that you have been putting up with.

After a few weeks of this, you will be won over. You may even go to your church organist and ask him or her to play, if not a Brahms symphony (since that requires a large orchestra to do it justice), at least something of comparable musical value. And there is plenty. Bach, Mendelssohn, Franck, and

Brahms, to name only a few—all wrote magnificently for organ, and their music is highly appropriate for use in church.

There is More to Music than Listening

But listening to music is not the only way to enjoy it. Even more rewarding is the experience of making music. Of all the uses of leisure, very few are more enjoyable and worthwhile than the practice of music through singing or playing an instrument. Aside from the example of a consistent Christian life and a sound education, parents can give children few more lasting gifts than the opportunity to learn a musical instrument. And, contrary to American custom, let boys as well as girls have their chance at lessons; significantly enough, *all* the great composers have been men. Only a tiny minority of children will become professional musicians, and very few indeed will become highly accomplished amateurs. Talent is inevitably selective, and the gifted alone will continue. Yet even limited experience of making music is beneficial.

Moreover, adults should not rule out their participation in music. Many a man or woman finds joy in even very modest competence on an instrument. And membership in church choirs and in some fine choral organizations enables one to take part in bringing alive the glorious pages of works such as Handel's *Messiah*, Haydn's *Creation*, or Mendelssohn's *Elijah*.

Let us stop feeding our musical sensibilities on ashes. In our lives and in our worship let us have music that is worthy of the Lord who bought us with his precious blood. He is the Author of life, and he is the Master Composer whose music flows through the men he has inspired. Let us rejoice in the gift of music, and let us learn to use it more fully to the glory of God.

How the Few and the Many Use Music

C. S. Lewis

Christians believe that all they do is for the glory of God. Their abilities, gifts, and activities are a form of service to God. Applied to the arts, this attitude leads Christians to be alert for ways in which music or literature or art can be channeled into the cause of religion.

There is nothing inherently wrong with this attitude. Anyone who has thrilled to the majesty of Milton's Paradise Lost *or Mendelssohn's* Reformation *Symphony or the great architecture of a cathedral knows how marvelous it is when a work of art is simultaneously a monument to art and to religion. Yet the use of art in the service of religion has inherent dangers. It runs the continual risk of short-circuiting the work of art. When we look for what we can use for religious purposes, we then ignore the other elements present in the work.*

The following critique of the syndrome of "using" music, excerpted from C. S. Lewis's An Experiment in Criticism, *is not concerned with the specifically Christian use of music that I have cited above. But the analysis is particularly relevant to the Christian scene.*

In music I suppose that most of us, perhaps nearly all of us, began life in the ranks of the many. In every performance of every work we attended exclusively to the 'tune'; to just so much of the total sound as could be represented by whistling or humming. Once this was grasped, all else became practically inaudible. One did not notice either how the composer treated it or how the performers rendered his treatment. To the tune itself there was, I believe, a twofold response.

First, and most obviously, a social and organic response. One wanted to 'join in'; to sing, to hum, to beat time, to sway one's body rhythmically. How often the many feel and indulge this impulse we all know only too well.

Secondly, there was an emotional response. We became heroic, lugubrious, or gay as the tune seemed to invite us. There are reasons for this cautious word 'seemed.' Some musical purists have told me that the appropriateness of certain airs to certain emotions is an illusion; certainly that it decreases with every advance in real musical understanding. It is by no means universal. Even in Eastern Europe the minor key has not the significance it has for most Englishmen; and when I heard a Zulu war song it sounded to me so wistful and gentle as to suggest a *berceuse* rather than the advance of a bloodthirsty impi. Sometimes, too, such emotional responses are dictated quite as much by the fanciful verbal titles which have been attached to certain compositions as by the music itself.

Once the emotional response is well aroused it begets imaginings. Dim ideas of inconsolable sorrows, brilliant revelry, or well-fought fields, arise. Increasingly it is these that we really enjoy. The very tune itself, let alone the use the composer makes of it and the quality of the performance, almost sinks out of hearing. As regards one instrument (the bagpipes) I am still in this condition. I can't tell one piece from another, nor a good piper from a bad. It is all just 'pipes,' all equally intoxicating, heart-rending, orgiastic. Boswell reacted thus to all music. 'I told him that it affected me to such a degree, as often to agitate my nerves painfully, producing in my mind alternate sensations of pathetic dejection, so that I was ready to shed tears, and of daring resolution, so that I was inclined to rush into the thickest part of the battle.' Johnson's reply will be remembered: 'Sir, I should never hear it, if it made me such a fool.'[1]

We have had to remind ourselves that the popular use of pictures, though not an appreciation of the pictures as they really are, need not be—though of course it very often is—base or degraded in itself. We hardly need a similar reminder about the popular use of music. A wholesale condemnation either of this organic or this emotional response is out of the question. It could be made only in defiance of the whole human race. To sing and dance round a fiddler at a fair (the organic and social response) is obviously a right-minded thing to do. To have 'the salt tear harped out of your eye' is not foolish or shameful. And neither response is peculiar to the unmusical. The *cognoscenti* too can be caught humming or whistling. They too, or some of them, respond to the emotional suggestions of music.

But they don't hum or whistle while the music is going on; only in reminiscence, as we quote favorite lines of verse to ourselves. And the direct emotional impact of this or that passage is of very minor importance. When they have grasped the structure of the whole work, have received into their aural imagination the composer's (at once sensuous and intellectual) invention, they may have an emotion about that. It is a different sort of emotion and towards a different sort of object. It is impregnated with intelligence. Yet it is also far more sensuous than the popular use; more tied to the ear. They attend fully to the actual sounds that are being made. But of music as of pictures, the majority make a selection or précis, picking out the elements they can use and neglecting the rest. As the first demand of the picture is 'Look,' the first demand of the music is 'Listen.' The composer may begin by giving out a 'tune' which you could whistle. But the question is not whether you particularly like that tune. Wait. Attend. See what he is going to make of it.

---

1. Boswell, *Life of Johnson*, 23 September 1777.

Yet I find a difficulty about music that I did not find about pictures. I cannot, however I try, rid myself of the feeling that some simple airs, quite apart from what is done with them and quite apart from the execution, are intrinsically vile and ugly. Certain popular songs and hymns come to mind. If my feeling is well-grounded, then it would follow that in music there can be bad taste in the positive sense; a delight in badness as such just because it is bad. But perhaps this means that I am not sufficiently musical. Perhaps the emotional invitation of certain airs to vulgar swagger or lacrimose self-pity so over-powers me that I cannot hear them as neutral patterns of which a good use might possibly be made. I leave it to true musicians to say whether there is no tune so odious (not even *Home Sweet Home*) that a great composer might not success-fully make it one of the materials of a good symphony.

Fortunately the question can be left unanswered. In general the parallel between the popular uses of music and of pictures is close enough. Both consist of 'using' rather than 'receiving.' Both rush hastily forward to do things with the work of art instead of waiting for it to do something to them. As a result, a very great deal that is really visible on the canvas or audible in the performance is ignored; ignored because it cannot be so 'used.' And if the work contains nothing that can be so used—if there are no catchy tunes in the symphony, if the picture is of things that the majority does not care about—it is com-pletely rejected. Neither reaction need be in itself reprehensible; but both leave a man outside the full experience of the arts in question.

In both, when young people are just beginning to pass from the ranks of the many to those of the few, a ludicrous, but fortunately transient error may occur. The young person who has only recently discovered that there is in music something far more lastingly delightful than catchy tunes may go through a phase in which the mere occurrence of such a tune in any work makes him disdain it as 'cheap.' And another young man, at the same stage, may disdain as 'sentimental' any picture whose subject makes a ready appeal to the normal affections of the human mind. It is as if, having once discovered that there are other things to be demanded of a house than comfort, you then concluded that no comfortable house could be 'good architecture.'

I have said this error is transient. I meant transient in real lovers of music or of painting. But in status seekers and devotees of culture it may sometimes become a fixation.

The Christian and Music

Frank E. Gaebelein

Etienne Gilson wrote in The Arts of the Beautiful *that "a universe having no other function than to be beautiful would be a glorious thing indeed." This premise underlies all of the arts, but is preeminently true of music.*

Music (that is, music without words) is the most abstract of the arts, and least laden with rational ideas. This gives music at least one distinct advantage over literature and the visual arts: music is allowed to exist as an artistic phenomenon—a source of beauty—and is not treated as philosophy or theology or sociology or psychology.

The experience of beauty, whether it consists of appreciating a sunset or a symphony, can become a religious experience when a person receives it as a manifestation of a quality of God himself. According to Jonathan Edwards, "All the beauty to be found throughout the whole creation, is but the reflection of the diffused beams of that Being who hath an infinite fulness of brightness and glory; God . . . is the foundation and fountain of all being and all beauty."

The religious potential of music is the overriding theme of the following essay. A great deal of the focus of this book is summed up in Dr.

Gaebelein's remembrance of listening to Beethoven's Violin Concerto *after his father's funeral.*

All Truth Is God's Truth—In Music, Too

What kind of music has a place in the Christian's life? What kind of music belongs in Christian education, in the home, in the church? The foundation upon which our answers to these questions must rest in this: *All truth is of God*. Therefore, music that has integrity is part of God's truth and belongs in a Christian's life. Truth is not confined to the spoken and written word and to such fields as mathematics and science; it relates to the arts also.

If music is a valid part of God's all-embracing truth, it follows that we must break down the misleading distinction between sacred and secular music. What, after all, is sacred music? According to common practice, it is music linked either to religious words or music written for religious use. Thus there are Christians who, while suspicious of all so-called secular music, attend with clear conscience performances labeled sacred concerts in which a good deal of third-rate, sentimental music has been baptized, as it were, by association with Christian verse; or in which tawdry, tasteless hymn arrangements, false to any real musical integrity, are deemed religious.

But is the principle of sanctification by association a valid criterion for the distinction, so common in evangelicalism, between sacred or Christian and secular or worldly music? Certainly not. Rather the only defensible criterion for the fitness of music for service as a handmaid of the glorious truths of the Gospel is its own inherent quality, provided that it meets first of all the test of truth.

"And what," someone asks, "is truth in music?" Consider it negatively, first of all. Music that is pretentious, music that is vulgar, music that reeks with sentimentality, that shows off by resorting to empty, ear-tickling adornment (witness the so-called evangelistic style of piano playing) lacks integrity. As music it is not true, even though doctrinally it may keep the best of company.

And what, positively considered, are some of the elements of truth in music? Are they not honesty of expression, sincerity in the sense of avoidance of the cheap and contrived? Surely also they include such elements as simplicity and directness. But on the other hand they do not rule out either complexity or sophistications as opposed to artless simplicity. Bach wrote some enormously complex music, yet there is no higher musical truth than his. Honesty and integrity in music are not confined to the simple and naive.

In point of fact, there is a vast body of music that has truth and integrity, yet is not fitted for church use, although Christians may enjoy it, because it is part of God's truth. For example, the Chopin polonaises or mazurkas, beautiful as they are, do not convey religious feeling. They have a place in the Christian's enjoyment of music but not in church.

Is There a "Religious Music"?

Is there, then, music that as music, quite apart from words or religious association, is compatible with spiritual worship? Surely the answer is a clear yes. Music is not spiritual only by association. On the contrary, there is music that is innately uplifting in its appeal. To be sure, it cannot by itself convey doctrine and thus is not specifically sacred or Christian, but in its feeling and effect it is spiritually elevating.

Not all of Bach's religious music was written for church use. Some of the preludes and fugues, such as the great E-major Prelude and Fugue in Book II of *The Well-Tempered Clavichord*, are deeply spiritual. Unquestionably many of Beethoven's slow movements, such as the wonderful *Arietta* and variations of the last piano sonata *(Op. 111)*, speak with a transcendental, almost heavenly voice. One of my abiding memories is that of listening after my father's funeral to the "Adagio" of Beethoven's *Violin Concerto*. The Scriptures had indeed given me their unique comfort, yet music also spoke its lesser and wordless language of comfort. Mendelssohn's *Reformation* Symphony has its religious moments and not just because of the use of "Ein' feste Burg." But the César Franck symphony without any such reference is also religious, even mystical, in spirit. The firm majesty of Handel, so compatible with faith, is not confined to the *Messiah*. Witness the universally familiar "Largo" which, though composed for secular use, has found such wide religious acceptance. Or take a piece like the brief Mendelssohn Song without Words, called "Consolation," which we have in our hymnals under the name "Communion"; or the Schumann "Nachtstück," which we know as the hymn tune "Canonbury." Granted that personal taste enters into comments like these, still the point is clear that there is a wealth of absolute music that in itself is conducive to worship.

My own feeling is that more of this kind of absolute music should be used in our churches, not self-consciously but unobtrusively. The question may sound radical, but is the practice of always printing on our church bulletins the names and composers of preludes and postludes and offertories a good thing? Certainly we desire to develop understanding of fine music. But a church service is not a course in music appreciation. We must be careful in reaching out for a higher level of Christian music that we do not foster what Don Hustad calls "spectatorism" in which the people look upon parts of the church musical service as a performance.

Consider an illustration from painting. A distinguished artist had finished a canvas of the Last Supper. All was done with great skill, and the chalice in particular had been portrayed most beautifully. As one after another of the artist's friends looked at the painting, they said, "What a beautiful cup!" Then the artist realized that he had diverted attention from the Lord. Taking his brush, he painted out the gorgeous chalice and substituted for it a more quietly beautiful but far less obtrusive one. So should it be with music in worship. It should not call attention to itself nor monopolize the center of attraction that belongs to the Lord alone. And it may well be that the use, almost anonymously, of some first-rate music that, while unfamiliar, is in itself spiritual, will help the atmosphere of worship.

What Type of Hymns Belong in the Church?

But what about gospel hymns? Must all of our church music be classical? The questions come out of a chief point of tension in evangelical Protestant worship today. Surely, when it comes to gospel hymns and their more formal companions, it is not a matter of "either-or" but of "both-and." The criterion for gospel music must be the truth, just as the truth is the criterion for theology. Christians ought not to tolerate a double standard in worship—namely, zeal for the truth in doctrine and disregard of the truth in art.

God's truth is wonderfully comprehensive. Some of the truest music ever written, music of greatest integrity, is folk music. Think, for example, of the nobility of some Negro spirituals. It is a mistake to confine truth in music to the classical, to the sophisticated, or to the old. Christians ought not be suspicious of music just because it is new or unfamiliar. Our respect for the classics must not obscure the fact that good music is being written in our time. And there are gospel hymns—and the number is not inconsiderable—that in sincere, artless expression are honest music. They belong in our worship and education. Included among them are hymns like "What a Friend We Have in Jesus," "Blessed Assurance," or "Saviour, Like a Shepherd Lead Us," a tune, by the way, that Dvořák wove into the last movement of his *Violincello Concerto*.

One gets a little weary of extremists who say, "Away with gospel music; it's all trash"; or of those who say, "Away with all the older hymns; they're all staid, doleful, and joyless." The antitheses are false. Not all the old, standard hymns are staid and somber; and even the best denominational hymnals contain some hymns of negligible value that are hardly ever sung.

As for classifying all gospel music as trash, this is nothing less than obscurantism. It is more difficult to be thoughtfully discriminating than to fall back upon sweeping generalization. Nevertheless, discrimination according to the truth is the only responsible answer to the tension between gospel hymns and standard hymns.

In point of fact, there is a far greater threat to the musical integrity of our evangelical worship and education than the gospel hymn. This threat is the invasion of Christian music by certain techniques of the entertainment world. With the almost universal use of TV, radio, and stereos, the primary, God-ordained center of education, the home, has been infiltrated by the musical devices of Hollywood and the night club. What does the habitual use of such music do in a home? The plain answer is that it debases taste and cheapens the gospel. An editorial in the *Sunday School Times* was absolutely right in its slashing attack upon the dressing up of gospel melodies in the garments of show business. If the state of music among evangelicals leaves a great deal to be desired, then records in which the precious doctrines of our redemption are unequally yoked with the movie theatre organ or sung in the mood of cocktail hour ballads have much for which to answer.

As a matter of fact, some forms of jazz may have more musical integrity than this kind of Christian music. As Professor Wilson Wade of Dartmouth has said, there is a type of jazz that expresses honestly the spiritual lostness and rootlessness of modern man. And while many evangelicals would dissent from his conclusion that the integrity of jazz in reflecting the predicament of man today entitles it to a place in worship, there are those who would think its use as a spiritual medium to be less questionable than that of some of the shoddy music that finds acceptance among us. Paul's exhortation, "Don't let the world around you squeeze you into its own mold" (Romans 12:2, Phillips), is an aesthetic as well as moral imperative; and it applies as much to some of the music so popular among many Christians as it does to jazz.

The Formation of Musical Taste

Now we come to the heart of the matter, which is the formation of musical taste. Alfred North Whitehead has this noble sentence: "Moral education is impossible apart from the habitual vision of greatness." Let us paraphrase it thus: "Musical education is impossible apart from the habitual hearing of greatness." Here is the key to the place of music in the Christian's life.

Look again at the home. And permit me a bit of autobiography. It is my privilege to be the son of a great Bible teacher, one who stood firmly upon the Word of God and who preached the gospel fearlessly wherever he went. Why am I a Christian today? Because of God's grace in using the witness of my parents in my home, the place where, as a small boy, I received Christ as my Savior. And why am I a musical person today? Again, because of my home. Among my earliest memories is that of hearing my father and my oldest brother playing Beethoven's *Fourth Symphony* in a four-hand piano arrangement. Or I recall waking up on one of the Sunday mornings when my father was not out preaching and hearing him play Mendelssohn. This was long before the day of radio and stereos. Yet we had music in our home. My father and brother were only amateur pianists, but they loved and played good music. Yes, musical education is impossible apart from the habitual hearing of greatness—not necessarily in great performance, for that was not nearly so available in my boyhood as it is now, thanks to records, but in constant hearing of even unskilled performance of great music.

What of musical education in school and college? Here, too, the same principle holds. Whatever else we do, we must expose young people to greatness in music. Moreover, we need to tell them the difference between the good and the bad, between the worthy and the unworthy. Today one of the watchwords in education is the pursuit of excellence. Christian education, committed to that which is most excellent of all, the truth incarnate in Him who is altogether lovely, can do no less than seek excellence in music, as in everything else.

The key to better things in Christian music is the habitual hearing of greatness in music not only in school, not only in college and Bible institute, but in Sunday school also. For the music that younger children hear exercises a formative influence on their taste. Not even the smallest child may safely be fed a diet of musical trash.

The Christian Musician

Music is a demanding art. To achieve excellence in it requires hard discipline and unremitting work. Yet with all his devotion to it, a Christian musician must keep his priorities clear. God is the source of all talent. When He gives talent, including musical talent, He gives it, not to be made an idol of, but to be used to His glory. You may remember how humbly Haydn summed up his musical life. "I know," he said, "that God appointed me a task. I acknowledge it with thanks and hope and believe I have done my duty and have been useful to the world." Music is indeed a great gift; but it is the Giver, not the gift, who must have the first place in the teaching and practice of music in Christian education.

In his own account of his conversion, the church father Jerome tells of a dream that led to his conversion. He dreamed, he says, that he appeared before the judgment seat of the Judge. Asked who and what he was, he replied, "I am a Christian." But He who presided said, "Thou liest; thou art a follower of Cicero, not of Christ." For Jerome was a rhetorician and his consuming interest and first love was his study of Cicero.

So the Christian musician must take care that the art to which he is devoted does not usurp the place that belongs to the Lord alone. He must be a Christian first, which means that everything without exception must be brought into captivity to the obedience of Christ, who in all things, music among them, must have the preeminence.